Culture and Power in Revolutionary Russia

The Intelligentsia and the Transition from Tsarism to Communism

Christopher Read

Lecturer in History
University of Warwick

M

MACMILLAN

First published 1990

Published by
THE MACMILLAN PRESS LTD
Houndmills, Basingstoke, Hampshire RG21 2XS
and London
Companies and representatives
throughout the world

Typeset by Wessex Typesetters
(Division of The Eastern Press Ltd)
Frome, Somerset

Printed in Hong Kong

British Library Cataloguing in Publication Data
Read, Christopher
Culture and power in revolutionary Russia: the
Intelligentsia and the transition from tsarism to communism
1. Russian Revolution, 1917 & Russian Civil War. Role
of intellectuals
I. Title
947.084′1
ISBN 0–333–49792–9

For Françoise, Alexandra and Natalia

The fact is that, when an intellectual decides to take the intelligentsia as an object of reflection, it is usually as a subject for a confession, curses, or a sermon and not as an object of study.

Régis Debray, *Teachers, Writers, Celebrities*

Contents

Preface

The book here offered to the reader is not the one the author set out to write. The initial ideas underwent more than the usual transformation as the research information accumulated and the task of writing progressed. In its first incarnation it was intended as an investigation of the problem of how the vibrant pre-revolutionary intelligentsia was turned into the cowed, unquestioning technical intelligentsia of Stalin's day. It was assumed that the story would focus on the pre-war period and the 1920s. After all, ten years ago the period from 1917 to 1921 was underestimated by almost everyone in discussions of the evolution of Soviet Russia. These years were thought of as an understandable aberration, given the immensity of the crisis Russian society underwent during them. It appeared that only when less stressful times emerged, during the supposedly freer atmosphere of New Economic Policy, was the normal business of revolutionary and cultural transformation taken in hand and the direction taken under war communism reversed. In any case, it seemed that sources for the years of revolution and civil war were too thin to sustain any serious argument, particularly about cultural life. Only the works of a few individuals of the symbolist and avant-garde schools were very well known and widely discussed. Pioneering works by Western scholars, of whom Sheila Fitzpatrick occupies the most prominent position in the area of cultural politics, appeared to have exhausted all that could be said on the basis of the evidence available.

As the research began to take shape, however, I discovered (as have many others now working on the period) that the 'lost' years were the most important ones. Far from being an interlude, they were crucial. Closer inspection showed that, though there were undoubtedly formidable problems in finding sources about key areas (particularly top-level decision-making), the pool of available information was expanding. Soviet secondary works released a steady drip of new facts. Archives became more accessible to Soviet and foreign scholars, including the present one, whose feel for this period was completely reconstructed as a result of using the archives of Narkompros, Proletkul't, Sverdlov University, cultural trade unions etc., in Moscow. The result was that the whole focus of the work moved from the 1920s to the years of civil war and the transition to

NEP. It emerged from close observation that, by 1922 (rather than 1932), the underlying principles of the new Soviet government's policies towards culture and the intelligentsia had already emerged. The transformation of the pre-war intelligentsia was already well advanced. Consequently, this book is largely devoted to substantiating this view and demonstrating that NEP was not so much based on a relaxed attitude to culture but on increasingly systematic control of intellectual life. NEP was not a step away from repression towards greater toleration but a step in the direction of more extensive cultural intervention by the Soviet authorities. While it is no part of the present argument to suggest that 'Stalinism' was inevitable, it is the case that what might loosely be thought of as a sort of 'proto-Stalinism' was increasingly important in these years and that certain foundations of 'Stalinism' were laid.

Because of the chronic unevenness of source material for this period the technique used in the present work may be thought of as resembling geological method. Given the lack of complete, systematic evidence covering the whole area being studied, a series of boreholes have been drilled, determined partly by accessibility. This means that Proletkul't, Moscow University, aspects of Narkompros's activity, *Smena vekh*, the *rabfaky*, the work of various individuals such as Bogdanov, Lunacharsky, Andreev, Berdiaev and Chagall, have been looked at in relative detail and an attempt made, on the basis of an examination of these core samples, to make a map of the strata of the area as a whole. In addition, an effort has been made to concentrate on less well-known aspects, the corollary of this being that better-known ones – the artists and poets of the avant-garde above all – have been all but ignored since there is already an extensive literature on them to which the present author is very much indebted. But, while this study is far from exhaustive, it is to be hoped that boreholes sunk elsewhere will either reveal results consistent with the main picture embodied in the present analysis, or that the present hypothesis, where it is inadequate, will stimulate the formation of a more accurate picture of the subject. In any case, every reader will no doubt judge for her or himself whether I have struck diamonds, oil, coal or fool's gold.

Whatever its value, this book would not have been possible without considerable material assistance. While responsibility for its vices rests with me, any virtues it may possess flow, above all, from the help I have received from many quarters. In particular, I should like to thank the British Academy which, through its Soviet Exchange scheme and its Small Grants in the Humanities fund enabled me to undertake extended research visits to Moscow, New York, Cambridge (Mass.), Berkeley and Palo Alto. My thanks go also to the University of Warwick for granting the study leave that enabled me to make these journeys. I am very much in the debt of the librarians and personnel of the Lenin Library, Inion and the History Department of the Soviet Academy of Sciences in Moscow; the History Departments of the Armenian, Estonian and Siberian Academies of Science; Columbia University Library; the New York Public Library; the Widener Library, Harvard; Berkeley University Library; the Hoover Institution Library; the British Library; the Bodleian Library, Oxford; Birmingham and Warwick University Libraries. I am particularly grateful to the archivists of the Central State Historical Archive and the Central State Literary Archive in Moscow; the Bakhmetev Collection at Columbia; the Houghton Library at Harvard and the Hoover Archive at Stanford. I was very glad to have had the opportunity to present some of my thoughts to Russian seminars at CREES (Birmingham), LSE, SSEESS (London), Essex, Columbia and Paris universities. I learned a great deal from these encounters and they have all had a most beneficial effect on my ideas. I also gained a great deal from conversations with specialists in the field. In particular, I should like to thank the following: Professor Richard Pipes; Dr Zenovia Sochor; Dr Avrahm Yassour; Dr S. A. Fediukin; Academician M. P. Kim; Professor Yurii Lotman; Dr L. Ginzburg; Professor V. L. Soskin; Dr K. Khudaverdian; and, finally, members of the Study Group on the Russian Revolution. I also wish to record my thanks to Mrs Kay Rainsley and Mrs Sam Hundal for word-processing my much-amended typescript.

More informal debts to individuals are too numerous to record and I must beg forgiveness for not mentioning them all by name. I cannot, however, overlook the friendship offered by Lucy Lezhneva, Slava Nemodrug and their daughter Julia. Selflessly and graciously, they helped me to sustain my morale during several enervating visits to Moscow in winter. Sunday skiing with them in Izmailovsky Park was essential to my survival. Nor can I fail to thank Anne Kurepalu for her friendship and help over the years and for all that she has taught me about her beloved Estonia. These, and many other Soviet friends, showed me that the best traditions of the intelligentsia are still alive and well.

Above all, however, I am most happy to thank my wife Françoise for all her help, encouragement and legendary patience, as well as for undertaking the extra family duties my work has forced on her, particularly since the arrival of our daughters Alexandra and Natalia, without whom this book would, undoubtedly, have been completed years earlier. That, however, would have been no recompense for not having them.

C. R.
Coventry

1 The Making of the Russian Intelligentsia

And if it is a despot you would dethrone, see first that his throne erected within you is destroyed.

Kahlil Gibran, *The Prophet*

When the Bolsheviks came to power in October 1917 their aim was not simply to reform the old regime or institute a new political and social order. Their ultimate goal was to reshape human nature, or, more precisely, to release it from the pressures that were distorting it. Freed from the tyranny of the ruling class and its enslaving fetish of private property, people would begin to live, for the first time, free and integrated lives. The revolution would bring to an end what Marx had called, referring to all that had happened until then, the pre-history of human society.[1] Like many of the deeper purposes of the Bolsheviks, this aim was not widely known at the time of the revolution and had attracted serious attention from only a handful of party activists. None the less, it was a real dimension of the revolution and was, even for those who paid little attention to it, the unexamined matrix into which the actual revolution had to be fitted.

To some extent Bolshevik expectations in this respect can be traced back to Marx, for whom, arguably, thoroughgoing cultural revolution – meaning a revolution of consciousness and values – was the essence of the revolutionary process and the means by which alienation was to be overcome. But this would only be one chain of explanation. A second has to be added; one related to the particular historical circumstances of Russia. By comparison with their eastern counterparts, west European Marxist parties of the period were much less ambitious in this respect and we cannot explain the Russian revolutionaries' concern with this dimension of Marxist thought solely by tracing it back in a linear fashion. Marxist ideas are no less subject to a form of conditioning by historical circumstances than any others. While one might disagree with his reasoning, the approach of the former Marxist Nicholas Berdiaev, in his book *The Sources of Russian Communism*, was quite correct to the extent that he attempted to show a particular appropriateness of revolutionary communist ideas to the Russian cultural tradition. The first step in unravelling this

1

relationship is to examine the roots of one of the most frequently noted features of pre-revolutionary Russia, the particularly close links that existed between politics and culture.

POLITICS AND CULTURE IN LATE TSARIST RUSSIA

The intertwining of culture and politics stretches far back into Russia's past. In the absence of a stable national territory and as a result of the ebb and flow of invasion and the periodic weakness of the central state it was a cultural institution – the Orthodox church – that became the predominant focus of Russianness in pre-Petrine Russia. The complex relationship between church and state was, apparently, simplified in 1700 when Peter allowed the office of Patriarch to lapse and the church was placed under firm state control. In the nineteenth century the church was used as a weapon of the declining tsarist state in an effort to exert its authority over an increasingly turbulent population.

Two ministers, in particular, stand out in this respect. First, Sergei Uvarov (1786–1855) who was Minister of Education from 1833 to 1849 and, secondly, Konstantin Pobedonostsev (1827–1907) who, as Procurator of the Holy Synod from 1880 to 1905, was the lay head of the Orthodox church. He was also adviser and tutor to the last two tsars. While different in many ways, each shared the same task of shoring up the sagging edifice of tsarist ideology in their respective periods. Summarising his first decade in office, Uvarov commented that 'In the midst of the rapid collapse in Europe of religious and civil institutions, at the time of a general spread of destructive ideas . . . it was necessary to find the principles which form the distinctive character of Russia, and which belong only to Russia.'[2] His chief focus in this respect was on the church which, he suggested, 'the Russian has of old considered the guarantee of social and family happiness'.[3] Though himself an atheist, according to S. M. Solov'ev, Uvarov had wasted no time, when he came to office, before issuing a circular firmly attaching the well-being of the regime to the reinforcement of the influence of the church. In it he wrote to his provincial officials that

Our common obligation consists in this that the education of the people be conducted, according to the Supreme intention of our August monarch, in the joint spirit of Orthodoxy, autocracy and nationality. I am convinced that every professor and teacher, being permeated by one and the same feeling of devotion to throne and fatherland, will use all his resources to become a worthy tool of the government and to earn its complete confidence.[4]

Uvarov's circular marked an important turning-point in tsarist cultural policy in that he was the first to engage in the task, worthy of King Canute, of holding back the tide of liberal ideas (in which Uvarov himself had once, and maybe still, believed) pouring in from western Europe. Conservatives quickly penned encomia to the new trinity of virtues, but underneath the process of encroachment and erosion continued all the same. As the century progressed it was precisely from among professors and teachers, and to an even greater degree their students, that a minority came forward which was not in the least willing to 'use all [its] resources to become a worthy tool of the government'. The consequences of the policy of pure conservatism and refusal to compromise with change, of which education policy was only one aspect, were so stifling that Alexander II, who reigned from 1855 to 1881, was forced to embark on a risky policy of reform, embracing serfdom, the judiciary, education and the armed services, the net outcome of which was a new series of contradictions between conservatives and radicals. The dangers of reform had become plain long before Alexander was assassinated in 1881 by members of the revolutionary movement, which had achieved take-off in the conditions obtaining during his reign. For the quarter century following this event the survival strategy of the autocracy was guided above all by Pobedonostsev.

Pobedonostsev detested reform as firmly as he detested parliamentary government. He found a ready audience for his lugubrious denunciations of these evils in the person of the heir to the throne, the Grand Duke Alexander, to whom he was tutor and companion. The reforms were, he said, 'a whole bazaar of projects'.[5] The tragic circumstances of his accession can only have reinforced Pobedonostsev's warnings in the mind of the new Tsar Alexander III. The leitmotif of his reign from 1881 to 1894 was the attempt to cleanse once more Holy Russia's shores of the pollution of profane ideas flowing from western Europe. Strengthening the police force, sending longer trails of political prisoners into exile, turning a blind eye to anti-Semitic mobs, using the army more frequently to suppress social disorders in the villages and closing off many of the fragile channels of contact with the outside world were prominent aspects of this process. At the heart of it, Pobedonostsev encouraged Russification as a means of drawing the increasingly multi-cultural empire together. There was an aggressive policy of substituting Russian as the official language of instruction in schools in minority areas, but the centrepiece of Russification was the Orthodox church. Non-Orthodox subjects, particularly Jews, were encouraged to convert to Orthodoxy by enforcing severe constraints on their rights of residence, occupation, access to education and so on, if they refused to do so. Conversion from Orthodoxy was an offence punishable at law. The fusion of tsar and people in the ancestral faith was the dream that Pobedonostsev was attempting to realise. 'However powerful the State may be, its power is based alone upon identity of religious profession with the people; the faith of the people sustains it; when discord once appears to weaken this identity, its foundations are sapped, its power dissolves away.' The advantage of this, for the rulers at least, was clear to Pobedonostsev. 'In spiritual sympathy with its rulers a people may bear many heavy burdens, may concede much, and surrender many of its privileges and rights.'[6] To ensure the continuity of these sound principles Alexander ensured that Pobedonostsev should inculcate them in his own son. When Nicholas succeeded to the throne in 1894 the liberals hoped the pendulum would swing towards them once again, but in an important speech of January 1895, in which the hand of Pobedonostsev could be clearly distinguished, Nicholas II dismissed such aspirations as 'senseless dreams'. Pobedonostsev remained a vital figure in the new Tsar's administration, continuing to root out heterodoxy and stifle the dreaded reform impulse and allow 'another very effective force – inertia' to play its role. 'As the ballast in a ship, inertia sustains humanity in the crises of its history, and so indispensable has it become that without it all measured progress would be impossible.'[7] By 1905 the Russian ship of state had, it seems, completely run out of ballast, and as a consequence Pobedonostsev's strategy had completely failed: at the age of 78, he was dismissed. The dams he had tried to erect served only to add to the force of the torrent when the flood season inevitably came around and burst them all.

Incredibly, the 1905 revolution signified to those at the heart of the autocracy simply that the labour of Sysyphus had to be undertaken once more. The weapons for rolling back change – anti-Semitism to the point of proto-Fascism and widespread application of martial law – were becoming more clumsy and were continuing to show diminishing returns. The church remained the keystone of this process and in the words of one of its historians 'Instead of an inner renewal of the Church, the years after 1906 brought an *increasing* identification of the official Church with political reaction.'[8] Even those who tried to save the autocracy from itself, notably Stolypin, were distrusted and their position was undermined by those frightened even by the limited changes they had tried to introduce and protect, particularly the increasingly circumscribed semi-parliament, the Duma, which had been forced out of the autocracy when it was at its most vulnerable in 1905.

It is beyond the scope of the present work to analyse all the forces making the path of reaction so difficult but one of the most important aspects of change, the demand for more education, is central to our study and is the best possible illustration of the autocracy's predicament in its last half century or so. In order to preserve itself, the autocracy needed internal and external strength, which were becoming increasingly bound up with economic, particularly industrial, growth. A higher level of education was an essential prerequisite for this, but education itself was one of the most persistent forces eroding the foundations of the autocratic edifice. Tsarism was thus caught in a vicious circle. The end of securing its position could only be achieved through means which undermined that end. In the broadest terms, the history of the regime after the Crimean War (1854–6) was one attempt after another to balance these ultimately incompatible pressures and to evade the inexorable logic of their interaction.

The difficulties experienced by Russia in the Crimean War had been decisive in persuading the regime to grasp the nettle of reform. Russia's backwardness in comparison with her great power rivals had been exposed. In addition to institutional reform attention began to be paid to practical problems such as the state of the country's strategic communications. Surfaced roads were extremely rare despite the vastness of the Empire. It had taken some troops more than twelve months of marching to redeploy from Siberia to St Petersburg and Poland during the war.[9] The slowness this imposed on Russia's ability to concentrate its enormous military forces was an increasing risk to the security of the regime both from external enemies and from internal ones such as the Poles, who had rebelled in 1830 and again in 1863. After decades of delaying the introduction of railways, for fear that they would create unwelcome mobility and social change, the government decided that not having them was, after all, the more dangerous course and the foundations of a railway network were laid down in the 1860s. From about 1000 kilometres in operation in 1855 the total rose to over 18,000 kilometres in 1874.[10] The effort involved in this stimulated growth in other areas of the economy.

Rapid industrial growth was, however, a late-blossoming feature of tsarist Russia and it was only in the late 1880s and particularly the 1890s that it began to reach significant levels. The mainstay of Russia's economy remained her agriculture but the stability brought about by her grain exports to western Europe, which created a favourable balance of payments, left some flexibility for industrial expansion. Investment in Russian industry, particularly from France, Britain and Germany, became an increasingly important element in the Russian economy. During Sergei Witte's term as Minister of Finance (1891–1903) industrial growth reached annual rates of 10 per cent in key sectors like mining and chemicals. Railway construction continued at a rapid pace. A decade of such growth was not sufficient to effect a complete transformation of Russia but it did appreciably increase its wealth, as the rapid growth of capital and banking shows. While harsh exploitation of the peasantry and the migrant workers of the growing cities was the foundation of this expansion, new wealth began to flow through certain parts of the middle and upper classes. The agrarian sector as a whole did not share in this boom, in fact quite the reverse as competition in the world grain market, particularly from North America, brought a fall in grain prices which Russia, with its outdated methods and labour-intensive cultivation, was ill-equipped to meet. But alongside the old land-owning élite, a new class of industrialists began to compete for status and influence.

These developments, which continued after a major depression from 1900 that precipitated the 1905 revolution, affected the cultural life of Russia in two ways. First, direct patronage from these newly rich entrepreneurs helped fuel the cultural dynamism Russia showed in this period which is examined below.[11] Less directly, but more importantly in the long run, it created an unprecedented demand for qualified professional, technical, managerial and clerical personnel. This could only be satisfied by a major expansion of the ramshackle educational system, which, beyond a small number of élite schools, colleges and universities, traditionally dominated by the sons of wealthy landowners, did not make much contribution to Russia's needs, though the absence of a mass education system no doubt assisted in preserving social stability for the time being.

The expansion of higher education in tsarist Russia was particularly intensive from 1900 onwards. The most authoritative source suggests that the total number of university graduates produced in Russia from 1859 to 1900 was 60,000 while in 1900 there were 85,000 people with higher-education qualifications and equivalent.[12] In most areas the output of qualified people between 1900 and 1917 was greater than the total for the preceding four decades. Available figures for various major sectors of higher education tell the same story. Higher technical colleges produced 18,356 graduates in the period from 1901 to 1917 compared with 11,830 from their origin in the 1860s up to 1900.[13] In the academic year 1913–14 these colleges had an enrolment of 27,010 students.[14] University law faculties produced 22,400 qualified people in the second half of the nineteenth century, while in the four years 1910–13 they produced 11,421.[15] In the same four years university history/philosophy faculties awarded 1951 certificates of completion compared to 4850 for the second half of the nineteenth century. Finally, in physics/mathematics faculties there were 4405 certificates of completion issued from 1900 to 1913 compared to a total of 10,432 in the second half of the nineteenth century.[16] Though the types of course and qualifications changed over the years and the rates of growth differed from one area to another – showing least growth in the relatively well-established pure sciences and the less economically 'relevant' and, politically, more dangerous humanities – there can be no doubt that the number of students and graduates in higher education was increasing in a wide range of fields.

Precise figures for the total number of higher-education students, and even the number of institutions, varies considerably according to precise definition, the status of private institutions and the exact national boundaries used. None the less, the general picture of mass expansion is clear. One careful compilation gives a total of 9344 students in seven universities (excluding Warsaw) in 1881 and 6100 in institutes of higher education in 1880. By 1903 the fifty-five institutes of higher education included in the figures of the Central Statistical Committee had 42,884 students of whom half were in universities. By January 1914 this had risen to 71,921 students in the state sector. Other figures, including a wide range of private institutions, give a total of 90,000 higher-education students in 1909 and 125,000 (of whom 30,000 were women) in ninety higher-education institutions by the middle of World War One.[17] Whatever the precise figures, they all point in the same direction and show the same rapid rate of growth.

Elementary and middle education show a corresponding expansion in this period. Using the number of teachers as a guide, which also serves as an indicator of the growing size of the intelligentsia itself, there were 10,000 teachers in middle schools at the turn of the century.[18] By 1914 the number was about 30,000. Immediately before the revolution it appears to have been over 40,000.[19] The majority of these were graduates, many of them women. Middle-school teachers represented a relatively prosperous layer receiving a moderate salary and having the right to a pension paid according to their length of service.[20] By comparison the elementary teachers (*narodnye uchiteli*) were underqualified and underpaid. The government's aim, adopted in 1906, of establishing universal elementary education put considerable pressure on this sector. The increases were very striking. In 1900 there were about 60,000 teachers in elementary schools. In 1906, Ministry of Education schools employed 72,000 teachers, of whom 69,200 were in rural schools and 2800 in urban schools. By 1914 the number had risen to 131,500, of whom 128,000 were in rural schools and 3500 in urban ones. Despite these increases a recent Soviet scholar has concluded that the government was unable to keep up with the demands its target called for.[21]

While the scope of these changes in education was limited compared to the total population of the country (about 170 million in 1913) it had a much more significant effect on modifying the outlook and structure of the élite and particularly of the major metropolitan centres – Kharkov, Warsaw, Kiev, Moscow and, above all, St Petersburg – in which the higher-education institutions were concentrated. Here, the overall effect of these developments is incalculable. However, certain aspects can be singled out for comment. In the first place, there was a noticeable and quantifiable broadening of the social base of higher-education establishments. Well into the late nineteenth century, Russia's wealth and institutions were dominated by a tiny élite of landowning hereditary nobles plus a significant office-holding caste whose titles, and often functions, were also hereditary since families had worked their way up through the Table of Ranks to achieve hereditary noble status. This tiny group was, however, unable to reproduce itself sufficiently rapidly to meet the demand for more and more skilled and educated personnel. The proportion of sons of hereditary nobles enrolled in Russian universities declined at a particularly striking rate from 23.2 per cent in 1880[22] to 7.6 per cent in 1914.[23] The fact that this steep decline in the proportion of hereditary nobles masks an increase of 25 per cent in the actual numbers (since 23.2 per cent of the approximately 9000 university students in 1880 is 2088 while 7.6 per cent of the 35,000 or so university students of 1914 is 2660) illustrates the dilemma of a narrow élite caught up in economic expansion. It was unable to rely on its own resources for the necessary expansion of skilled pesonnel required and this opened up the road to limited meritocracy. In Russia's case the beneficiaries of this process were, first, the children of personal nobles (that is, the ranks immediately below the hereditary nobility) the proportion of whom went up from 23.4 per cent in 1880[24] to 28.8 per cent in 1914;[25] secondly, the children of middle- and lower-class backgrounds, the proportion of whom went up from 31.5 per cent in 1900 to 35.7 per cent in 1914; and, most of all, the children of peasant and cossack background, the proportion of whom rose from 5.3 per cent in 1900 to 13.3 per cent in 1914.[26] There is no certainty, but one might speculate that these students of peasant background may well have come from the families of wealthier peasants favoured by Stolypin's agrarian reform policies.

Many of the new graduates being produced at this time, particularly those in the main academic disciplines, were going on to become teachers in the influential middle-school sector. In 1906 there were 11,647 graduate teachers in Ministry of Education schools. By 1914 there were 21,000. In both cases, more than half of them were in grammar schools for girls, suggesting there may have been a significant number of overqualified women turning to teaching as a career. Figures for elementary-school teachers also show the women among them to be more highly qualified than the men. Altogether, including private and commercial colleges, there were over 27,000 middle-school teachers with higher education.[27]

This process of expansion clearly stretched the traditional controls over the ideas and outlook of students and pupils. It remained compulsory for all schools to have religious education instructors (*zakonouchiteli* – literally 'teachers of the law') and in 1914 Ministry schools employed some 3800 of them.[28] While political turbulence was an intermittent feature of life in the tsarist school, there is no systematic evidence of its increase or decrease during the last quarter century before the revolution, though there is obviously a correlation with the peaks and troughs of political activity in the country as a whole. In any case, it was not in itself a serious problem for the government. Higher education, however, was a very different matter and it had always threatened to slip out of the grip of the autocracy. Even the relatively timid advances of the 1860s had frightened the government as ideas corrosive of traditional values took hold. Hegel, Comte, Darwin and Spencer formed the basis for various radical schools. University teachers such as Peter Lavrov became spokesmen for the developing populist movement, itself largely university based. It was a Professor at the University of Kiev, Danielson, who began the study of Marx's ideas in Russia and made the first translation in any language of *Das Kapital* in 1872. The censor's comment in approving it for publication in Russia – that it was 'difficult and hardly comprehensible' and that 'Few would read it and still fewer understand it' – has become a minor legend. The government's response to this ferment had been to appoint Count Dmitri Tolstoy to limit the damage, which he sought to do by swamping student's free time, which it was feared they spent in developing subversive theories and engaging in revolutionary plots, with vast quantities of cramming for exams in classical languages. The efforts of Tolstoy and his successors were not without success in that tsarist universities remained bastions of conservatism and careerism, though this was increasingly tinged with liberalism as the century progressed. However, headlong expansion in the early twentieth century put irresistible strain on the hegemonic values of Orthodoxy, autocracy and nationality.

Ultimately, the challenge to those values, within the universities and in the wider society beyond, derived from the absorption, on a hitherto unprecedented scale, of principles, methods and means, from western Europe. To say that, however, is not to say very much in that 'Western' influences were far from homogenous. Indeed, in the areas of Russian life most directly affected they were contradictory. On the one hand there was the growth of industrial capitalism and the beginnings of a 'Western' style bourgeois class often influenced by certain features of liberalism. The influx of enormous amounts of foreign capital and corresponding numbers of foreign professional, technical and managerial personnel clearly contributed greatly to this process. On the other there was the continuing development of a critical radical intelligentsia and an organised labour movement. Poised somewhere between these two contradictory aspects of what might be considered one process, there was a dynamic artistic intelligentsia which was the energising force of a blossoming of Russian high culture particularly in the years after 1900. It was the interaction between these forces and those of 'traditional' tsarism that created the specific characteristics of the period. It should, however, be stressed that this was not a straightforward dispute between Westernising and Slavophile forces. Even those areas of Russian life most affected by the outside world were not imitations of that world but mediations of it, imposing a Russian flavour on them. Russian philosophy, painting, music, liberalism, socialism, political parties, trade unions and so on were distinctive formations often showing considerable differences from their foreign originals.

Defenders of the autocracy continued the long and increasingly ineffective struggle to prevent reform, to withdraw it where it had had to be conceded and to quarantine those elements carrying the disease of progress. The attempts to do this can be seen everywhere. There were bizarre experiments to set up trade unions with a pro-tsarist ideology which were to be controlled by police and clergy. There was the quintessentially medieval spectacle of the royal pilgrimage to Sarov, attended by 400,000 people, on the occasion in 1903 of the canonisation of a local saint, Saint Serafim. After 1905 the government reversed as many of the concessions extracted in that crisis as it thought it could get away with. Clearly, exploitation of peasant ignorance, credulity and religiosity was the key to the possible success of this strategy. Nicholas II, for instance, retained a touching faith in the loyalty of simple peasants almost until the end of his reign, by which time he thought they had rather let him down. When, in December 1916, the British ambassador, Buchanan, suggested he should regain their confidence, the Tsar's reply was that it was up to the people to regain his confidence.

The rapid dismemberment of China at the end of the nineteenth century was, however, a timely reminder that relying on isolation and backwardness was not enough. Some degree of reform and economic growth continued to be necessary at least to maintain the nation's defences. This called for exactly the opposite of what the regime wanted. It required even more contact with the outside world and, amongst other things, continual expansion of education at all levels, including the popular, to create a more productive labour force. The fifth column of this process was the still weak but increasingly influential group of Russian capitalists and industrial entrepreneurs, plus an educated 'Westernised' professional class – often quite conservative in their politics – which formed the core of a growing bourgeoisie. The interests of this group were directly opposed to those of the autocracy, which was based on a land- and office-holding nobility. Up until the end the autocracy held these people at arm's length and did its best to circumvent the reforms they had managed to achieve, such as the Duma system which they hoped would give them a voice in national politics. These people were no revolutionaries and appeared ever ready to compromise with the autocracy, but the government showed no desire to accommodate their wishes or to share power with them. Even the shared fear of revolution from below was unable to change this confrontation. As late as 1915 and 1916 the Progressive Bloc in the Duma, composed largely of these Russian bourgeois, was treated with contempt by Nicholas II and his advisers. Far from showing the effects of liberalisation after the revoultion of 1905 it was clear that the regime had gone into its bunker and was fighting off liberalisation as hard as it could. There appeared to be no possibility of a compromise with the bourgeoisie and its European backers. At the same time, its own survival was dependent on these forces. Thus it was engaged in a hopeless struggle against history. On the one hand it was engaging in an ideological struggle against imported ideas and on the other it was pursuing diplomatic and economic *rapprochement* with the sources of those ideas. Not unlike its successors, it was trying to pursue ideological cold war and confrontation at the same time as *détente* and coexistence in practical affairs.

As a result there were two Russias, each with its own subdivisions and contradictions. On the one hand there was 'medieval' tsarist Russia, composed of the old élite relying somewhat uncomfortably on the acquiescence of the ignorant peasant masses, ensured, it was hoped, by the administering through the church of large doses of Christian humility, acceptance of suffering and pie in the sky, with a powerful reserve of diversionary anti-Semitism and martial law if the first line of defence should fail. On the other was the weak, but increasingly restless, bourgeoisie, whose interests coincided with powerful external forces, whose outlook and principles were founded on a post-Enlightenment type of education based on science and reason. To a degree, this group shared some of the interests of its work-force in that both opposed aspects of the status quo, and in 1905 some employers financed workers' organisations and even strikes to use them as a battering ram against the intransigent regime. Some of them also wanted to see at least some better-educated workers who might become as 'civilised', pliable and productive as those in Britain. The norm, however, was for exploitation of labour to be particularly intense.

THE EMERGENCE OF THE INTELLIGENTSIA

It was on the field of battle laid out by the forces of tradition, feudalism and backwardness in their slow-burning, century-long confrontation with rationalism, capitalism and industrialisation that Russia's cultural life also grew and developed. Even those parts of it considering themselves above or outside politics were affected, particularly in crisis years such as 1905. This environment provided appropriate conditions for the two most important features of Russian high culture at this time: first, the growth and development of a unique social group, the intelligentsia, and, secondly, the unprecedented wide-ranging cultural dynamism and creativity that Russia showed during the period from 1900 onwards, which continued inside and outside Russia after 1917. Almost all the political ideals and principles found across the whole spectrum of revolutionary life can be seen to have incubated in this period and many of the leading figures, on all sides, matured intellectually at this time, as a closer examination of each of the two phenomena will show.

If the general question of the role of the intellectual in politics is a disputed one then that of the specific nature of the Russian intelligentsia is especially fiercely argued. Its members have been idealised for their heroic qualities by subsequent revolutionaries and radicals, excoriated by conservatives as purveyors of the pollution of rationalism and upbraided by liberals as irresponsible and immature juveniles whose ill-thought-out radicalism upset the calculations of the moderate and sensible advocates of controlled change. For Dostoevsky they were 'Devils'; for Solzhenitsyn they were the forerunners of all twentieth-century terrorist and revolutionary groups; for contemporary Western scholars they are forerunners of student radicals of the 1960s and 1970s who, allegedly, engaged in political demonstrations and related activities because they had been spoiled and egocentric children. Even some Soviet scholars have begun to reinterpret some of them in a similarly unfavourable light, defending Dostoevsky's view of them, for example, on the grounds that at the time he was writing the radical movement was composed of petty-bourgeois intellectuals comparable to the 'infantile' leftists' denounced by Lenin in 1918.[29] There are very few points of agreement. One tends to be that the intelligentsia is undefinable, a second that, for all its value as an example of subsequent goods or evils, it is unique. Both of these assertions need to be carefully qualified.

Despite its small size, the breadth and variety of the intelligentsia makes the problem of definition particularly difficult. To define it sociologically as the educated class, as the graduates of higher education, or as the class of mental labourers is far too wide. Such definitions could include tsars, aristocrats, army officers, government ministers, schoolteachers and clerks without discrimination. It would also exclude the small number of members of the intelligentsia who lacked formal education and lived by manual labour. A rather more promising route towards a definition is to identify the intelligentsia by its cast of mind. An essential prerequisite for membership of the intelligentsia was the possession of a critical spirit, particularly in relation to the principles and practice of tsarism as it actually existed. On this basis one might define the intelligentsia as the verbally articulate opponents of tsarism. This definition has a number of advantages. In the first place it is sufficiently broad to include people with a wide variety of intellectual and political positions: Slavophile, liberal and socialist. It can also be stretched to include many creative intellectuals whose art was implicitly rather than explicitly critical of tsarism. This definition would also be sufficiently broad to include people without a formal education who come within its orbit. A second advantage is that it excludes certain types of people and certain kinds of activity. For instance, active opposition to the status quo through strikes and stealing firewood, let us say, is not in itself intelligentsia-type activity even though *intelligenty* (members of the intelligentsia) might engage in it. Verbal exhortation to this kind of act would, however, often fall within this definition, so that propaganda and agitation, whether carried on by a working-class trade unionist, a peasant or a university graduate, could sometimes be considered as an activity consistent with membership of the intelligentsia. This would enable one to extend the term to cover the more articulate but less educated leaders of the popular movement who formed a sort of people's intelligentsia. This group was to become very important in the formation of the post-revolutionary equivalent of the intelligentsia. This definition would also usefully exclude the majority of educated people who either actively supported the regime or were passive and apolitical. Thus the managerial class, artists, doctors, careerists in the state bureaucracy who were not critical of the regime would be excluded.

Among the prominent weaknesses of this definition is the fact that it conflicts with self-ascription. People who might be included within it were themselves critical of and distanced themselves from the intelligentsia. From very different outlooks, Dostoevsky, Chekhov and Lenin come immediately to mind in this respect. There would also be problems arising from accommodating the sometimes protean development of Russian *intelligenty* so that a man like Peter Struve, a vigorous Marxist in the 1890s, an author of the Social-Democratic party programme, who became a monarchist and an imperialist by 1908, would appear to be within the definition at one time but outside it at another. In addition, the key terms within the definition – 'verbally articulate' and 'tsarism' – are themselves open to diverse definitions and value judgements. At what stage is one 'articulate' as opposed to 'incoherent'? Is criticism of certain aspects of Orthodoxy, for instance its attitude to divorce, equivalent to criticising 'tsarism'? Thus, a wide variety of grey areas are left, as is the case with all the other definitions that have been proposed. Despite this, the present definition does point to certain key characteristics the others omit and cuts the area of application down to avoid the confusion that follows from attempts at 'objective' definitions of the intelligentsia based on their occupation (as mental labourers) or educational level (higher-education graduates). Such approaches can result in the lumping together of disparate groups such as secretaries and conductors of orchestras who would appear to have little in common other than the fact that they are not manual labourers. In this way it illuminates contemporary usage of the term in tsarist Russia.[30]

With regard to the question of the intelligentsia's uniqueness there is a certain amount of truth in the view that in the late nineteenth century it was unique, even though comparable, but not identical, groups have become more frequent in the twentieth century. The essential characteristics of the intelligentsia identified above, its oppositional outlook, its high degree of political or artistic awareness and frequently, though sometimes intermittently, its commitment to social change, arise from the unique circumstances of Russia. Tsarism was a distinctive and as yet imperfectly analysed social formation. In part, and this is very much reflected in the make-up of the intelligentsia, tsarist Russia was analagous to an underdeveloped country and has some claim to being the first country that could be so described. It was one of the first nations to become conscious of the growing gap between its own wealth and power and that of the rapidly industrialising societies further west. It was the problem posed by this increasing awareness that dominated the minds of the intelligentsia, left and right, and their function in society was, among other things, to bring out the implications of this situation. Much of the discourse of the intelligentsia, notably the Slavophile–Westerner debate discussed below, was underpinned by this question.[31] Clearly one cannot push this analogy too far in that tsarist Russia had certain features not normally associated with an underdeveloped nation, notably a strong and independent state, a long-standing status as a great power and, important in the area of concern to the present study, a mature élite culture in the European tradition. None the less, the Russian intelligentsia has numerous distant relatives in the twentieth century among the conservative, liberal and radical intellectuals of Third World countries, particularly in those such as Argentina, Brazil and the Middle East which, like nineteenth-century Russia, have a high cultural level and are developing relatively rapidly. Like their Russian predecessors, Third World intellectuals show the same range of responses from the reassertion of traditional values against the import of foreign ways of life – shown most vividly today among Islamic intellectuals who bear more than a passing resemblance to Slavophiles in this respect – through to revolutionary socialism, which, in its predominant Marxist–Leninist form, traces its descent directly from part of the Russian intelligentsia. Thus, the Russian intelligentsia's uniqueness has to be seen against this background.

Since the intelligentsia itself was a product of the peculiarities of tsarism and its position in the European political and economic system, and since it exists at the intersection of important social, economic and cultural forces, it is no surprise that its development bore a close relationship to the continuing interaction of those forces. Even a cursory survey of the origin of the intelligentsia and its development up to the end of the nineteenth century illustrates the importance of these fundamental features of its existence.

There is no unanimity about precisely when the intelligentsia, as understood in the present study, could be said to have come into existence as a separate group. Its precursors can be found at least as early as the end of the eighteenth century. One of the most notable founders of the intelligentsia way of thinking was Alexander Radishchev (1749–1802) who, in 1792, published a description of *A Journey from St Petersburg to Moscow* which, in a dignified and restrained but none the less powerful fashion, portrayed the suffering and hardship of the serfs he met on his way. The government, its nervousness and vigilance heightened by the revolution taking place in France at that time, reacted strongly to the criticism, attempted to suppress the book completely and had Radishchev imprisoned. The Russian state was already proving itself incapable of tolerating anyone who illuminated the dark areas of Russian reality. It was not, however, able to control the spirit behind Radishchev's act. In the introduction the author explained that he could not be happy when so many of his fellow men were suffering. This was the first important expression of the moral impulse motivating the growing number of so-called 'repentant nobleman' who gradually formed the core of the emerging intelligentsia. His comment could apply to many privileged people in the world today who are equally sensitive to the plight of the impoverished.

The flowering of Russian literature that took place in the first half of the nineteenth century was marked by this impulse and, not infrequently, showed a sometimes subtle fusing of political as well as literary concerns. The lyric poet Aleksandr Pushkin (1799–1837) was deemed a sufficient threat to Russia's stability to be carefully supervised by Tsar Nicholas I himself and, when that failed to intimidate him, his death in a duel was engineered by his enemies with possible government connivance. Like many artists of the Romantic era, from Wordsworth to Beethoven, political concerns in the form of an awakening liberal-democratic nationalism formed an important matrix for Pushkin's writing. Even a writer as apparently unpolitical as Ivan Turgenev (1818–83) fell foul of the authorities in an affair very reminiscent of that involving Radischev. In the form of simple descriptive episodes, published under the title *Sketches from a Hunter's Notebook*, Turgenev committed the unpardonable offence of portraying the serfs as human beings and, what is more, as people with a rich culture and world of their own. Its publication in 1852, shortly after revolutions had rocked central and western Europe and the Tsar had acquired notoriety as the hangman of Europe, ensured that they would attract official disapproval and Turgenev, too, was imprisoned for a time and afterwards spent much of his life abroad. The situation had, however, changed since Radishchev's time. In place of a few individual conscience-stricken noblemen, a wider (though still, of course, very small) group of educated people had come together in intellectual salons and circles (*kruzhki*). These groups discussed largely philosophical topics and literary criticism and became vehicles for veiled discussion of political issues. Thus, by the mid-century the encoding of political questions in 'Aesopian' language had become a widespread convention through which official disapproval and censorship could be partially circumvented. The pre-eminent performer at these *kruzhki* was Vissarion Belinsky (1810–48) whose intense and committed essays became a source of inspiration for a variety of Russian liberals and radicals in subsequent generations. In addition, more overtly political groups began to appear. The best known is the Petrashevsky circle to which the young Fyodor Dostoevsky belonged. In essence, it was little more than a clandestine study group that discussed French socialist ideas and developed grandiose dreams of a Utopian future for Russia. However, the government was not prepared to tolerate even this in the current climate and in 1849 it was broken up and some of its members sentenced to death. Dostoevsky was reprieved only at the very last minute with the firing squad assembled and the bandage ready to cover his eyes.

In addition to this Utopianism of the left, a kind of conservative Utopianism, focused around a romantic myth of the unity of throne and people, was also taking shape. Though its hierarchical and paternalist assumptions were welcome to the government its vision of an idealised past that had been undermined by Peter the Great's policy of 'Westernisation from above' led them to criticise certain aspects of existing tsarism in the name of its supposedly superior pre-Petrine form. In this way, some of this group could be seen to fall within our definition of the intelligentsia. They also show a fusion of culture and politics. Not only did they see the Orthodox church as the focus of national Russian identity, their ideas also began to be reflected in literature, criticism and philosophical and religious essays. Perhaps the most striking embodiment of their outlook came in the form of a flowering of Russian orchestral music and operas glorifying the majesty of Russia's past. Here conservative Utopianism began to shade into the officially sponsored principles of autocracy, Orthodoxy and nationality. However, to see these conservative, nationalist Utopians as merely the embodiment of hegemonic political ideas would be to oversimplify their position.

By the middle of the nineteenth century, a small but diverse intelligentsia was coming into existence. Its maturity was heralded by the wide-ranging debate between its radical and conservative wings, conventionally referred to as 'Westerners' and 'Slavophiles' respectively. In the broadest terms, the Westerners wanted to adopt what they saw as basic features of the western European way of life, notably the intellectual values of the Enlightenment and the economic and material advances of the Industrial Revolution. The Slavophiles, on the other hand, wanted to preserve as much of Russia's specific tradition and culture as possible from the onslaught of imported ideas and practices (among which some of them included the modernising aspirations of tsarism itself), which, they thought, would disturb Russia's stability and tranquillity. This is not, however, the place to go into a detailed examination of the issues separating them. This has been done elsewhere.[32] Some general comments are, however, necessary since certain important features of the debate can be traced even in contemporary Russian and Soviet thought. In the first place, the two schools are not completely distinct in that there are few, if any, individuals who could be considered pure adherents of either school. This is particularly true of the so-called 'Westerners', whose position is especially complex in that there is no clearly defined set of 'Western' values and practises which they were, allegedly, devoted to introducing in Russia. In addition, they were themselves the product of the Russian culture that they sought to modify and embodied some of its characteristics. As a result, in the eyes of western Europeans, even 'Westerners' appeared to have many peculiarities derived from their Russian background. Personalities as diverse as Herzen and Trotsky show this clearly. Perhaps the most distinctive principle shared by Westerners and Slavophiles was an idealised view of the 'people', usually meaning the serfs or peasantry but later also applied to the urban working class, echoes of this usage surviving even to the present. It is, of course, no surprise that each wing of the intelligentsia admired diametrically opposed characteristics that each claimed to detect in the peasantry. For the Slavophiles, it was imperviousness to reason, loyalty to the tsar, acceptance of the social order and apparent closeness to the church that were admired. For most Westerners, it was peasant rebelliousness, which they hoped to harness into a force capable of liberating Russia from its antiquated social and political institutions, that commended itself. Even where they admired the same supposed features of the peasant outlook, notably the collectivist mentality exemplified in the ancient institution of the commune (*mir*), they did so for incompatible reasons. The Slavophiles admired it because they liked to think of Russia as something akin to a vast family rather than as a society divided according to class, and they saw the commune as an important link in this social cohesion. For the Westerners, of whom one of the first to propose the idea in this form was Alexander Herzen (1812–70), the commune appeared to be the germ of a future collectivist society in which property would be held in common. Both sides, however, were agreed that it was a welcome bulwark against the dreaded Western disease of individualism. They also shared some other significant principles. For instance, though Westerners admired foreign ideas they were by no means uncritical of existing west European societies. Slavophiles and Westerners were thus able to unite in criticising industrialism, capitalism and the middle class. They found common ground in abominating bourgeois values, especially vulgar materialism, preoccupation with money making and the hypocrisy of liberalism. Both sides also, given the prevailing conditions in Russia, expressed their ideas in works of fiction, literary criticism and philosophical and religious tracts rather than in direct political language. Thus for both sides culture and politics were intertwined at the intellectual and practical levels. As a result a certain potential for dialogue and synthesis was built in to the argument, and indeed as the century progressed it became increasingly difficult to find unadulterated pure examples of one school or the other. One needs to look no further than the two towering figures of late nineteenth-century Russian culture, Fyodor Dostoevsky (1821–81) and Lev Tolstoy (1828–1910), who represent complex blends of principles from both schools.

Two other general points about the dispute should also be borne in mind. Most important, the conventional labels tend to disguise the fact that the decisive differences between them lay not solely in their respective attitudes to Russia's past and future and to Europe in the present, but to the underlying philosophies of the two groups. The Slavophiles based their views on philosophical idealism, usually connected with Orthodox Christianity, while the Westerners tended to be materialist in their philosophical position and based their outlook on rationalism, positivism and atheism. Once again, we may note the intense fusion of culture and politics these positions represent. In the second place, the Slavophiles cannot be equated simply with conservatives in the most frequently used sense, that is upholders of the status quo, since their ideal was not directly to existing tsarism but to an historical myth of tsarism, a kind of medieval golden age deemed to have existed before the time of Peter the Great. Whatever the accuracy of this vision it did mean that their loyalty was not necessarily to existing tsarist institutions since they could be seen to have been polluted to some extent as a result of reforms that had taken place since the late seventeenth century.

From this core debate, which has been repeated in different forms in other countries in the process of beginning to learn from and suffer the impact of European and industrial capitalism, a wider intelligentsia came into being, embracing the arts, music, philosophy, literature, science and politics. While the old matrix of Slavophile and Westerner tendencies remained, it was overlain with other categories of debate – conservative, liberal, radical and so on – that do not coincide exactly with the older divisions. By the turn of the century, the beginning of our period proper, the intelligentsia had become more extensive, as a result of the educational and other changes in tsarist society mentioned above, and more mature and complex in its outlook. The best way to appreciate these changes is to turn to an examination of the intelligentsia in the last decade and a half of tsarism when it enjoyed one of its most creative and productive periods.

CULTURAL DYNAMISM IN EARLY TWENTIETH-CENTURY RUSSIA

No previous period in Russian cultural history can compare with the last decade and a half before World War One in terms of range and breadth of achievement. Areas in which Russia had already been strong for a half century or more – science, political thought, literature and music being the most notable – continued to flourish on a wider basis than ever. In addition significant achievements were being recorded in quite new areas. Perhaps the most remarkable of these was painting where a whole generation of influential artists were embarking on their careers at this time. Chagall and Kandinsky are the best known but a wide range of immensely talented people – Tatlin, Malevich, Larionov, Goncharova, Naum Gabo and others – were beginning to make their mark. Russian ballet became a world standard under the guidance of Sergei Diaghilev, who was the centre of a gifted group of dancers, designers and choreographers. Bigger audiences and greater material facilities – theatres, presses, journals and so on – were at the disposal of the expanding creative intelligentsia. A wider range of schools in all fields began to flourish to create an unprecedented degree of intellectual pluralism. In addition, links between high culture and popular culture, which became of particular significance after 1917, were strengthened in this period.

While this flowering might be said to lack any individual figures of the highest stature, Tolstoy's survival until 1910 only serving to underline his unchallenged pre-eminence to which none of the younger intellectuals could even aspire, the period was notable for the unprecedented range of intellectual forms that it encompassed and for the maturity, variety and richness of the fundamental principles on which intellectual discourse was based. Both of these characteristics are deserving of a little attention.

The most cursory glance is sufficient to illustrate the range of forms. While one of Russia's traditional areas of excellence, literature, continued to be a major driving force of this renaissance, there was an explosion of talent in a wide variety of areas. Visual arts, philosophy, political ideas and religion showed particularly striking development. Prior to 1900 Russia had been little noted for its visual arts. Medieval traditions of icon painting and architecture had died out long before and, especially since Peter the Great, it had become normal for major state and aristocratic projects, including buildings, monuments and laying out of parks, to be supervised by foreign experts. St Basil's, the buildings and gardens of the Imperial summer palace at Tsarskoe Selo, the Bronze Horseman, were all the work of west Europeans. Official portrait painting was also the province of foreigners.[33] Even as Russians began to take over some of these skills they were, by and large, pupils and imitators of foreign taste rather than adaptors and innovators. It is all the more surprising then that in these years distinctive and more independent talents should emerge. Conventionally, the secession from the Academy in 1870 by a group of artists who came to be known as 'The Wanderers' (*Peredvizhniki*) because they held exhibitions in a wide variety of venues is seen as the starting point of this process. Rebelling against the canons of official taste, they began to bring new life and new themes into their painting. Like many creative artists of their day their work showed a subtle interweaving of themes – Slavophilism, Westernism and populism – rather than strict adherence to any one of them. Many of them showed a deep love of the Russian countryside and celebrated its inspirational qualities in affectionate landscapes capturing a multitude of its moods and aspects. An interest in Russia's past, a theme that was especially strong at the turn of the century, brought out their gentle nationalism in a series of re-creations of historical events and legends. The arrival of the Slavs on the Dnepr, medieval warriors (*bogatyri*), saints and tsars, including Peter the Great, were the subjects of some of the finest paintings of the period. Russia's medieval architectural heritage was rediscovered and depicted against its natural background. While rarely overtly political, some of the works of this school and its descendants did entail implicit judgements about Russian society. This is exemplified in the career of Il'ia Repin (1844–1930), one of the original Wanderers. From the 1870s he turned his attention to painting scenes from the lives of the ordinary people. Poverty and destitution were displayed in his paintings. One of them, *A Religious Procession in Kursk Guberniia* (1883), includes cripples and beggars prominently portrayed. His *The Boat-Haulers* (*Burliaki*) of 1873 presented the reputed dregs of Russian society, those who were employed almost as animals to use their brute strength to haul barges up the Volga. In the revolutionary years of the early twentieth century Repin did turn his attention back to the very élite of Russian society, the State Council, a body that drew together the leading members of the royal family, the richest nobles and the most powerful ministers including Pobedonostsev and Witte, under the chairmanship of Tsar Nicholas II himself. When the painting was first shown it caused no little surprise. Repin had a reputation for being able to produce extremely vibrant, action-filled canvasses, such as *The Zaporozhets Cossacks*, but the painting of the State Council seemed vacuous and limp. Then it began to dawn on the critics that this was the genius of the painting, Repin had simply drawn what he had seen. It was, in its way a revolutionary painting.

While, in the field of themes, Wanderers such as Repin could be thought of as mildly revolutionary, in aesthetics they were conservative, remaining resolutely realistic. By the turn of the century, however, the domination of realism in the visual arts was beginning to break down. Mikhail Vrubel's brilliant and underestimated series of paintings on the theme of the Demon penetrated a subconscious world of anxieties, fear, hope and beauty presented usually in an imagined landscape of misty mountain peaks and gloomy valleys recalling dreams and nightmares rather than external reality. Everywhere the veil of 'the real' was being lifted a little to show what was underneath. This could be seen in a variety of artists such as Alexander Benois (1870–1960) who produced a series of semi-caricatures based on Russia at the time of Peter the Great, Dobuzhinsky (1875–1957) who turned his beloved St Petersburg into a timeless, almost fairytale, city and Nikolai Rerich (1874–1947) and Bilibin (1876–1942) who produced historical fantasies often in the style of illustrations to children's books. They did not always use their talents in an innocuous way. Bilibin was briefly imprisoned in 1906 for producing what looked from its background and framing as though it was going to be a picture of the Tsar, but putting an ass in the centre instead of the august royal personage.

While these were the established masters of Russian painting, a younger generation, destined to become much better known and to achieve prominence partly through the revolution, was also growing up. Many of them, such as Chagall (1887–1984) retained that balance between realism and, in his case, whimsical imagination throughout their careers, while others, notably Kandinsky (1866–1944), were in the forefront of purely abstract painting from very early on. His career, among others, is a pointer to the fact that Russian painting had developed to such an extent in such a short time that it could no longer be said to be derived from foreign models. Indeed, for the first time the reverse was coming true and Russian art became an innovative force in European art, a feature that, although it became more obvious after 1917, had already begun before World War One.[34]

Intimately linked with this expansion into new forms of intellectual endeavour was a burgeoning of the range of Russian intellectual discourse through the multiplication of schools, their increasing complexity and more subtle interaction with each other. While Russian intellectual life had never been uniform, the impression given by this period is that of a much broader intellectual atmosphere, a pluralism that had not been achieved before on such a wide scale and has not been repeated since. Conflict between and within schools of thought was very extensive. Broad categories of conservative, liberal and radical, each of them by this time containing significant elements of both Slavophilism and Westernism, can be distinguished in all fields. Indeed, these political categories are perhaps the most coherent ones that can be used at this time even in areas apparently distant from politics, because one effect of the 1905 revolution and its aftermath was to present the political issue in such an acute form that it was almost impossible to ignore it. Some of the less overtly political figures in the intelligentsia were drawn in. Such things as a focusing on the virtues of Japanese culture while the Russo–Japanese war was at its height, as the symbolist journal *The Scales* (*Vesy*) did in its October–November issue of 1904, could only be seen as a political gesture. The poet Aleksandr Blok, while certainly a populist in his writings, had had little contact with the ordinary inhabitants of St Petersburg before 1905 and was caught up in a wave of political euphoria which even led him, on one famous occasion, to carry a red flag in a demonstration. The censure this act drew from his protector Briusov, who upbraided him for demeaning the vocation of the poet by taking to the street, was itself an implicitly conservative act. Naturally enough, many intellectuals threw themselves whole-heartedly into the political struggle at that time, which is no surprise since the *raison d'être* of the intelligentsia was opposition to despotism and assistance to the downtrodden.

An understanding of the complexity of intellectual life at this time is particularly important for an appreciation of post-revolutionary developments in that the wide range of groupings that had matured by then became the basic foundation of almost all the intellectual positions taken up in the arguments immediately after 1917. One can even see links between the principles argued about before 1917 and those present in contemporary Russian intellectual life as exemplified by different groups among dissident intellectuals. Partial freezing of Russian development at this level, since this was the last phase of its more or less free, spontaneous, 'natural' growth, makes it all the more vital to appreciate its fundamental features.

In terms of innovation much of the running was made by a group that could loosely be described as symbolists. In painting and literature they began to adapt and adopt the principles of French symbolism. Tending towards the esoteric and the mystical, they inhabited an aesthetic world that many of them considered to be self-contained, a world devoted to art for art's sake. They gathered in small salons that exuded a distinctively Olympian atmosphere. They formed groups and factions revolving around publishing ventures and journals, of which the most significant was *World of Art* (*Mir iskusstva*), which was published from 1899 to 1904. While intellectual journals were nothing new in Russia, *World of Art* was unique in its concentration on fine art and literature to the apparent exclusion of vulgar topics such as politics. The impossibility of remaining oblivious to such issues, in a situation such as that in which Russia found itself during the years of *World of Art*'s existence, was one of the reasons contributing to the journal's decline. It broke up and some of its former contributors moved into areas that were more prepared to enter into dialogue with the 'problems of the day', as they tended to be called. None the less, they tended to remain a small and isolated group that existed on the Bohemian fringe of the monied classes, attracting substantial patronage and allowing its more successful members to live the high life of the metropolitan cities even though the most 'respectable' elements of élite society held them at arms length. Circulation of their journal and its successors remained low, as did the print runs of most of their publications: *Vesy* had 845 subscribers, *Zolotoe runo* (*Golden Fleece*) 934 in 1906. Their impact on the intelligentsia proper was slight though their very existence might be construed as an early sign of growing *embourgeoisement* in the intelligentsia. One could also question their credentials for being considered part of the intelligentsia, in that one might have to force them into the category of 'articulate opponents of tsarism', since

Nicholas II was one of the patrons of *World of Art*. The fact that he ceased to make financial contributions, as a result of which the journal folded in 1904, might, however, put them into our classification after all.

Despite their undoubted élitism, it would be quite wrong to see the symbolists as an interesting but ultimately unproductive byway in Russia's intellectual development. Though leaders of the group were happy to style themselves as decadents and take on a fashionable *fin-de-siècle* millenarianism and to see themselves as being self-consciously isolated from 'society', their pretensions in this direction should not delude us into accepting them at face value. The revolutionary year of 1905 found many of them bringing their political attitudes out into the open, almost always in terms of some kind of appeal for reform of the status quo. Many of the leading *World of Art* contributors produced cartoons and satires on the regime. One of the most conservative decadents, V. V. Rozanov (1856–1919), was moved to write about the potential for a kind of happy anarchism and child-like innocence which 1905 revealed in a book called *When Authority Went Away (Kogda nachal'stvo ushlo)*, which compared the experience to that of the mischievous behaviour of a child in the absence of a strict parent.[35] A second reason for taking them seriously is that their aesthetic influence over subsequent generations and schools was very extensive. Arguably, even those who reacted against them owed no little debt to them for putting Russia much more firmly on the European artistic map, particularly in painting. Also they opened the door to the break with realism that many subsequent groups took advantage of. Thus their influence spread in numerous ways. On the one hand, a talented younger generation of symbolists, led by Aleksandr Blok (1880–1921) and Andrei Belyi (1880–1934), retained many of the aesthetic principles of the movement while fusing them with a form of populism that had social and artistic dimensions, while on the other, breakaway groups opposed to the earlier symbolists formed themselves into the schools of futurism and its successors (some of which fed directly into post-revolutionary art) but retained numerous features inherited from the older generation.[36]

While the symbolist avant-garde and its successors have attracted the bulk of Western scholarly interest in recent years, the much larger school of realist writers has been somewhat looked down on.[37] The differentiation of interest between west and east cannot be explained in exclusively aesthetic terms nor solely by official control of scholarship in the Sovet Union. While certainly less interesting from the point of view of artistic innovation and aesthetic originality, from the point of view of intellectual history the realists (again a rather imprecise general term) have to be given full weight. Their publications were produced in tens of thousands where those of the symbolists were produced in hundreds. The most popular intellectual journals of the day published realist rather than avant-garde works. Many sections of the intelligentsia, from the liberal professionals of the Kadet movement such as Miliukov to the professional revolutionaries such as Lenin, who disagreed about so much else, shared a deep dislike of what they saw as the self-indulgence, irrelevance, élitism and gross insensitivity to suffering of the avant-garde. In their view, this was no time for frivolous, aesthetic escapism. While their judgements in this were not untouched by philistinism, their view was shared by the vast majority of the intelligentsia. After all, the great Russian writers of the nineteenth century were realists, and the greatest of all, Tolstoy, was still around to thunder out denunciations of the avant-garde for their lack of moral seriousness. The most popular of the younger writers, Maksim Gorky (1868–1936), was realist in aesthetics and political, specifically socialist, in outlook. His serialised novels were eagerly anticipated month by month by a wide variety of intelligentsia readers and by some working-class ones. It is impossible to escape the conclusion that the realist school was the dominant one of the intellectual life of Russia throughout this period, a fact having considerable bearing on its eventually dominating position in the post-revolutionary intellectual world.

It would be an oversimplification to see Russian intellectual life being divided into symbolist and realist camps. While this had a degree of truth in 1900, subsequent developments blurred the issue. In the forefront of these was the growth of the so-called new religious consciousness which had an impact on both groups. It took a variety of forms and was composed of a number of sources. Its main manifestations were in the form of vague, intuitive mysticism, clearly related to the symbolist principles of the limits of reason in the face of truth and the need to go beyond it by means of the unconscious into the realm of the inexpressible. In this sense 'religion' tended to mean the acknowledgement of the existence of a largely unknown higher reality. Links were made with eastern religions as much as with Christianity and it led to the emergence of highly unconventional mystics such as Gurdjieff and P. D. Ouspensky, who enjoyed a certain vogue among the Russian emigration in Paris after the revolution. The new religious consciousness also had more conventional aspects, opening up for the first time a dialogue between parts of the intelligentsia and parts of the Russian Orthodox church in the St Petersburg Religious and Philosophical Society, presided over by the leading symbolists Dmitri Merezhkovsky (1866–1941) and Zinaida Gippius (1869–1945), the twin gatekeepers of the new literary orthodoxy. Some members of the intelligentsia began to fuse Marxist principles of social organisation with philosophical idealism and subjectivism, while others went over from socialism to liberalism as a result of this process. As a result a fascinating range of combinations of socialist, liberal and Christian ideas can be found among prominent figures of the intelligentsia at this time such as Sergei Bulgakov (1871–1944), Nicholas Berdiaev (1874–1948) and Peter Struve (1870–1944). The new principles penetrated even further into the realist camp, particularly after the 1905 revolution, when leading realist and social democrats, such as Gorky and Anatoly Lunacharsky (1875–1933), who later became Soviet Minister for Education and as such became an important arbiter of post-revolutionary intellectual life, toyed with religious philosophy. Lunacharsky argued that socialism should be understood as the last, all-embracing, great religion, bringing together all that was good in previous human culture and liberating man from humiliating dependence on a mythical other world. Gorky was also attracted to religion as metaphor and as emotional and spiritual cement for the socialist endeavour. This tendency, known as God-building, met up with the intelligentsia mysticism, known as God-seeking, but was very distinct from it, retaining a more rational and positivist foundation than that of the God-seekers.

    The best encapsulation of the intricacies and diversity of intellectual life as it was affected by these developments came in the furore that broke out, against the authors' expectations, around a volume of essays entitled *Landmarks* (*Vekhi*), which was published in 1909. Among the contributors were Bulgakov, Berdiaev and Struve. Though far from united in their own outlooks, the *Vekhi* group, if such it can be called, have become a symbol of reaction, timidity and treachery from within the intelligentsia. The book was assailed in this vein from all sides. Liberals, radicals, conservatives, all weighed in to denounce it for being either too conservative or too radical. Journals, newspapers and lecture halls were filled with discussion and debate about the volume. Of the hundreds of reviews and articles about it, only a handful show even a cautious welcome for its basic assertion that the intelligentsia had overemphasised the life of society and the laws on which society was thought to be governed and had underemphasised personal life, creativity and individual action towards overcoming Russia's backwardness. The rather delicate and subtle principles of most of its contributors were easy to caricature, and their viewpoint was drowned in a welter of uncomprehending denunciation, not to mention the equally uncomprehending support it received from a few unwanted admirers such as the notorious anti-Semite Archbishop Antony Volynsky. What both he and the critics of *Vekhi* shared was an assumption that the volume marked an important step in intelligentsia development away from revolution and towards conservatism and even reaction. While the later career of some of its contributors, notably Struve, partly bears this out, other contributors, notably Bulgakov, Berdiaev and the volume's editor Mikhail Gershenzon (1869–1925), remained vigorous opponents of tsarism and even proponents of what they saw as a more profound revolution of consciousness as an important element of any potentially successful revolutionary process. Arguably, the main weakness that they identified in mainstream intellectual assumptions in Russia about social and political change – namely the lack of attention to the subjective dimension, the question of consciousness and ultimately, though they did not use the term, cultural revolution – turned out to be prophetic as this dimension was found to be more intractable for the revolutionaries than institutional and social revolution. Be that as it may, the debate itself did show up some of the main features of intelligentsia life, including its continued hostility to the status quo, deep-rooted populism and tenacious positivism, as well as its flirting with new ideas. The result was an unusually wide diversity of principles though the debate made it pretty clear that, if this was a potential turning-point of the kind the intelligentsia had encountered before, around 1860 and 1890, for instance with the adoption of positivism and Marxism respectively, then the new principles of subjectivism and idealism had a long way to go. The debate showed also a kind of generation gap in that within the major groupings of liberalism and radicalism a positivist old guard, led by Miliukov among liberals and Plekhanov and Lenin among the Marxists, much as they disliked each other, at least shared a hostility to all attempts to undermine what they saw as the heroic principles of scientific rationalism on which Russia's revolutionary tradition had been built since the 1860s. Both were contemptuous of the younger generation (the term being used here in the intellectual and not necessarily the physical sense) to the extent that Struve, not without justification, wrote a powerful article in which he denounced the intelligentsia for its conservatism and lack of openness to new ideas.[38]

The *Vekhi* debate, as is the way with such phenomena, was inconclusive in the short term and did little to change the main features of the situation that it had illuminated so well. The intelligentsia remained as it had been, the debate faded and by the second anniversary of the publication of *Vekhi* attention had become focused elsewhere. From 1911 onwards a return to instability within Russia and in the international system made directly political issues more prominent once again. The lengthening shadow of European war and, eventually, the experience of war, naturally affected members of the intelligentsia. Even so, despite practical difficulties, the process of creativity and innovation continued, though at a reduced tempo.

One area of considerable significance to the evolution of post-revolutionary intellectual life did develop in these years. Russian painting continued its rapid differentiation into schools and people who took a leading role in the 1920s began to emerge into the forefront of innovation at this time. In particular, the avant-garde attracted attention. The centrepiece of it was futurism – which, of course, also affected other arts – and on the eve of the war Russia had a school which, as with the symbolists, could stand comparison with its counterparts in the rest of Europe. The avant-garde took its place among all the other groups and schools in the increasing diversity of Russian intellectual, artistic and spiritual life. Even though the avant-garde artists in particular tended to inhabit a small, introverted and self-contained world, they are of importance not only on account of their creative dynamism but also because of the weight they carried in the immediate post-revolutionary years when, under the protection of the Ministry of Education, avant-garde artists attempted to make their works accessible to all on a grand scale. The divisions between them, which were endemic from the origin of the movement, became battles for control of Soviet art. The roots of the bitter faction fights in many artistic fields in the 1920s, as rival groups tried to obtain access to the only real patron, the state, can be traced back to the pre-revolutionary years. Thus, although before 1917 the avant-garde remained ultra-élitist, afterwards it came to occupy a central position in Russian cultural politics.

But avant-garde and élite culture did not have a monopoly on creativity at this time. Even though detailed studies of education and popular culture in this period are few and far between, there are numerous indications that there was a deep, unslaked thirst for knowledge in early twentieth-century Russia, though the number of people who shared it is open to question.[39] Some light is thrown on the topic by an extensive, though unfortunately unsystematic and even contradictory survey written by L. M. Kleinbort. Originally intended as a series of articles in one of the social-democratic 'thick' journals (see pp. 35–6), Kleinbort's study grew into a two-volume history devoted mainly to worker education between 1905 and 1916 but offering some evidence of the situation prior to that.[40] There was, he said, a great thirst among the workers for 'facts, facts, facts'.[41] According to the information he presents, this had been confined to a tiny minority in the 1890s but had developed rapidly after 1905 and reached a peak around 1912. In the 1890s, he says, distrust of workers' newspapers and immersion in the gutter press were characteristic of most of the working class.[42] There were some exceptions. A barber, of a somewhat philosophical turn of mind is quoted as asking, not surprisingly given his profession, 'Do we have heads on our shoulders just to put our hats on?'[43] Kleinbort suggests that at this time it was the workers in more established factories who enjoyed a high level of culture, pointing to the Morozov factory in Tver' as an example. There the workers had their own library and theatre, although the younger ones were more interested in getting drunk than reading.[44] Since the Morozovs were well known as liberal and paternalistic employers this factory may well have been an exception. Kleinbort goes on to argue that the period after 1900 was one of great growth for the independent working-class movement in all respects, the field of worker education sharing in this development particularly after 1905. In Kiev in 1912, for instance, of 12,300 people who attended lectures organised by the Society for the Diffusion of Education among the People, 9656 were workers. In St Petersburg a similar society had 1000 members and a library of 1000–2000 books.[45] There were seven other, smaller societies of this kind in the city.[46] Eighteen to twenty-three year olds were the most prominent age group among the members, with very few over forty taking part.[47] Kleinbort's scattered evidence suggests the predominant taste among readers in these societies was for fiction rather than works of what he calls a 'serious' kind. 'Even among metalworkers 80% of books issued were fiction.'[48] Most surveys showed Tolstoy and Gorky to have been overwhelmingly the most popular with Turgenev, Chekhov, and Dostoevsky also frequently read.[49] After fiction, political economy and natural science were favourite topics. Party newspapers built up a regular readership in these societies.[50] As well as libraries these organisations organised excursions and an important function was to celebrate the anniversary of a notable thinker or writer with an 'evening' or 'morning' devoted to his ideas. 'All the educational societies', says Kleinbort, 'devoted evenings and mornings to Karl Marx.'[51] The tiniest infringement of the rules could, he says, bring about the closure of such societies by the authorities.[52] A final piece of evidence presented by the author serves as a warning not to overestimate the penetration of working-class circles achieved by such organisations. In one region of St Petersburg the library of the Metalworkers' Union (a union noted for its militancy and relatively highly conscious membership) was used by only 160 out of 1000 members in a given year and only 732 books were issued.[53]

While the evidence presented by Kleinbort and others is unsatisfactory, particularly because it is unsystematic, it does all point in the same direction. A small core of the *narod*, more prominent in the cities than in the countryside, was becoming more aware of the outside world, and traditional ideas were, for these people, being replaced. The fact that fiction rather than political literature was more popular should not be allowed to hide from us, given the close links between fiction and politics in Russia, the fact that a higher level of social and political consciousness was being created. The fact that Tolstoy was the most widely read author, in town and countryside, shows this in that Tolstoy's writings comprise a blend of imagination, philosophy, history and politics that spoke precisely to the current situation in Russia. His influence among the *narod* was very great, not only among those devotees who formed Tolstoyan communities based on pacifism and opposition to the state, but among many who were less committed to his principles. Tolstoy was the moral teacher not only of a generation of privileged intellectuals but of a wide cross-section of the Russian community in a way that was not paralleled by any other writer, with the possible exception of Gorky whose works also appear to have been absorbed by the *narod*. Gorky, too, was a writer for whom politics and ideas were the essence of his work, fiction merely the form. It is interesting to note that Gorky himself came from a humble background and was very close to being a writer from among the *narod* himself. Throughout his life he encouraged working-class and peasant writers. The first signs of the existence of such a group were becoming visible in the pre-war period and Gorky himself was instrumental in the publication of works by some of them.[54]

It is relatively easy to identify and describe periods of cultural creativity such as that which Russia was undergoing in the early years of this century. It is much more difficult to provide an acceptable explanation for them. Types of explanation tend to revolve around two poles. On the one hand, the view that the key to understanding lies in the subjective mysteries of individual creative genius. On the other, intellectual creativity is seen as being heavily bound up in social processes rather than individual ones. Any attempt to explain the roots of any period of cultural flowering must take both dimensions into account. It would be as foolish to interpret art as being above society, as it would be to see intellectual life as being wholly determined by social forces and the individual being no more than the instrument by which those impersonal forces express themselves. This may seem obvious to us today, but in Russia at the time there was bitter argument around the two positions. It would take an exceptionally bold spirit to attempt any general explanation of cultural development equally applicable to all its occurrences from Athens and Egypt through the Renaissance to the present. Such was the nature of Russian intellectual life that such comprehensive explanations were, in fact, bandied about freely by mystical anarchists, liberals, Marxists and so on. The only feature these bold general theories, produced at the drop of a hat, shared with one another was that they tended to remain very unconvincing. Liberals, such as Gershenzon, saw the individual as the sole source of creativity, while Marxists, notably Plekhanov, saw individuals as the product of their environment to the extent that the historical role of the particular 'great men' we are familiar with would have been played by a substitute had they not existed. Attempts to stretch this view of the individual into the field of culture were particularly unsatisfactory.

Individual genius is the most obvious feature of intellectual creativity. Works of art, literature, philosophy and so on are produced by gifted individuals. The cult of the individual genius was, in fact, at one of its high points in late nineteenth-century Europe. Its central figure was Friedrich Nietzsche, whose unashamed espousal of the greater worth of the talented person over the apparently less talented was enormously influential over a wide range of philosophies from violent anarchists, through socialists to liberals, conservatives and, ultimately, fascists. The Nietzschean image of cultural life was that of lonely geniuses conversing with one another from the mountain tops while the herd remained, unenlightened and uncomprehending, in the valleys below, a prey to the 'weakening' influences of love and compassion, dispensed by Christians, socialists and women alike, which prevented them from scaling the heights. The ramifications of

Nietzsche's bleak vision and its effect on Russian thought at this time were extensive. Even social-democrats like Gorky and Lunacharsky were affected by it, at least to the extent that they believed the achievements of high culture were worth preserving and cultivating, sometimes at the expense of egalitarianism. Mystical anarchists such as Vyacheslav Ivanov (1866–1949), who were of a much different cast of mind politically, were heavily influenced by Nietzsche and wove his principles into their own cult of the unbridled ego. They were particularly impressed by his contempt for Christianity and feminity. Leading figures of the older generation of symbolists and decadents, such as Merezhkovksy and V. V. Rozanov, shared Nietzsche's evaluation of genius, indeed Merezhkovsky's best known work was an historical novel based on the life of Leonardo da Vinci as an example of the ideal.[55]

However, the most obvious factor is not necessarily also the most decisive. While the existence of talented people, and the long tradition of intellectual achievement in Russia including people of the calibre of Pushkin, Dostoevsky and Tolstoy, cannot be overlooked, the social structures defining the channels of that creativity – such as patronage, the nature of the audience, the level of technology, style, and the wider social and economic environment including the nature of the economic system and social and political institutions – also have to be given due weight. All of them impinge on the 'absolute' freedom of individual creativity, coinciding and interacting with economic and political upsurge. The underlying contradictions of tsarism, particularly its attempts to educate technical, managerial and administrative personnel to facilitate economic growth, were creating acute tensions that certainly helped to inspire intellectuals of all types. Looked at in this way, Russia's 'Silver Age', as it was called, reflects not only a crisis of values within a putatively 'self-contained' artistic world but also shows up the wider crisis of values going on in tsarist society as a whole. As has been pointed out already, the matrix of this wider crisis lies in the fundamental conflict of the period between the decaying values of tsarism and the developing values of a capitalist society. The struggle between the two gave an edge to intellectual life in these years.

In addition, it is particularly important to recall here that the expansion of education widened the social stratum receptive to ideas. The thinness and fragility of the traditional élite was forcing it to recruit outside the ranks of its most reliable members and to reach down into the lower strata of society, to men and women from families of minor functionaries, the increasingly important professions and what might be thought of as petty-bourgeois intelligentsia backgrounds. Many of these newly educated were dedicated to reform and revolution. They were increasingly recruited to the cause of 'modernising' Russia economically, politically and intellectually. They stood for the values of science 'almost synonymous with atheism for most of them), rationality, openness to the outside world, legal order and democratic, constitutional government, the very things the die-hards who dominated the decisions of government wanted to prevent. Despite differences in other respects, most members of the intelligentsia (according to the working definition in use here) and less committed intellectuals tended to side with the growing 'modern' values rather than the decaying 'traditional' ones. Rational education was ensuring the development of the latter despite the Canute-like efforts to stem the tide through such things as compulsory religious instruction. Social-democrats, liberals even decadents and symbolists, stood for change and reform. Even conservatives among creative intellectuals had little sympathy for the church and often, as men-tioned in the case of Rozanov, an ambiguous attitude to the regime, which was not cherished but had to be recognised as its protector. Indeed it was one of the supposedly less political and more conserva-tive intellectuals, Dmitri Merezhkovsky, who in 1907 best expressed the dimensions and root of the crisis of values and the intellectual task of the opponents of tsarism. Tsarism, he said, pretended to terrestrial and celestial power, to material and spiritual authority. It was a theocracy. As such, he concluded, it had to be combated in the intellectual and spiritual sphere as well as the material, political one.[56] This is exactly what the intellectuals of the time were largely engaged in, even though some of them would deny political signifi-cance to their actions.

A more tangible link between social and intellectual processes at this time is provided by considering the increased wealth of Russia as a result of her economic growth and the vastly expanding numbers of highly qualified men and women. Taken together these provided the material resources essential to support the cultural activities of the period. They provided the audience for artistic endeavours and the readership and contributors for the impressive and unique 'thick' journals which were produced in profusion. These journals are perhaps the truest measure of the intelligentsia at this time. They tended to share major characteristics in that each was associated with one or other political tendency, each produced some 500 pages per month, which were usually evenly divided between a literature and criticism section, and a 'social thought' section, which included political and social analysis from home and abroad and articles on developments in philosophy and ideas of all kinds.[57] Though their roots go back to the mid nineteenth century these journals flourished as never before in the early twentieth century and enjoyed greater freedom than ever after the virtual abolition of censorship that they forced out of the government in 1905. No more impressive evidence of the breadth and maturity of the intelligentsia, as well as of its radical and oppositional frame of mind, can be mustered than that provided by these publications.

While these journals provided a kind of widespread mass patronage for writers of all kinds, the growing wealth of the country also expressed itself in a growth of individual patrons, not only from traditional landowning backgrounds but also from increasingly affluent industrialists pursuing prestigious forms of conspicuous consumption and investment. Painting in particular tended to benefit from this and its healthy growth at this time depended on the patronage received. An early sign of this was the acquisition of the Abramtsevo estate, near Moscow, by the railway speculator Savva Mamontov who purchased it from the Slavophile intellectual K. Aksakov. Mamontov's desire to preserve some of the Slavophile ambience strengthened the mild nationalism and medievalism of the artists in all fields who became associated with the artistic colony formed there. By the 1890s the focus had shifted to the journal *World of Art* which was also funded by Mamontov and by Princess Tenishcheva. The gap created by its demise was later filled by *Golden Fleece*, patronised by another industrialist N. P. Riabushchinsky. A major theme of this journal was contact with western European artistic development, a process facilitated by the fact that newly wealthy Russians were among the major purchasers of Post-Impressionist paintings. Their collections formed the core of later Soviet art galleries. The most extensive private collection was that of Sergei Shchukin which by 1914 included 54 works by Picasso, 37 by Matisse, 19 by Monet, 13 by Renoir, 26 by Cezanne, 29 by Gauguin, 20 by Derain and 7 by Rousseau.[58] Interestingly enough, Franco–Russian relations were developing in all fields at this time, reaching a peak after 1905 when diplomatic *entente* and massive French loans were central to the autocracy's domestic and foreign policies. Major exhibitions of Russian art were held in Paris in 1901 and 1906. The public relations effect of them softened criticism in France of the government's policies of bailing out the most despotic major power in Europe from the consequences of its self-inflicted, and cruelly suppressed, revolution. In this process we see the interweaving of individual, social and political themes in the development of artistic creativity. If Russian art had, by 1914, become self-confident and outward-looking, as well as retaining a traditional core looking back to peasant arts and crafts and the tradition of icon painting, it was in no small part due to the interaction of these various forces.

The resultant of all these forces, in Russia as a whole, was an intelligentsia packed with creative, energetic and vibrant people. In art, literature, science and politics Russians were making names for themselves at the top of their fields. The Russian contribution to European and world culture had never been higher. To see this as an adornment of tsarism, as part of a process of evolution of the autocracy, would, however, be mistaken. While this diverse intelligentsia was pregnant with all sorts of different possibilities for Russia's future, the autocracy and its agents were doing their best to repress them. Tolstoy was excommunicated. A purge of even mildly liberal professors in Moscow University was conducted by the reactionary education minister, Kasso, in 1911. For obvious reasons, many of the radical political intelligentsia were in exile. The incompleteness of the repression was not the result of tsarist toleration, but of the regime's inability to realise the promptings of its deepest instincts. It should also be borne in mind that if anything united the new intelligentsia, it was its opposition to the autocracy. Indeed, this very characteristic is an essential element in its definition. This was reaffirmed by the debate around *Vekhi* in 1909 and 1910, which showed that the intelligentsia was still in no mood to accept the autocracy. On the left, Economism, a kind of Bernsteinian revisionism which called for priority to be given to economic rather than political struggle, made no major inroads. Mensheviks (often wrongly thought of as themselves harbouring quasi-Bernsteinian principles) and Bolsheviks fought resolutely against the Economists. They vigorously defended the proposition that the first step in changing the situation had to be the overthrow of the autocracy and the convening of a Constituent Assembly. Populists shared this view. The liberals, though more ambiguous about preserving the monarchy, wanted its autocratic powers abolished. If anything, this burgeoning intelligentsia and the elements of an independent civil society that it represented are evidence of future problems for tsarism not of a peaceful evolution. Indeed, there was a growing mood of impending catastrophe. This was felt, especially after 1905, in the gloomy pessimism of the ruling circles, the increasingly inflammatory denunciations of the status quo by the revolutionaries and in the prominence of apocalyptic themes among creative intellectuals. What was not foreseen, however, was that the catastrophe, when it finally came, was not initiated in the form of an internally generated revolution but of an external disaster – World War One. The immense economic and social upheaval that the war entailed ensured that, when it came, the expected revolution was not so much a political revolution with social consequences as a social revolution with political consequences. The stresses of the war began to erode all the social, institutional and economic underpinnings of Russian life in general and of intelligentsia life in particular. Education, publishing, theatre, concerts and exhibitions were all affected. Audiences and patronage dried up. It is important to recall that the revolution – at least in so far as it affected the intelligentsia though the same might be true of the rest of society – was not simply a question of changes in consciousness, in attitudes, but was accompanied by, even powered by, a complete transformation of the social and economic conditions that had brought the intelligentsia into existence. Similarly, the political tension generated by its deep opposition to tsarism was also transformed. The war and the resultant revolutions presented the intelligentsia with a completely new set of problems that existed alongside of, and sometimes replaced, those with which it was more familiar. Turning to the world war and the revolution and their effects in the sphere of intellectual life, one has to bear in mind that a very complex interplay of social forces is always at work in shaping creativity, the life of the mind, consciousness.

2 The Intelligentsia in War and Revolution

In spite of everything, life fermented irresistibly in mankind.

Marc Bloch

The conditions under which the intelligentsia had been formed and matured were not immune from the upheavals of war and revolution. On the contrary, between 1914 and 1921 its life was as thoroughly restructured as any other aspect of Russian society. In addition to the long-term influences examined in the previous chapter, shorter-term, but extremely intensive and influential, pressures were brought to bear on it.

Before discussing this process, however, it is worth noting that the turning-points in intellectual life did not coincide precisely with political developments. The atmosphere of the first months of the 1917 revolution was one of trying to carry on as normally as possible. Given that the idea of revolution had been of great importance to the intelligentsia its reaction in 1917 seems odd. Where one might have expected it to be at the centre of the development of the revolution, it actually moved in the opposite direction. It became preoccupied with its own life and its own world. In this world surprisingly little changed after the February revolution. There was no immediate sign of a great upsurge in activity or thoroughgoing change in its way of life. Naturally enough, the political intelligentsia operated under quite different conditions. The possibilities for political organisation were, of course, unprecedented. But the new opportunities in this sphere were much more dramatic than those presented to the rest of the intelligentsia and the two areas should not be confused. Most members of the intelligentsia were not full-time politicians and were only involved in politics as a secondary activity. This mean that, for the majority of the intelligentsia, the revolutionary year of 1917 and the early months of the Soviet government were more of an interlude than a phase in which significant cultural changes took place. It was only with the outbreak of civil war in 1918 and the terror following the abortive anti-Bolshevik manoeuvre of the Left Socialist Revolutionary party in summer of 1918 that the revolution began to have a serious impact on cultural life. For a considerable part of the intervening period, however, the intelligentsia lived a life of relative normality (with the emphasis on 'relative') and institutions such as schools, universities, theatres and presses continued to function as best they could. There is little evidence of serious disruption to them before October 1917. Even immediately afterwards, with the exception of the newspaper and journal presses, the Soviet government appears to have tried to keep existing institutions viable for as long as possible, providing that they did not constitute what the government construed as a direct threat to its existence.

THE FIRST STAGE OF TRANSFORMATION: AUGUST 1914–MARCH 1918

This is not to say that nothing of importance happened in the first fifteen months of the revolution. They are significant for two reasons. One is that the emergence of the Provisional Government marked a major step forward in the process of 'Westernisation' in Russia in that, despite profound political differences between the victors in other respects, the February revolution marked the irreversible defeat of tsarist ideology and tsarist values as nurtured by Pobedonostsev and others. The declining autocracy had finally succumbed and, for a while, the industrialists, the capitalists and the professional intelligentsia were in the ascendant. In previous moments of crisis these rather weakly developed groups had timidly formed an alliance with tsarism against the rebellious peasantry, the urban workers and the revolutionary intelligentsia. The foundering of tsarism left them to face this danger alone. The period of the Provisional Government was, then, a test of the Western-oriented middle class and their liberal and reformist values. Secondly, the absence of a strong central authority in these months led to a higher degree of spontaneity in all walks of life, the intelligentsia being no exception. All sectors of Russian society appeared to see this period as one in which they could promote their favoured projects with a minimum of interference from outside. This was as true of the liberal professors who took over control of Moscow University as it was of peasants who took over estates and workers who took over supervisory functions in the labour process. Thus these months became revealing of tendencies and aspirations in the cultural sphere, even though no solutions emerged to the conflicts that came to the surface.

The Provisional Government could not be said to have had anything resembling a cultural policy. It instituted piecemeal reforms and began inquiring into the possibility of more consistent involvement but did not get round to achieving it. In its early weeks there were some inspired rumours that it was planning to set up a Ministry for the Arts. Even this relatively innocuous proposal stirred up a hornets' nest. There was considerable trepidation at the prospect since it was seen as a step not towards the liberation of art but to its re-enslavement by the fledgling state. An articulate assessment of the proposal appeared as an editorial in the first post-revolutionary edition of the influential journal *Apollo* (*Apollon*). The author reached the conclusion that art did not need more bureaucrats but rather a chain of base communities spreading its values through the entire population. Art, the author argued, should follow the path leading to the creation of 'individualised artistic cells in Great Russia, to a democratic, really all-embracing, rebirth of our artistic culture'.[1] As the year progressed this kind of language became confined to the left, but it is interesting to note that populist aspirations of this kind could, initially, be found among the 'moderates'.

These views were also infused with another widespread characteristic of the intelligentsia outlook at this time, namely the desire to allow a spontaneous, grass-roots flourishing of initiative. All the ambitions for change that had been repressed under tsarism began to assert themselves. The few voices that, rather unromantically, pointed out the need for order and discipline if the revolution were to survive were very much in the minority. Typically, Peter Struve was quick to remind the readers of his journal *Russian Thought* (*Russkaia mysl'*) that 'without the army a structured, organised, united new Russia will perish'.[2] However, most liberals were carried away by the blissful alliance which, for the time being, included everyone from tsarist generals to Bolsheviks. This brief period was one in which it was naïvely thought that a hundred flowers would be able to bloom safely. This aspiration to pluralism increasingly developed into an unrestrained pursuit of ultimately conflicting interests by different groups in society in which the strong eventually crushed the weak.

An illustrative example of this process can be found in the cultural sphere, namely the question of higher education reform. The universities entered the revolution still smarting from reactionary measures of late tsarism, which had culminated, in 1911, in the dismissal or enforced resignation of a number of professors who were thought to be too liberal for the taste of the Ministry of Education. The first thing the academic establishment did once tsarism had gone was to reinstate those who had been blackballed. Beyond this, the professoriate saw the revolution as an opportunity to consolidate its own interests and its own control of the university system. It was in this light that it understood the idea of 'reform'. As a result, the government commission on higher education, chaired by the rector of Moscow University, M. M. Novikov, found it difficult to agree on anything very significant other than that universities should be autonomous and that women should continue to be excluded.[3] Professorial insistence on academic freedom and the preservation of the highest possible standards of research and study cut across the desire of more radical reformers to open up the university system to a wider constituency. This sharp conflict was beyond anything the Provisional Government could control, indeed even the Bolsheviks shield away from it for some time after 1917. In the meantime the universities, particularly Moscow, became strongholds of the Kadet version of liberalism and their hostility to radical reform tended to increase rather than diminish as the revolution progressed. Very few sympathisers with Bolshevism were to emerge from the university establishment.

Mainstream cultural and artistic life went on in 1917 as 'normally' as it could. Publishers published, painters painted, exhibitions were held, critics criticised as best they could. All this has been confirmed by Lapshin's indispensable account of artistic life in Moscow and Petrograd in 1917.[4] Reading through that account one can only agree that the picture suggests that cultural life was continuing, as the Russians say, 'from inertia' or that people were simply going through the motions. As an extremely rough indication of the relatively even tenor of artistic life through 1917, Lapshin's chronology of events devotes about the same amount of space to each month of the year except for August, which is much shorter, presumably as a traditional vacation period. The impression given by other sources is very similar.

The one major exception to the picture that intelligentsia life only changed gradually in 1917 is to be found among those intellectuals who set out to educate the ordinary people. This was an area in which the fall of tsarism had a clear impact. While the autocracy existed, societies for adult education among the urban poor were very suspect, the slightest infringement of the rules could result in closure.[5] However, the overthrow of the police system in the February revolution led to growing possibilities in this area. Both the Provisional

Government and the Soviets became involved. Many Soviets (one cannot say precisely how many) had cultural sections. Political parties organised parallel activities of their own. One of the best known activists in this area was, of course, Nadezhda Krupskaia, who had a lifelong interest in worker education. Her first meeting with her future husband, Lenin, had been at a committee for literacy in the 1890s. In 1917 and after, Krupskaia continued to work in this field. After she and Lenin returned to Petrograd from Switzerland she threw herself into work at the grass roots in the Vyborg district, which she much preferred to the boring tasks she had been assigned in the Bolshevik secretariat at Party headquarters in the Ksheshinskaia mansion. So successful was she that, at a Petrograd city conference, Krupskaia claimed to have upstaged the provisional government deputy minister Countess S. V. Panina. The latter's report admitted the Provisional Government's plans for education were not being fulfilled, while Krupskaia claimed that the Bolsheviks and the people themselves had great achievements to their credit.[6]

Ideas began to develop about bringing all this work together and achieving co-ordination. One attempt was made by the Moscow Soviet in the summer of 1917. An appeal was made to 'Painters, sculptors, artists, poets, musicians and architects' who were called upon to respond to the enthusiastic upsurge of interest in and opportunities for cultural growth. It was hoped that, in the special circumstances of what is called the sin of a great war between peoples, that those responding to the appeal would throw art a lifebelt.[7]

Initiatives of this sort led to the formation of Proletkul't in the days immediately preceding the October revolution. Its chief luminaries, Bogdanov and Lunacharsky, had been involved in cultural-educational work in a variety of ways. Lunacharsky's most notable contribution was in the form of mass lectures in the Cirque Moderne. His favourite theme was scientific explanation of various religious cults and practices. On 16–19 October the first Petrograd conference of proletarian cultural educational organisations was held, under the auspices of the Central Soviet of Factory Committees, and it was from this that Proletkul't grew. In addition to Lunacharsky and Bogdanov, Krupskaia showed some interest but never played a significant role. The Central Committee of Proletkul't met for the first time on 17 November 1917 and established the different departments that the organisation retained throughout its existence. These were theatre, literature, clubs, lectures, fine art, music, school and extramural education.[8]

It should, however, be emphasised that the 'normality' that ran into and through mainstream intellectual life was the 'normality' of the war years, not of the pre-war period. August 1914 had marked a larger demarcation in intellectual life than either February or, in the short term, October 1917. The effect of the war had been to create a sombreness and thinness in intellectual life in general. Conscription had drawn many younger intellectuals into the armed forces. Enrolment in universities fell. A glance at any of the intelligentsia journals shows the effects vividly. They ceased to be 'thick' journals and became physically thinner, the quality of paper deteriorated but the range of contents narrowed even more spectacularly. Europe was, of course, divided into three intellectual blocks, one centred on Paris, one on Vienna–Munich–Berlin and, a poor relation, one on Moscow and St Petersburg. Contact between them was sparse. Very little news filtered through. Interchange between them, such a vital part of intellectual life, was very restricted. Only a few enclaves of contact – Switzerland and, for a while, Italy – survived. Like the radical political intelligentsia, the Russian artistic intelligentsia, and its young avant-garde above all, was itself divided among these groupings. Kandinsky, Altman, Chagall and Tatlin had recently returned from the West and were caught within the virtual cultural blockade, while Bakst, Goncharova, Larionov, Lipchitz and Soutine were at the heart of the Russian avant-garde emigration in Paris.

The result was that an unaccustomed parochialism descended on Russian intellectual life. Editors strained to make something of any local events. Reports of happenings abroad were usually brief and often based on unreliable sources. The only areas to benefit, if that is the right word, were war art and the beginnings of official poster art which are to be found in the war years rather than in 1917 or after.

Most of these effects are well known from, for example, the last few pages of the memoirs of Benedikt Livshits – *The One and a Half Eyed Archer* who brilliantly describes the transition from peace-time Petersburg to war-time Petersburg. He describes his own willing transformation into a soldier, the division mobilisation made in the community and the disruption to other areas of life. The university, for instance, was handed over to the garrison. In Livshits's words 'The university became (not in the metaphorical sense but in the literal sense of the word) a nidus of infection.' This came about not least because, as he describes, soldiers seemed to get a particular pleasure out of defecating on the main staircase. This, not unnaturally, tended to put a damper on the life of the university.[9]

The increasingly chaotic conditions of the war thus wrought their own transformation of Russian intellectual society. With a few notable exceptions (such as the Tramway V and 0.10 exhibitions in 1915 which are well known, not least on account of a supposed exchange of blows that took place at the latter between its two leading exhibitors, Tatlin and Malevich[10]) the creative energy of Russia appeared to have been subdued by the long catalogue of horror and an increasing sense of the irrelevance and superficiality of high culture in the face of reality. By the autumn of 1916 the Petrograd art exhibition season, one of the highlights of the cultural year, could not arouse the critics. While it was, perhaps, a miracle that exhibitions were held at all, the comments tended to point to the lack of originality. One critic commented that the majority of exhibitions gave the impression that everything had 'been said yesterday'. Surveying the season in February 1917, a correspondent in the newspaper *Moskovskie vedemosti* said that one of the major exhibitions, that of the Union of Russian Artists, 'gave the impression that it had been hung the year before. The whole year and everything that had happened had not brought about any significant changes. The subjects were the same, the names were the same, they were even in the same places.' Another writer commented that the Wanderers were 'repeating what had been said long ago'.[11]

The February revolution did little to improve this situation. The number of visitors to exhibitions fell in the spring season of 1917 and hardly any of them purchased anything.[12] Reports of the first exhibition of the season, that of the Petrograd Society of Artists, somewhat contradict this, however, in that paintings were quickly snapped up in late September by people eager to turn their paper money into something that might hold its value in the prevailing inflationary conditions.[13] However, critics commented on the irrelevance of the exhibits in the worsening conditions of the time. One of them said that, looking at the paintings in this exhibition, one could not tell it was no longer the age of Nicholas. The reaction of another was that the paintings were extraordinarily apolitical, that there was not one painting on a contemporary theme, 'not an echo, not a reflection'. A third concluded that 'it is hard to believe that in the volcanic atmosphere which surrounds us that painters can occupy themselves with such trivialities.'[14] By and large, the continuation of wartime conditions was blamed. Indeed, things had become much worse. The fall of Riga on 2 September (NS) meant that Petrograd was now feared to be in the war zone. Those who could began to leave. The evacuation of art treasures from the Hermitage and elsewhere began. The political crisis precipitated by Kornilov and the continuing economic chaos were not conducive to intellectual activity. Maiakovsky spoke for many when he said 'It is impossible to paint pictures in the chaos in which we are living.'[15] Thus, even before the Bolsheviks took power, even before they appeared to be a serious threat, the intellectual life of the capital had been seriously undermined. The October revolution, when it came, only appeared to be an extension of these conditions. The exhibition season continued as best it could despite additional practical hazards. For example, painters were very reluctant to entrust their work to the railway system for transportation so exhibitions tended to be increasingly local. Even so, nine exhibitions, about half the number of the previous year, opened in Petrograd and Moscow in October and November.[16] The indicators are that, in the immediate crisis, they were little visited by viewers but that, by Christmas, crowds were once again filling the halls. Inside the scene was little different, according to Lapshin, from what it had been 'before the war and even before the revolution'.[17] It is possible that this had, by then, become an attraction in that the exhibitions may have had a certain nostalgia value in being 'islands of the old life'.[18] While the visitors may have been impressed, and even continued to buy paintings, the critics were not. The old complaints about the outdated and irrelevant nature of what was on display continued to be heard.[19]

The immediate inheritance of the Bolsheviks in the field of culture was, then, as unpromising as in other areas. Crisis had already set in and the October revolution took some time to make a real impact on events. In the early stages such attention as was paid to intellectual matters tended to be based on the assumption that there should be some kind of reconciliation with those members of the intelligentsia who were opposed to the revolution. With this in mind, a major public meeting was organised in Petrograd for late 1917. Accounts differ as to what exactly took place and why, but the overall picture can be discerned. The meeting, on the theme 'The Intelligentsia and the People', was to be addressed by Lunacharsky, Alexandra Kollontai, Blok, Ivanov-Razumnik, Meierkhol'd, Esenin, Petrov-Vodkin, Rurik Ivnev and other leading intellectuals. When the moment came, however, almost all the invited intellectuals absented themselves. Only Lunacharsky, Kollontai and Ivnev spoke. Their main theme was that to desert the Bolshevik revolution was to abandon the fundamental intelligentsia impulse of service to the people, since the October revolution was that revolution of the people (*narod*). Ivnev's assertion that if Tolstoy had been alive he would have supported the October revolution was apparently greeted with applause by part of the audience while the remainder 'whistled madly'. The official explanation for the lack of intelligentsia support for the meeting was that it was the result of unusually bad weather, inexperience on the part of the organisers and the fact that the tramway was not functioning that day. Another explanation appears, perhaps, more likely. In a letter published a few days after the fiasco in *Izvestiia TsIK* Ivnev complained that the newspaper had claimed that it was necessary for intellectuals to work 'under the supervision of the Soviet authorities' whereas most intellectuals recognised only the supervision of their own tastes and opinions. If this clash was the real reason for the failure of the meeting then it was a foreshadowing of the shape of relations between the new government and the intelligentsia for many years to come. Also the main reason put forward by Lunacharsky and others as to why intellectuals should side with the revolution, namely that only by doing this could they remain faithful to their aim of serving the people, echoed through all the ensuing disputes.[20]

The depth of hostility felt by many intellectuals was clearly too great to be patched up by a badly organised public meeting. Opposition to Bolshevism went back long before the revolution itself and, like other aspects of the situation, what happened in the early months of the Soviet government's life was only a continuation of what had existed before. A good barometer of the opinions of a wide variety of the intelligentsia at this time is provided by the journal *Reports from Literature and Life* (*Biulleteni Literaturyi i zhizni*)[21] which, as a digest of the press with a slant towards intelligentsia interest – symbolised by its masthead, which proclaimed that 'The task of the moment is the building up of Russian culture' – provides a range of sources from the now scarce newspaper and journal press of the day. Its issues around the time of the October revolution were infused with foreboding. In place of the sentimental image of the benevolent peasant, an equally distorted vision of the peasant as nothing but looter and pillager had begun to grow. There were many warnings that the radicals were destroying everything for which the progressive intelligentsia (that is, the educated, Westernised, liberal intellectuals) stood. An impressive range of charges, though with little supporting evidence, was laid at the door of the revolutionary socialist intellectuals in a number of articles, mostly reprinted from the liberal and socialist-revolutionary press. For instance, one writer accused the intelligentsia of being responsible for 'national suicide' by weakening the state through continuing to spread hostility to the regime at a time of external threat.[22] This, like other criticisms, was reminiscent of *Vekhi*. One of *Vekhi*'s authors, Nicholas Berdiaev, was also quoted to the effect that Bolshevism, with its dogmatism, intolerance and comprehensive spiritual ambitions, was deeply rooted in Russian religious psychology.[23] The sociologist Pitirim Sorokin associated Bolshevism with Slavophile messianism, the idea that it was the mission of Russia to 'save' the West, presenting as evidence the use of slogans portraying Russia as the avant-garde of world socialism.[24] For another writer, Bolshevism was intimately tied up with the immediate circumstances of collapse in which Russia found itself. Its rejection of the slightest compromise and its 'demand for blind partisanship [*priamolineinost'*] and deaf absoluteness [*bezotnositel'nost'*]' could only thrive in the current moment of cultural–historical crisis.[25] In a later issue another writer argued that, with its irresponsible incitement of the lower classes, who were plunged in 'darkness' (*temnota*) as opposed to the creative vision characteristic of the intelligentsia, the revolutionary intellectuals had 'sown the wind and reaped the storm'.[26] The Bolshevik intelligentsia in particular was accused of being out of touch with Russia as a result of long emigration abroad and the inward-looking nature of the communities its members had lived in, which allowed all kinds of fantasies to breed,[27] and of exploiting the popular movement by attempting to harness it as a force to carry out their own hidden agenda. By, for instance, promising land to the peasantry when they actually opposed private ownership of land on principle, the socialists were, continued the author, aiming to be 'carried on the backs of the peasants to where they could not go by any other path – into power'.[28]

These early skirmishes, constituting an ambiguous phoney war, continued until late March 1918 when a debate was organised by the Union of Writers in Petrograd. On the one hand, the theme of the debate, 'The Tragedy of the Intelligentsia', implied that the current situation and prospects were disastrous and represented the destruction of decades of populist aspirations. On the other, as the correspondent of a non-Bolshevik Petrograd newspaper described it, the appearance of the meeting gave the impression 'that no such "tragedy" had befallen either the intelligentsia or Russia as a whole. The same people were on the platform and the audience had hardly changed.'[29]

Speakers and participants came from a broad range of the intelligentsia spectrum including Kadets, socialist-revolutionaries and Mensheviks. No Bolsheviks appear to have been present though V. A. Bazarov, a long-standing friend and colleague of Lunacharsky, who was now the Commissar for Education, did attend. The main speaker was A. Red'ko and his views, also published in one of the surviving 'thick' journals, provide an interesting example of the themes and preoccupations of the rather traditional populist-minded intellectual at this time. Red'ko had three main concerns. One was the apparent disappearance of the intelligentsia from view, the second was the role of the intelligentsia in the production process and the third, and most traditional, the one that provided a matrix for the others, was the relationship between the intelligentsia and the people. His central point was that for 130 years the intelligentsia had considered itself to be outside or above class and to be in the service of the whole people. 'The revolution', he said, 'showed this to be a laughable self-deception.'[30] Instead, 'suddenly it turned out that there was nothing but the proletariat and the bourgeoise'[31] because since the February (*sic*) revolution everything had been divided into 'productive' and 'unproductive', the former embodying all virtue, the latter the capitalist heritage.[32] According to current terminology, he argued, only physical labour created anything.[33] In this way the revolution had 'brought the intelligentsia an unusual present, a hat which had the power to make its wearer invisible'.[34] Because its role both in the revolutionary movement and in the economy had been hidden from view as a result of this process, the workers put the intelligentsia in the camp of their enemies in the class war. The intelligentsia it seemed, simply shared in the fruits of the exploitation of the working class.[35] Behind this phenomena, Red'ko continued, a struggle was taking place for the control of mental labour power.[36] He pointed out that the situation was not a new one for the intelligentsia since the old regime, like the new one, had aimed 'to make a slave of the creative intelligentsia'.[37] Red'ko's defence of the intelligentsia was twofold. The most substantial part of his article pointed out the productive nature of creative mental work, drawing on examples ranging from the development of the railway system in late nineteenth-century Russia to the prevalence of legends of the sacred art of the smith in sub-Saharan Africa.[38] 'Without the intervention of creative thought and knowledge, (that is the intelligentsia) nothing would be done.'[39] The second line of defence was the traditional one pointing out the devotion of the intelligentsia proper to the people's cause. This had been characteristic of it since the 1860s.

> The difference began with the choice of school. You went to the medical-surgical academy to serve the people, to the technical school to serve yourself.[40] To belong to the intelligentsia was not a right, but an obligation which imposed the weighty fulfillment of political duty.[41]

To be at the top of the intellectual tree was not, of itself, sufficient to guarantee this title.[42] In conformity with the old ideals, Red'ko himself concluded with a call for co-operation rather than class struggle, the latter being an idea which, he said, bore the imprint 'Made in Germany'.[43]

Red'ko's ideas thus represent a fusion of old principles with new emphases brought into prominence by the experience of the year of revolution. In addition to the defence of the intelligentsia's role as defenders of the people, Red'ko added the idea of its importance in the production process. In this way he amalgamated the tradition of the intelligentsia with its specific economic, material interests, which, as we have seen, had been emerging rapidly in the pre-war years. As presented by Red'ko there was no incompatibility between the intelligentsia's own class interest and its claim to serve the people. The intelligentsia served them not only through its political heroism and sense of duty but also through application of its mental labour power to economic, technical and managerial tasks. While the idea of service of the people through 'small deeds', usually as doctors, teachers, agronomists and so on, had long been part of the intelligentsia tradition, Red'ko was now making a case for its crucial role in industrial society. While not necessarily incompatible, there was an obvious possibility of tension between idealism and class interest with the former being increasingly debased simply to the level of ideological camouflage for the latter. This possibility had been predicted nearly twenty years earlier by Jan Vaclav Machajski.

The second major speaker in the debate, A. N. Potresov, echoed some of Red'ko's themes but used them, in a *Vekhi*-like way, to accuse the intelligentsia of contributing to the 'tragedy' through its own shortcomings. Potresov had always had certain ideas in common with *Vekhi* and had been referred to as a 'Vekhist among the Marxists'.[44] Certainly his speech gave out distinctly Vekhist resonances. His main point was that the Russian intelligentsia had not devoted its talents to the building up of a national state. It had not been involved in routine creative work in the way that its counterparts abroad – he specifically mentioned Germany – had been. Russian society lacked awareness of the importance of the state and was not cultured. The function of the intelligentsia should be to overcome these faults. Loud applause greeted his central statement that the intelligentsia should 'assert the independence of Russia and transform her poverty into wealth'.[45] Thus, Potresov, too, had an eye on the economic role of the intelligentsia and saw its function in a developing industrial society to be one of constructive labour rather than destructive criticism, though he and all the other participants in the debate were asserting their right to criticise. It was not clear what relationship Potresov and others saw between these two functions. Primacy of the former would lead to the intelligentsia becoming tame servants of industrialism – capitalist or socialist – whereas the latter would prolong the current unsatisfactory situation that they hoped to remedy.

INTELLECTUAL LIFE DURING THE CIVIL WAR

This debate was held at the time of the negotiation and signing of the Brest–Litovsk treaty, a coincidence that accounts for a great deal of the passion surrounding it. It was also the time when the relative 'normality' of intellectual life began to be eroded much more rapidly than hitherto. The ensuing period, that of the civil war, thus became a highly complicated one with respect to the intelligentsia. By carefully choosing parts of the evidence and ignoring or dismissing other parts, two quite separate interpretations of the period can be arrived at. At the root of this is the fact that intellectuals underwent an extremely wide variety of fates in these years and it is easy to mistake the part for the whole. At one extreme a group of intellectuals benefited from the revolution. New artistic vistas were opened for them and, at least for a time, they enthusiastically embraced the new conditions. The most notable of these are Blok, Belyi and Maiakovsky the poets; the artists Chagall, Malevich and Tatlin; the novelist Gorky. At the other extreme were the victims of the system. Rozanov and Khlebnikov died as a result of the privations of these years, as did many other intellectuals in all areas of activity. Many went into exile rather than live in the new Soviet Russia. Some were expelled. A few were executed – such as Nikolai Gumilev in 1921 – or persecuted and killed. A further complication arises from the fact that people like Blok welcomed the revolution at first but may have come to reject it later. As a result of this, quite contradictory accounts of the period exist. One set of explanations emphasised those who gained from the revolution, though even within this school there are those who give priority to the growth of working-class and socialist art and culture, and others who see the period as a golden age of the avant-garde élite. On the other hand, many of the *émigrés* and those associated with them, and some of the survivors within Soviet Russia, have pointed to the terrible conditions prevailing in these years. The period as a whole can only be understood by taking both of these extremes into account as well as remembering that there was a great body of intellectuals who did not fit neatly into either camp but simply tried to extend the conditions of normality as best they could in an increasingly piecemeal fashion.

Before looking at the experience of some individuals and groups in this period, a glance at the factors affecting all areas might help to throw some light on the contradictory evidence. In the first place, those policies of the new government that bore directly on the intelligentsia tended to be conciliatory. While Lenin himself had been very hostile to the intelligentsia, once the party came to power he was quicker than many of his colleagues to come to the conclusion that the revolution could not survive without extensive, though carefully controlled, collaboration with intellectuals and managers of many kinds. As early as February 1918 Lenin embarked on the policy of trying to encourage as many skilled administrative and executive personnel to work for the new government as could be encouraged or cajoled to do so. While this policy had enormous implications for the Bolshevik party and for the bureaucratisation of the new state system, as far as the present study is concerned, it is sufficient to note that it had a primary sorting effect. The intelligentsia was immediately divided into the necessary and the unnecessary, those who were deemed to be economically productive or who had indispensable skills and those who were superfluous. Needless to say most of the intelligentsia proper fell into the latter category but a relatively fortunate minority gained a small degree of protection through this. For those who were less favoured by this policy, notably the cultural élite, the main source of protection was the new Ministry of Education and its founding head, Lunacharsky. Here, too, conciliatory policies were applied that extended to a wide range of writers, artists and academics many of whom were not Bolsheviks, indeed some were very hostile to it. None the less, the basic aim of this policy was to preserve the élite of the creative intelligentsia in the hope that its leading members could be won over to the task of constructing the new socialist order. Lunacharsky's work in this area is well known and does not need to be emphasised here.[46] For present purposes it is sufficient simply to point out that here too, the only other area in which policies impinging directly on the intelligentsia were being applied in these early days, conciliation was the order of the day. Needless to say, it is these two areas of policy that are stressed by the defenders of Soviet policies of this period. It is, however, misleading to comment on them without bearing in mind that more powerful *indirect* forces were also bearing on the situation and that they were working in the opposite direction. The evidence suggests that the intelligentsia suffered greatly as a result of the side effects of other policies and of the general crisis of these turbulent years.

Among the policies of the Soviet government that were not aimed at the intelligentsia but severely damaged it none the less, three were particularly prominent. From the earliest days of the revolution the Bolsheviks began the systematic harassment and repression of their opponents. Particularly damaging to the intelligentsia was the closing down of newspapers and journals. By early 1918 most of the bourgeois and a large proportion of the socialist and anarchist press had been circumscribed. Naturally, this deprived many intellectuals not only of opportunities for self-expression but also of sources of income. Also, since intellectuals played a leading role in nearly all centre and left-wing parties, they were prominent among the victims of political arrests.

Secondly, as the revolution deepened, the theme of class struggle came to the fore. It is likely that here, too, intellectuals suffered disproportionately. In addition to political arrests, anti-parasite laws and compulsory labour obligation fell heavily on the intelligentsia. The intelligentsia as a whole – cultural, professional and technical – began to fall into a role that was increasingly fatal to it. It was becoming a kind of surrogate bourgeoisie. Bolshevik ideology fanned the flame of class struggle in Russia but one of the prime requisites – a powerful and oppressive bourgeoisie – was missing. It was even harder to find in 1918 since those with wealth and property had, if at all possible, rifled their company safes, sold what they could, picked up the family valuables, deserted the Soviet areas and headed for White protection or emigration. That left white-collar employees and intellectuals as the only prominent components of the old élite within Soviet areas. If class struggle had to be prosecuted and the real class enemies – capitalists, bankers, landowners and so on – were on the run, then the intelligentsia were the best the militants could find in their place. Something of this dogged relations between the non-intelligentsia party left and the educated classes throughout the 1920s.

Thirdly, the Bolsheviks assiduously crushed the fledgling institutions of civil society in these years. The most notable victims of this process were popular institutions such as the soviets and the trade unions, which were fairly rapidly brought under party/state control. Intellectual institutions and professional organisations also lost their independence in these years. Some that had existed in tsarist times, like the Imperial Free Economic Society or the doctors' Pirogov Society, withered and died. New ones set up to combat the worsening conditions were wound up by the authorities or transformed into harmless and ineffective non-political organisations.[47] In many cases these were destroyed less as a deliberate act of policy than as a result of Bolshevik suspicion of all independent organisations. Clearly the party's aspiration to extensive control of Soviet society conflicted with the full application of policies of toleration, completely foreign to its nature, which were being pursued elsewhere.

Political processes alone, however, do not explain what happened. A major transforming effect came about through what perhaps one could call the *perestroika* – restructuring – of the economic base of intellectual life at this time. The political economy of the major intellectual institutions – the press, publishing, the theatre, concert halls, cinemas, universities, schools and so on – was falling to pieces. The chief sources of intellectual incomes – profits from performances; private patronage; sponsorship and purchase; the tsarist state budget, especially for higher education; the book market; newspaper and journal readership – were all breaking up and suffering from economic collapse themselves. Most *intelligenty* were not well paid and had few reserves to fall back on. Those that did have savings soon lost them in the collapse of paper money. This economic hurricane wreaked greater havoc among intellectuals than the direct political pressure of the fledging Bolshevik state. Many intellectuals were reduced to manual labour, to cultivating small plots of land, to flight, to starvation. Where the economic situation was particularly bad, in Petrograd, for example, in 1919, the death toll among intellectuals appears to have been enormous. Eminent, elderly and undernourished scholars had little resistance to cholera and typhus. Memoirs recall the frequency of death and funerals in this period. Younger people, too, were affected, as Zamiatan grimly portrays in his story 'The Cave' in which the stove-god in the apartment of an unemployed intellectual couple swallows up their furniture, reduces them to stealing firewood and a few potatoes to live on. Eventually they give in and commit suicide. This fictional tragedy was being repeated in real life.

As late as the winter of 1921–2, by which time the worst had passed in the main metropolitan cities, reports were still coming in of severe hardship in the provinces. The independent writers' journal *Letopis' dom literatorov* (*The Chronicle of the House of Writers*) contained frequent accounts of such hardships. In the Crimea, for instance, it was reported that the poet M. A. Voloshin was 'in a very poor state of health and without means apart from the proceeds of occasional literary works and the sale of his paintings'. Two women writers were 'both ill and existed by making hats and handbags for sale'. I. S. Shmelev and his wife 'wanted to work in the vineyards but they did not have any boots'. All of them should have been receiving official supplies of rations 'but in fact they never received them'. The local officials in charge of distribution did not wish to give them rations and were very hostile towards them, treating them like idlers who were allocated a ration for no reason. It was also reported that they had difficulty in purchasing goods from the peasantry for money (presumably because the peasants, in the circumstances of massive inflation, preferred barter).[48] Although hard to quantify precisely there can be no doubt that the creative intelligentsia in particular was often defenceless against the harsh conditions and the hostility of minor officials who, like those in the Crimea, saw them only as useless mouths to feed, as a drain on scarce resources that should have gone to the working people. All the scattered and unsystematic pieces of evidence point in this direction.

However, one of the key features of intelligentsia life in these stormy years was that the effects of political and economic pressure were far from even. Some intellectuals suffered heavily, some hardly at all; a few thrived and prospered. Some semblance of traditional intellectual life survived in the most unlikely oases. This was partly because of pure chance, particularly for those in the provinces where local attitudes can be expected to have had more influence than central policies; partly as a result of intelligentsia self-defence against the situation; and partly as a result of those government policies and decisions that offered some protection to parts of the intelligentsia.

The overwhelming impact of these factors was that intellectual life was subject to arbitrary and capricious forces. They added up to an uncontrolled and violent storm that everyone reacted to in their own way and tried to survive as best they could. Not surprisingly the first victim was the fragile unity of the intelligentsia. Even at the best of times factionalism had been strong, though, despite differences, a show of unity in the face of the common tsarist enemy was usually possible for the bulk of the intelligentsia before 1914. However, in these years the intelligentsia split apart, never to be reunited. The main cleavage was between those who, in the jargon of the time, in some sense or other accepted the revolution and those who rejected it. Within each of these categories there were those who were more active and those who were relatively passive. In this way, four major groupings, of unequal size, can be discerned in the intelligentsia. First there were those who actively opposed Bolshevism. For these most intransigent opponents, underground organisation, regrouping in non-Bolshevik areas and, eventually, emigration were the most characteristic practical responses. Secondly, what was probably the largest group (though quantification is hazardous) was made up of those who neither supported Bolshevism nor actively opposed it, but continued to try and make their way as best they could under the abominable conditions. This group took less dramatic steps. For them, the central aim was to preserve as much as they could of traditional intellectual life and values. This often took the form of setting up professional, cultural and, increasingly, trade union type institutions for the defence of their interests. In addition, defence of existing institutions, notably universities and the Academy of Sciences, or even working within the new Soviet institutions, was chosen by these relatively passive opponents of Bolshevism. More wholehearted collaboration with the new government, or at least seeing promise in the new situation, characterised the activities of the third grouping, which was made up of those who, to some extent, sympathised with the Soviet government without fully absorbing its ideology or joining the party. Finally, the Bolsheviks themselves were led by people who had been moulded in the intelligentsia tradition and were part and parcel of it. Naturally, their activity was bound up with the new party and state institutions. It goes without saying that, given the complexity of intellectual life, these compartments are far from watertight. The remainder of this chapter is devoted to the first three of these groups. The next chapter looks at the fourth group, the intelligentsia Bolsheviks.

ANTI-BOLSHEVIK ACTIVISM

Active anti-Bolshevism appealed to a wide stratum of intellectuals.[49] No one of them is typical but a glance at the evolution of the anti-Bolshevik opinions of one of them, Leonid Andreev, serves to remind us that such ideas were not as straightforward as they sometimes seem. Andreev, for instance, had always been a bitter opponent of tsarism and greeted the February revolution without any reservations. In his view the Romanov dynasty, and Nicholas in particular, were tyrants responsible for untold quantities of innocent blood. Their fate was, if anything, too good for them. Their existence had prevented healthy development in Russia and had hampered the war effort. Now a freer and more democratic path was open. February, he thought, was not the end of a process of revolution but its beginning. He had long predicted a revolutionary outcome to the war and it was this hope that had turned him from being an internationally famous pacifist into an enthusiastic supporter of the war because he thought it would lead to the defeat of militarism and the founding of a United States of Europe. The old dynasties, the Romanov's and the Hohenzollern's, were, Andreev argued, the chief obstacle to this and their removal would be a great step to the democratisation and liberation of Europe. The contradiction of an alliance between the autocracy and the Western democracies was, for Andreev, unsustainable. Russia would have to liberalise and a new era would open up. The bedrock of Andreev's optimism was his belief that the Russian *narod* would respond to the opportunity and grow into free citizenship – a key concept for Andreev. This optimism even extended to the army. Contrary to most of those who shared his enthusiasm for February, Andreev was prepared to envisage the democratisation of the army adding to its effectiveness as a fighting force rather than detracting from it. The *narod* in arms would no longer be a collection of automatons dehumanised by tsarist discipline, but would, he thought, become a powerful creative force motivated to fight by 'love for its own people, love of freedom and faith in future brotherhood'.[50] It would fight for the principles of the French revolution. It was precisely here, however, that Andreev's dream began to fall apart. Rapid disillusion set in. The real *narod*, instead of acting as he had hoped, appeared to him to be falling into chaos and anarchy. In an increasingly shrill voice he began to urge it to conform to the role he had assigned it. His earlier optimism gave way to bitter denunciations of the degenerating situation and the collapse of the army. 'Where', he asked the intelligentsia as early as May 1917, 'is the *narod* you served so tirelessly and honestly? It has forgotten you.'[51] In July, in 'To You Soldier!', he denounced the ordinary soldiers for deserting the people's cause. He appealed to them to remember what they had been in February and return to their earlier nobility. 'The motherland is dying. The motherland calls out to you. Arise, dear soldier!'[52]

As the situation got out of control he began to make a distinction between 'revolution', which he saw as idealistic, creative, uplifting and honourable and which he never forsook, and *bunt* – riot or, loosely, social revolution – which was, for Andreev, materialistic, selfish, short-sighted and destructive. He also remained faithful to the ideal *narod*, but this was ever more tenuous. He hated the left and the 'revolutionary democracy', which he associated with German money and influence, and was so despondent about the situation by September that he called the allies to engage in a massive joint military venture to 'save' Russia from the threat of Lenin. Once the Bolshevik *bunt* had succeeded, this theme of calling on the allies to save the revolution from them was central to his outlook and he maintained it for the remaining two years of his life.

By this time Andreev had, like many others, gone into exile, although in his case this was mitigated by the fact that his home in Finland was in territory that the Soviet authorities did not control. Not all opponents of Bolshevism were so fortunate. Many of them fled. Of all the possible practical responses to Bolshevism, flight was perhaps the most obvious. The intelligentsia shared in the massive regrouping of the population that went on in these years. The exodus from the cities to the, hopefully, better-supplied and more self-sufficient countryside attracted many. Pasternak's fictionalised description of such a journey by an idealised conception of an intellectual in this period, Doctor Zhivago, could be multiplied innumerable times in reality. As with Zhivago, the end results were not always more welcome than the conditions bringing about the flight. Others might head for White areas not simply from political conviction, but from the hope that survival might be more probable. This, too, could be an illusion. The Crimea was a centre for this and for a while the Tauride University provided a focus for non-Bolshevik intellectuals who, although under White protection, were by no means all active in defence of the White cause any more than those in Red areas were all active Bolsheviks. At that time two members of the Academy of Sciences, V. I. Vernadsky and V. I. Palladin, and the theologian and contributor to *Vekhi*, S. N. Bulgakov, were on the university staff. The final collapse of White control in the area in 1920 precipitated an agitated debate as to whether the university should be evacuated from Simferopol'. The debate was said to have been 'stormy and prolonged', so prolonged, in fact, that given the legendary procrastination and lack of concern for detail of academics, by the time they reached their decision to go abroad, the last steamer had already left.[53]

The final phase of flight was, of course, emigration, and non-Bolsheviks of all kinds were forced into, or freely took up, this option. Naturally, those who were well known abroad, like Merezhkovsky, found this relatively easy. Many others swelled the *émigré* Russian intellectual communities in Paris, Prague, Berlin, Harbin and elsewhere. As the Whites were defeated, so many of their supporters and protégés preferred to take their chances abroad rather than in Soviet-held areas. By 1921 a figure usually thought to be of the order of one to two million Russians, including many intellectuals, had emigrated in this way. Their ranks were swelled by a wave of prominent intellectuals who had either attempted to work with the Bolsheviks or to remain neutral and had found their hopes dashed by the intricacies of political and intellectual life at this time. By 1920–1 almost all the organised non-Bolshevik and anti-Bolshevik intellectual groupings, including the leaders of political parties of the centre and left such as the Kadets, Mensheviks and socialist-revolutionaries had been forced into emigration. Some who remained in Soviet territory fell silent and came to be referred to as 'internal *émigrés*'. From the early years the emigration was a diverse and talented group.[54]

A second response, often leading to flight in the last resort, took the form of active resistance to Bolshevism in its home territories, including Petrograd and Moscow. By and large it was militants from the intelligentsia-led political parties suppressed by the Bolsheviks who took this route. For the most part their activity involved organising small groups to resist the Bolsheviks politically through speaking at meetings, publishing newspapers and, incessantly, formulating anti-Bolshevik action programmes. Efforts were made to produce a common anti-Bolshevik front among such organisations, but the breadth of interest and outlook prevented the attempts from being successful. For the first few months after October activities of this kind could be carried on fairly freely, but by the end of 1918, after the attempted assassination of Lenin and with the Civil War in full swing, resistance became more dangerous and was forced underground.

The atmosphere of resistance at this time is well expressed in the memoirs of two leading members of the small Popular Socialist party, S. P. Mel'gunov and V. Miakotin. In terms of political principles their party was rather more populist than the Kadets and rather more attached to the rights of the individual than the various socialist parties, so it occupied a small niche between liberalism and socialism. As Miakotin recalls, at first anti-Bolshevik activity was fragmented and hampered by over-confidence in that 'no one believed that Bolshevik power could be soundly-based and prolonged'.[55] The treaty of Brest–Litovsk, while confirming the potential weakness of the Bolsheviks since they were driven to such desperate lengths to retain power, also stirred up a common Russian nationalism that made agreement between opposition groups a little easier. Miakotin became involved in organising one such attempted united front, the Union for the Regeneration of Russia (*Soiuz Vozrozhdeniia Rossii*), which came into existence in April 1918. Miakotin makes clear that Russian nationalism was the most powerful factor bringing the groups together. 'We could not reconcile ourselves to the Treaty of Brest–Litovsk which made Russia dependent on the favour or disfavour of Germany; we could not see, without humiliation and shame, that the German ambassador, Graf Mirbach, was practically the overlord of Moscow.'[56] The aim of the organisation was to reform the alliance with the Western powers, reopen the Eastern Front[57] and to rebuild a unified Russian state, but on the basis of democratic principles through the convening of a new Constituent Assembly.[58] These somewhat Utopian principles, given the actual situation at that time, were not sufficient to paper over the differences between the participating groups. The two main ones, the Kadets and the Socialist Revolutionaries, were split over the issues of joining the Union. For the Kadet right the organisation was too radical and they leaned to a more conservative programme,[59] while the Socialist Revolutionaries involved had to keep the negotiations secret from their own membership, presumably for fear of an outcry if they were found to have been negotiating with the right.[60] Despite this continued chronic factiousness of the political intelligentsia some open activity was able to take place. In the summer of 1918, for example, it was still possible for Mel'gunov, A. V. Peshekhonov and others to address public meetings at Moscow University[61] and to continue to publish a newspaper. At first, when a newspaper was closed by the Bolsheviks it was easy to reopen it by the simple and traditional expedient of producing it under a new name.[62] Thus, while the activities of the Union itself were 'strictly conspiratorial'[63] there was, none the less, scope for public activity. This did not last for long. 'As time passed, so the Bolsheviks became stronger and such possibilities became more circumscribed.'[64]

By the middle of the summer of 1918 the Bolshevik terror began to make a rapid impact. All but the official press was closed down for good and the Union was only able to produce an 'Information Leaflet' once a week.[65] In July and August leading figures of the Union were either arrested or went underground, some in a rather comical fashion like the Kadet N. I. Astrov who considered it sufficient disguise to walk around Moscow in a peaked cap, which did not prevent any of his acquaintances from recognising him.[66] The flat in the Arbat, used by the Popular Socialists as their headquarters, was closed in August and the central committee escaped arrest because, by chance, they were meeting elsewhere on that particular day.[67] Various party members were arrested at the time, including Mel'gunov. Miakotin himself went underground for a while but the new situation in Moscow, combined with the growth of armed anti-Bolshevik movements in the provinces, opened up new perspectives, and he, and several leading figures of the Union, made their way through Bolshevik lines to join the Whites in the east.[68] There, if anything, the factiousness was probably worse,[69] though Miakotin says nothing of the problems of working with representatives of the pre-revolutionary establishment who formed the backbone of the White movement. Instead he refers to attempts to 'create an all-Russian state power which could give a lead to all anti-Bolshevik movements'.[70] The White movement proved incapable of achieving even that minimum of unity.

While the centre of gravity of resistance spread to the periphery, those left behind in the Red areas, like Mel'gunov, continued to defy the new Soviet authorities. He was arrested five times in this period. He was one of the defendants in the show trial of the so-called 'Tactical Centre' in August 1920 and was sentenced to death. This was commuted to a ten-year jail sentence. Under pressure from the Academy of Sciences and the veteran anarchist Peter Kropotkin he was released after serving one year and was eventually exiled from Soviet Russia in the mass expulsion of intellectuals in 1922.[71] Mel'gunov and those involved in the 'Tactical Centre' trial could consider themselves relatively fortunate. In another, more murky affair in August 1921, the so-called 'Tagantsev Conspiracy', some fifty defendants, mostly intellectuals and including one of Russia's leading poets, Nikolai Gumilev, were executed. A number of the victims were engineers and geologists with the Main Fuels Committee (Glavtop). The severity with which these victims were handled may be accounted for by the fact that the authorities wanted to make an unmistakable example of them in the aftermath of the Kronstadt crisis, but the details of these cases remain obscure.[72]

PASSIVE RESISTANCE, PASSIVE COLLABORATION

While active resistance provided an increasingly dangerous sphere of operations for a courageous and irreconcilable minority, the majority of the intelligentsia sought to protect themselves in a less heroic fashion either by building new organisations, often of a trade union type, or by strengthening and defending as best they could the traditional intellectual institutions such as the Academy of Sciences, universities, technical colleges, publishing houses, theatres and so on.

The appearance of organisations devoted to promoting the material interests of intellectuals resulted in part from continuation and expansion of tendencies already noted above. However, the appalling conditions of the early years of the revolution, when survival itself was at stake, plus the example of self-organisation going on, particularly among the urban workers, seem to have given much greater impetus to this kind of activity. Organisations of intellectuals took a variety of forms from relatively loose co-operative type institutions to full-blooded trade unions. The party and government took a particular interest in the latter type and attempted, not without some success, to assert its hegemony over them and use them as a front-line weapon in controlling certain sections of the intelligentsia. While an examination of these policies is best deferred until the next chapter, some examples of what these unions did are included in the current section.

In Moscow and Petrograd in particular some members of the intelligentsia turned from directly creative activities towards the commerce of culture as a surer way of earning their livelihood. Co-operative bookselling operations, often under the nominal authority of one or other of the many writers' organisations of the period, began to make their appearance. The Writers' Bookshop (*Knizhnaia lavka pisatelei*), which existed from September 1918 until 1922, was a pioneering example. The idea of setting up such an enterprise came to the Moscow intellectual Pavel Muratov after it became impossible to continue independent publishing on a significant scale.[73] Using the expertise and contacts of his circle, Muratov was able to launch his project. One of the participants, Mikhail Osorgin, recalled that 'during the hardest years it was not only the anchor of our personal safety, but also a small cultural centre for Moscow'.[74] It was, he said, a refuge for writers, artists, professors, teachers, for all those who did not wish to break their links with culture in the hard times they were living through. Meetings were organised, informal discussions took place with whoever happened to drop in at lunchtime. These events were probably not without distinction in that some of Russia's leading intellectuals, the writers Vladislav Khodasevich and Boris Zaitsev and the religous philosopher Nikolai Berdiaev, were associated with the enterprise for a time at least.[75] Osorgin believed that it was the only bookshop in Russia where anyone could buy any book on offer without requiring official permission.[76] The anomaly that allowed the enterprise to exist is hard to explain. Osorgin suggested that the main reasons for official tolerance of the bookshop were its co-operative structure, its links with the 'Writers' Trade Union', whose presidium came to include the shareholders in the bookshop, and the essential service it provided in giving advice and finding scarce books for state and municipal libraries and newly organised workers' clubs, schools, colleges and universities – given the fact that 'we know books while the new Soviet officials did not have the faintest idea about them'.[77] In addition, it is clear that, given the conditions of the time, the authorities were attempting to improve their links with the intelligentsia by permitting the bookshop to continue. It is more typical than supposed, as will be shown below, that, having survived the immensely difficult conditions of the civil war and war communism, the transition to the New Economic Policy, often interpreted as a more 'liberal' period in Soviet intellectual life, should have proved fatal. The bookshop had to be sold to a private trader, as the co-operative could not support the heavy weight of accumulated tax debts.[78]

Similar enterprises came to exist in the major cities in this period. The 'Petropolis' co-operative in Petrograd was also a cultural centre. It took advantage of improved conditions in Petrograd by 1921 to expand its efforts. Its biggest successes were editions of over a thousand copies of Anna Akhmatova's poems. 'Petropolis' was able to continue operating until 1923, but then it, too, fell victim of the

NEP tax provisions.[79] According to Osorgin, poets, artists and others set up similar enterprises in Moscow, Petrograd and the provinces (he gives an example of one in Kazan') which provided employment for A. Kizevetter, Iu. Vipper, S. Esenin and other leading intellectuals.[80] Like 'Petropolis' some of them were able to do a little publishing. The Moscow Writers' Bookshop, firstly as a joke but later as an important source of revenue for hungry writers, sold autograph manuscripts by poets and other writers for fairly substantial sums. The prices might reflect the dubious economic circumstances of war communism when barter was very extensive. Two of Osorgin's own humorous pamphlets were offered at a price of 'One pound of butter or a pound of sugar' in December 1920. The minor poet Vadim Shershenevich gave an explanation of how he arrived at the price of his manuscript on its cover. 'I took six hours to write this, that is $\frac{2}{3}$ of a working day. In a day I get through 1 jug of milk – 1800 roubles; $\frac{1}{4}$ pound of butter – 3200r.; dinner – 8000r.; 4 lumps of sugar – 2000r.; 50 cigarettes – 3000r.; loose change – 3000r.' This totalled 24,000 roubles (*sic*) to which was added the bookshop's cut of 12,000 roubles for a grant total of 36,000 roubles. Shershenevich generously allowed the purchaser a reduction of 25 per cent on account of his good taste.[81]

An additional focus of independent intellectual activity at this time was provided by the officially tolerated intellectual clubs, or *Domy* (houses). Like all such enterprises these thrived during the civil war but withered in the conditions of NEP, not least because they were deprived of their state patronage.[82]

Intellectuals also began to form more direct pressure groups for the defence of their interests, which were perceived as a decent income, or sufficient supplies to live on, plus creative freedom. These were not easy to achieve during the civil war. One such organisation, comprising a number of well-known writers including Gorky, A. Kuprin, Blok and Gumilev, was set up on the initiative of Fedor Sologub in March 1918 with a membership of forty, later to grow to 170 in April 1919.[83] The main aim of the organisation, called the Union of Belleslettristes (*Soiuz deiateli khudozhestvennoi literaturyi*), was to agitate for material assistance to its members, in particular supplies of food, heating and ensuring at least minimal opportunities to write and to avoid unemployment.[84] Since many of its members, and notably its president, Sologub, were very suspicious of the state, its relations with the authorities were very delicate. It was perhaps as well that Sologub left Petrograd, the centre of the Union's activities, in the summer of 1918, but even so the membership was divided about whether to accept the state's terms for allowing it to establish a publishing house in October 1918. According to its Soviet historian, P. P. Shirmakov, the Union was moribund for a while but showed signs of life again in the spring of 1919 when Gorky tried to amalgamate it with his own organisation 'Culture and Freedom'. Gorky's attitude is encapsulated in his comment of 3 January 1919 that 'The writer must take responsibility for his own affairs into his own hands – strong, conscious hands. The material means for this – money, paper, a press – should be taken from the Commissariat in the same way.'[85] Not surprisingly, in view of such attitudes, the organisation collapsed just as the merger was about to go through. Shirmakov's conclusion that internal bickering was at the root of this may conceal the role of the authorities who no doubt wanted to limit the influence of the old intelligentsia. Shirmakov's accusation that Gorky favoured the 'old' intelligentsia – Zamiatin, Merezhkovsky and Kuprin, for example – at the expense of the 'new', proletarian and revolutionary writers would no doubt have found its echo among contemporaries also.[86]

While organisations set up by established intellectuals on their own initiative were common and usually short lived as a result of official disapproval, the authorities naturally looked more favourably on organisations set up by their own supporters, sometimes under their direct supervision, which tried to organise the intellectual and cultural professions, defend their material interests and bring them closer to the spirit of the Bolshevik revolution. This was often achieved by aiming at the more 'proletarianised' elements of the cultural institutions, for instance print-workers and scene-shifters rather than writers and performers, who were thought to be more receptive to revolutionary ideas than many of the intellectuals themselves. One of the most ambitious projects in this respect was the Union of Workers in the Arts (*Soiuz rabotnikov iskusstv*), widely known as Rabis. This was an umbrella organisation having various federated subsections in each branch of the arts.

From the beginning, organisations such as Rabis combined, in so far as was possible, the twin functions of attracting members by defending their material interests with that of gradually trying to mould them to the tasks of cultural revolution as perceived by the Bolshevik leadership. In the early days the latter was played down, but as time progressed and the Bolsheviks became more and more sure of themselves, the propaganda element became increasingly pronounced. Thus the politics of Rabis in this period was characterised by a certain tension between the intelligentsia membership, whose chief concern was to defend their interests, and the administrators and organisers, backed by a few 'proletarian' intellectuals, who were trying to impose a particular vision of revolutionary cultural activity on a reluctant membership. This latter group, reflecting differences of tactics within the Bolshevik party as a whole, was itself divided between those who wanted to radicalise the intelligentsia at a relatively moderate pace and those who appeared to want all-out radicalisation as quickly as possible. The latter were often associated with local Proletkul't organisations, although the national leadership of Proletkul't did not always back them.

The gap between practitioners and administrators in Rabis is particularly striking if one compares the statutes proposed by the various subsections affiliated to Rabis, and the representations they made to the leadership, with the tone of the delegate and national conference of Rabis in 1920 and 1921. An early point of conflict came in June 1918 when the scene shifters in the Moscow area theatres tried to defend their Easter and Christmas holidays, threatened by the Bolsheviks' plans for secularisation.[87] The rules of the Moscow Union for Musical Artists, put forward in the late summer of 1918, showed how little had changed in the minds of its drafter in that its concerns were the traditional ones of securing minimum fees, unemployment benefit, health care, hostels and dining-rooms and other material advantages. The role of the Union was to take on 'the organisation and defence of the labour of its members and to concern itself with the improvement of their economic and legal standing'.[88] Two years later the pressure coming from the members was similar. The rules of the All-Russian Writers' Trade Union (*Vserossiiskii Professional'nyi Soiuz Pisatelei*), drawn up at its general meeting of the 6 April 1920, defined the union's role as 'the defence of the professional and spiritual interests' of writers. In order to achieve this the union should engage in 'economic struggle with publishers and employers'.[89] On 24 December 1919 the Composers' branch was complaining that its members were being deprived of the 'most valuable of human rights'. At a time when 'the most modest caretaker [*dvornik*] has the right to occupy himself with his own job, which he knows how to do and to which he is accustomed', composers were being forced to work as clerks, typists and accountants in various offices. They were, the resolution claimed, doing every sort of work apart from that for which they were most suited. To correct this, the resolution called for proper respect for authors' rights and a better system of payment for composers.[90]

The following day they also called for more administrative weight to be given to the membership at the expense of the bureaucrats by the setting up of commissions of qualified artistic and scientific workers of all schools and tendencies in the various fields on an equal footing with one another, plus obligatory participation of members of the central committee of the corresponding trade union.[91] The purpose of this was clearly to establish real representation of those actually practising the given profession in a way that could not be ignored by the *apparatchiki* running the organisations. Needless to say, no serious concessions in this direction were forthcoming.

All these examples show the continued attitude of hostility of much of the membership to the plans of the authorities and a regression to defence of immediate material interests in the face of the encroachments made by the Bolsheviks. No reference to the political and social duty of intellectuals towards the people is to be found in these statutes and resolutions. This is perhaps rather surprising given the ubiquitous populism of the intelligentsia up to 1917. Two reasons perhaps explain its disappearance. One is the fear, already mentioned above, that the people were completely hostile to the intelligentsia and threatened to destroy all that the intelligentsia held dear by way of higher cultural values. The second, and perhaps more immediate reason, is that the rhetoric of service of the people had been rapidly taken over as their own by the Bolsheviks after October, and any reference to this in resolutions and decisions of meetings was usually associated with support for radicalism, Bolshevik style.

A comparison of delegate and national conferences of Rabis in this period, occasions when the administrators rather than the members held the reins, clearly show signs of these processes at work. The first delegate conference of the Union, in May 1919, heard complaints from the floor about severe hardship being undergone by parts of the membership and about the iconoclastic excesses of some local Proletkul'ts, which wanted to do away with plays by Shakespeare and Molière. By June 1920, however, when the second national conference of the union was held, proceedings were dominated by the leading figure in the trade union movement, Tomsky, who ominously compared Rabis to the rest of the trade union movement with respect to the latter's role in removing the sectional prejudices of craft and artisan organisations. Applied to Rabis, this implied an equivalent conversion of waverers to Bolshevik cultural aims. Included in the resolutions based on his speech was a reference to Rabis standing 'on a platform of bringing about the communist system through the dictatorship of the proletariat' and of the membership 'going among the broad proletarian masses as teacher-comrades'.[92]

Appeals of this nature appear to have cut little ice with the bulk of the membership or with the established intelligentsia as a whole. For them, the defence of their own interests, perceived in a more traditional way, continued to be paramount and was increasingly seen as a parallel struggle to that of the working masses in general, as Red'ko had suggested in early 1918. It is interesting to note that intelligentsia 'labourism' of this type had developed to such an extent that it was even finding expression at this time among some of the more individualistic and radical of the *émigré* intellectuals. In Paris, the veteran poet N. M. Minsky (1855–1937) proposed a programme for a common struggle of mental and physical labourers against the ruling class, whether capitalist or socialist. All political parties, he suggested, aspired eventually to become a ruling class, living on the profits of the labour of others. 'We mental labourers must fight, together with the proletariat, against all ruling classes and parties because we do not want power to belong to those standing over labour or to the professionals of power, but to labour itself.'[93]

While institutions of this kind looked increasingly to the material welfare of the intelligentsia, other organisations and individuals concentrated on the preservation of its spiritual values. One of the most devoted activists in this respect, not just in these years but throughout his life, was Nicholas Berdiaev. As a self-proclaimed spiritual revolutionary who had had little time for the old order in Russia or in the materialistic bourgeois world of Western Europe, he found much to welcome in the revolution, though he was no Bolshevik, and had even prophesised that, should a revolution break out, it would be a cruel and barbarous one. A revolution, he wrote later, 'is a serious disease and a source of agony to those who undergo it'.[94] None the less, the revolution at least promised that a better world might emerge. 'Strange though it may seem', he recalled, 'I felt inwardly happier after the October revolution, in the Soviet period, than during the previous months.'[95] While this was partly attributable to his view that 'the Bolsheviks showed greater awareness of the situation and a greater courage in facing the revolutionary storm',[96] there was also a sense of stimulation that had not been present earlier. He had always been an active organiser of and attender at discussion groups and circles, but the early Soviet years were unprecedented in this respect. There was, he said 'something exhilarating in the atmosphere of post-revolutionary Russia'.[97] He was associated with several organisations at this time in which he engaged in 'an open war against the spirit [of communism], or rather its hostility to the spirit'.[98] One of them was the Writers' Union which, in conformity with the labourist spirit mentioned by Red'ko, had to be registered as an organisation of printers, there being no provision for organisations of writers.[99] His efforts to protect its members from arrest or the threat of eviction brought him into direct contact with Kamenev in his capacity as Chairman of the Moscow Soviet, who 'had a pleasant way with him' and 'invariably defended the interests of scholars and writers and did a great deal on behalf of the persecuted intellectuals'.[100] He also met Kalinin and, later, Dzherzhinsky, the head of the Cheka. In 1920 Berdiaev was elected a Professor of Philosophy at Moscow University and 'gave lectures in which I openly and without hindrance criticised Marxism'.[101] He was also associated with Osorgin's Writers' Bookshop, which provided his subsistence. It was, he confirms, 'something of a literary club, which apart from the opportunities it gave of meeting other people, provided food, warmth and light'.[102] He gave a number of public lectures on religious and philosophical themes at which debate was as wide ranging and lively as the cross-section of the population that attended. At one of them, on the topic 'Science and Religion', at which 2000 people were present, he had to explain that it was a condition of the lecture being permitted that there should not be any discussion of it, upon which one of those on the platform came forward and announced grandly 'In the name of the Cheka I declare the debate open.' The focus of his activities became the Free Academy of Spiritual Culture, which he set up on a legal but non-institutionalised basis. Lectures and seminars were held at a variety of venues that the authorities agreed to hire out, including, on one occasion, the Central Distillery. An article denouncing this meeting in *Pravda* apparently concluded with unaccustomed humour with a remark that it showed that there had always been a strong bond between religion and spirit. His activities brought him into contact with Dzherzhinsky at the time of the Tactical Centre trial in 1920 but he was released and 'for some months after this I lived comparatively undisturbed'. The situation, he recounts, 'began to change only in the spring of 1922'. He was arrested again and eventually deported with the group exiled in autumn of that year.[103]

On the practical side, Berdiaev experienced all the vicissitudes of the period. He performed compulsory labour but 'did not feel at all depressed and unhappy despite the unaccustomed strain of the pick and shovel on my sedentary muscles and the feeling of dizziness when engaged in hard physical labour. I could not help realising the justice of my predicament.' As far as hunger was concerned he recalled that 'in Petersburg and elsewhere the hunger became real starvation. The shortages in Moscow were less severe, though we were pretty hungry on the little bread and potatoes we were able to get. But all food tasted better than in the years of plenty.' Berdiaev received a small food ration even prior to the system of academic rations coming into existence. One can only agree with his conclusion about these years that the new system was 'full of contradictions and inconsistencies'.[104]

The kind of ideas that Berdiaev and those around him were discussing at this time can be sampled from the main collection of essays they were able to produce, *Iz glubiny* (*Out of the Depths*), which was suppressed on first being published in 1918, though the printers released a few copies illegally and a new edition, based on a copy that had found its way abroad, was published fifty years later.[105] Perhaps the most striking characteristic of the essays is their otherworldly quality. While a violent revolution was taking place the analysis of it in this volume was based on the writings of people such as Gogol' and Dostoevsky and rarely on observation of the actual events occurring at the time. For Berdiaev, popular revolution resulted from the diseases of the Russian soul diagnosed by these writers. Nowhere is there a reference to social injustice or material inequalities as a source for popular attitudes and activities. If anything, these essays show more of an ivory tower mentally than was the case prior to the revolution. Even so, none of the contributors doubted that Russia was undergoing a profound and irreversible change.[106]

Berdiaev was by no means alone in conducting activities of this kind. A large number of societies were set up by pre-revolutionary intellectuals to discuss religious, philosophical and theoretical issues. Andrei Belyi organised a 'Free Philosophical Association' in Petrograd from January 1919 to 1922. It was very similar in scope and outlook to Berdiaev's academy. Economists, sociologists and others organised similar circles in these years. They were to be found not only in Moscow, Petrograd and Kiev but in smaller provincial cities such as Kazan', Kostroma, Perm and Rostov, and even as far away as Tashkent and Chita.[107] In 1922 in particular, a number of these groups succeeded in publishing collections of articles comparable in format and content to those that had been such an important part of pre-revolutionary intellectual life. This proved, however, to be an Indian summer for both the groups and the publications. No such items appeared officially after that date and the leading activists were among those exiled in the autumn of 1922.

In addition to relatively new institutions such as co-operative bookshops and quasi-trade unions a great deal of energy was expended on the defence of longer established intellectual institutions, particularly those involved in the quintessentially intellectual occupations of teaching and research. Other creative intellectual institutions, notably the theatre, literary publishing and the new and increasingly important film industry, became focal points of struggle between the Bolsheviks and the non-Bolshevik intelligentsia. The ebb and flow of the struggles was far from even and no generalisations about this period are possible, apart from the fact that there was steady government encroachment on all fronts. Within that context resistance was more successful in some institutions than others. Moscow University, for instance, appears to have weathered the storm more easily than higher-education institutions in Petrograd. Medicine and science were somewhat better off than literature and the human sciences, though social science faculties – seen by the government as bridgeheads of Marxism in higher education – were set up in many institutions. Despite the relative success of some aspects of resistance, by 1921–2 all of them were much more firmly under government control than in 1919 and the foundations for more thorough integration into the party's cultural aims (once it got around to deciding what those aims were) had already been laid. In higher education, for instance, new methods, such as the establishment of Workers Faculties to give crash courses to the under-qualified, had been tested and Bolshevik personnel had come to dominate all the major decision-making bodies and were in place throughout the system. In the present paragraphs the focus is on the traditional intelligentsia's experiences as these processes unfolded. The policies themselves will be considered in the next chapter.

One of the centres wherein pre-revolutionary intelligentsia values were most successfully preserved was Moscow University. This is all the more remarkable given the formidable practical problems of the period, which were symbolised by the question of heating the university buildings. After a winter in which temperatures in lecture halls and laboratories had fallen to zero, and in some cases to −8°C, the authorities made heating a priority. The university's bursar was so successful in finding firewood that the temperature rose to a comparatively comfortable 7 or 8°C, enabling staff and students to thaw out after living in unheated apartment buildings. Not surprisingly 'the number of people taking part in university activities rose significantly'.[108] Even the Education Ministry, under pressure from its dependants to heat their buildings, tried to find the secret of how the university had been able to obtain its firewood.[109] Miracles were performed elsewhere in the supply field. Laboratory equipment, chemicals, books and so on were found so that some semblance of normal academic life could be carried on. Teaching activities were, in the words of the rector, M. M. Novikov, able to continue 'more or less successfully' although overcrowding on the initial courses brought a lowering of academic standards.[110] 'When one recalls now the intense teaching and, not infrequently, scientific activity going on at that time in the university, one can only marvel that it was possible under the distressing conditions of personal life.'[111] Although subject to arrest – Novikov himself having been caught up in the wave of arrests of September 1918 and sentenced to life imprisonment, which lasted until the amnesty of November 1918[112] – the staff were able to continue their work. Novikov even points out that despite Cheka searches and arrests, and collisions with and interference from the Education Ministry over specific questions, 'the general principle of autonomous administration of the university remained in force until autumn 1920'.[113] The struggle to preserve as much of that autonomy as possible continued right until the end. The professors even turned to the formation of trade union type organisations and tactics to defend their academic and material interests. In early 1922 a brief university strike, which quickly spread throughout higher-education institutions in Moscow, Petrograd and elsewhere, embarrassed the government when it was trying to put on its most acceptable face at the time of the Genoa Conference. Though there was a popular demand from the professors for 'Not twenty-five but two hundred and fifty roubles a month' the strike ended on a promise from A. I. Tsiurup, the acting chairman of the Bolshevik 'cabinet' (Bolshoi Sovnarkom), that a commission of inquiry, including freely elected representatives of the academic staff, would examine the grievances. The universities went meekly back to work and the inquiry commission produced little of benefit to the academics. The commission had a solemn meeting with Bolshoi Sovnarkom at which each side was able to put its point of view. Needless to say, in the end the Education Ministry's position was supported by the rest of the government. Rykov pointedly asked the delegation, referring to the professoriat in general, 'What have you done for the people?' At that time the academics had little to their credit on that score.[114] They were given little chance to improve their record as many of the Moscow University professors, who had mostly been supporters of the Kadets – Novikov, for example, having been a Duma representative for the city of Moscow – were prominent among the group of intellectuals exiled abroad at seven days notice in September 1922. Thus, even the comparatively successful and energetic resistance they had put up met with complete defeat.

The story of Moscow University was probably not typical. Other institutions found survival even harder. The Petrograd Institute of Technology, the leading institution in its field, fared much worse. Writing in 1928 the then Rector said that from the end of 1917 until the 1920–1 academic year normal academic life was impossible. Routine tasks of accepting students, giving lectures and even carrying out a little research continued 'from inertia' but preservation of self and institution were uppermost in everyone's minds. The number of graduating engineers, the institute's central teaching area, fell from 132 in 1917 to 28 in 1919. Problems of supply and finance were not dealt with as successfully as in Moscow University and it was only in 1920, when the Education Ministry was induced to take more interest, that the decline in the institute's fabric was halted and essential repairs undertaken. This coincided with the introduction of crash courses for former Red Army men, now demobilised as the civil war drew to a close. These courses were 'the bridge by which the October revolution first began to make its way into the Institute'. Intakes on the complete course also began to return to normal with 349 taken into the Mechanical Engineering faculty.[115]

The relative wealth, good connections and closeness of the decision makers whom it could, and did, lobby energetically, were advantages that helped prevent Moscow University in this period from falling into the moribund state of the Technology Institute. The difference may also reflect a generally harsher set of conditions in Petrograd during the civil war. The depopulation of the city affected the Institute and many members of staff left in 1918 as conditions became intolerable. Hunger, deprivation and epidemics began to take their toll,[116] though to what extent this was worse than in Moscow is difficult to judge. While student numbers fell at the Technology Institute they were breaking all records in Moscow, which admitted five times as many students in 1918 as in 1914, selected from nearly 6000 applicants.[117] Total numbers of students in Moscow University, according to its official report for 1917–20 submitted to the Ministry, rose from 6888 in January 1917 to 8682 a year later, 22,972 in January 1919 and 26,932 in January 1920. The increases were large in all faculties. The greatest beneficiaries of this expansion, however, were women, the total numbers of whom rose from 28 in January 1917 (when they were officially excluded) to a modest 202 in January 1918, reflecting the snail's pace of Provisional Government reform in this area, to 6566 in January 1919 and 10,253 in January 1920, comprising 38 per cent of the total.[118] The number of professors rose from 96 (1 January 1917) to 362 (1 January 1920) and total staff numbers from 717 to 829 in the same period.[119] In these respects, however, Moscow was clearly more typical of the country as a whole in that total student numbers in higher education in this period rose from 125,000 in 91 establishments in 1914–15 to a peak of 224,000 in no less than 244 establishments in the academic year 1921–2. Thereafter numbers began to decline as the central government got a firmer grip on this mushrooming growth and reclassified institutions to levels more appropriate to their functions and academic standards.[120]

Equally important to the material and spiritual well-being of the intelligentsia was the existence of press and publishing facilities. Here, although some independence was retained through this period, the situation was much bleaker than with respect to higher-education institutions. For the Bolsheviks, the newspaper and journal press was a vital element of the political struggle, and had been since the foundation of the movement when the newspaper *Iskra* was a bone of contention in the power struggle with the Mensheviks within the party. In the revolution itself, control of newspapers was equated with control of the organised activities of other political parties. Thus they had much more immediate importance than colleges and had to be watched very carefully and closed if they were thought to be too dangerous. Within a year of October the newspapers were all under government control, as were most journals. Private publishing of books and occasional journals of a non-political nature, in the everyday sense, continued to exist but on a very much reduced scale. In addition, some members of the intelligentsia, notably Gorky, were able to extract important concessions from the officially established state publishing houses and other authorities as a result of which some semblance of 'normal' intellectual life was able to continue. On the practical side, a certain amount of very limited patronage was available, which made a small contribution to the physical survival of some of the established intellectuals. Thus, in the field of book publishing as opposed to newspapers, the state monopoly did not come about at once but was mediated by the existence of private publishers and the involvement of non-party intellectuals in publishing ventures during the first phases of the transition period.

An early example of joint activity by party and non-party people at this time is provided by the literary-artistic committees set up in Petrograd and Moscow. As well as party and trade union members, the Petrograd committee included Blok, Benois, Morozov, Alt'man, Punin, Reisner and Shterenberg.[121] In Moscow, Veresaev, Briusov, Gershenzon, Grabar' and Sakulin sat on the committee. Several of them tried to protest against the proposed state monopoly of the publication of literary classics, which would take the most lucrative part of literary publishing out of the hands of independent publishers, but without success.[122] None the less, some private and co-operative publishing was able to continue. In 1918, over half of the titles published came from private publishers.[123] The largest such enterprise was the Writers' Publishing House (*Knigoizdatel'stvo pisatelei*) set up by Gershenzon on co-operative lines similar to the Writers' Bookshop mentioned above. It lasted from 1918 to 1923.[124] In the first year of the revolution it published 111 titles, ranging from works by A. A. Bogdanov to Rabindranath Tagore. This was by far the highest output of any private or co-operative publisher.[125]

Overall, then, as a group, the bulk of the intelligentsia remaining in Russia in this period tried to remain independent of both White and Red politics. The above examples all show how it gave increasing priority to its own immediate interests under the terrible pressures of direct political persecution and general deprivation resulting from the civil war and the collapse of the economy. This expressed itself through unions, co-operatives and traditional institutions. In all of them the sectional interests of the intelligentsia came to play a much more important role than the idealistic populist impulses that had been present in earlier times. Pure scholarship, the values of high culture, creative freedom, academic autonomy and preservation of academic standards became its dearest values. In a sense, the bulk of the intelligentsia had achieved its own specific class consciousness. As Red'ko put it in 1918, the idea that it was outside or above class was 'a laughable self-deception'. The terrifying harshness of war and revolution had squeezed out a great deal of the social idealism about service of the people in its populist form. In so far as it still existed among this group, this impulse was associated more with nationalism and making Russia strong, wealthy and powerful once more than with directly aiding 'the people'. The phrase 'the people' itself came to have a more and more ironic tone, formerly used only by rightwingers. It was not just Bolshevik prostitution (as they saw it) of the phrase but the outcome of a whole variety of experiences that led to the estrangement of intelligentsia from people, foretold ten years earlier by Gershenzon and Blok. It was not, however, that the people had uniformly turned on the intelligentsia. Even in prison Novikov had found common criminals, including at least one murderer, who had shown respect for his knowledge and, at their request, he had given them lectures on natural science.[126] The vast expansion of education at all levels also indicates a thirst for knowledge. However, the traditional intelligentsia did little to respond directly to this. Rykov's question, 'What have you done for the people?' was not simply a debating point. In the storm, the bulk of the intelligentsia had, perhaps understandably, turned to its beloved abstractions as a means of escape. It may be that hostility to it was increased by this apparent desertion. Certainly, the Bolsheviks used this line in anti-intelligentsia propaganda from the early weeks of the revolution.

Not all of the established intellectuals took this path. A minority, motivated more by populism than deep-rooted Marxism or Bolshevism, responded more directly and generously to the needs of the people. Some of them, like Belyi or Khodasevich, were far from being Bolshevik in any sense of the word; though they eventually lived in exile, they to some extent 'accepted the revolution', in the phrase of the time. Others were more wholeheartedly revolutionary.

ACTIVE COLLABORATION

The third major strategy among the non-Bolshevik intelligentsia was developed by those who were, to differing extents and for differing reasons, prepared to work with the new authorities. People pursuing this course often shared, to some extent, the professed aims of the Soviet government, though not its methods. Where the previous group was trying to build civil society independent of the state, this group was less reluctant to work within the framework of Soviet state structures. This group, like the two others we have examined, was wide ranging in its composition. At one extreme one could include relatively non-political scientific and technical workers who decided freely to work for the Bolsheviks, and at the other politically committed supporters of revolution, like the poet Vladimir

Maiakovsky (1893–1930). As a group, it was no more hermetically sealed than either of the others and it shades into the non-committed at one end and the Bolsheviks at the other. Passage across the always indistinct borders was not infrequent. None the less, one can identify the core of a distinctive response to the revolution characterising this group as a whole. They were distinguished from the non-committed by their greater willingness to work for the new system. For instance, where Novikov worked to try to limit Bolshevik influence in his sphere as much as possible, more active sympathisers at Moscow University, of whom the most notable was the biologist K. Timiriazev (1843–1920), actively promoted Bolshevik reform plans, though without going so far as other academics, such as the historian M. Pokrovsky (1868–1932) who was a very active and influential member of the Communist Party and of the bureaucratic apparatus controlling educational and cultural policy. Despite sharing this intermediate position, the atmosphere and attitudes of sympathisers from among the technical and scientific intelligentsia were different from those of the artistic intelligentsia and it would make for greater clarity to look at each of these groups separately.

While it is difficult to categorise any of the individuals and groups within the intelligentsia, this is particularly so with respect to the technical intelligentsia. In the early stages of the revolution they were as unsympathetic to the Bolsheviks as any other part of the intelligentsia, but they were won over more rapidly than any other section, not least become the Soviet government made this a priority. A glance at the scientific intelligentsia in these years will give an impression of the processes at work.[127]

One of the most representative conferences of the technical intelligentsia held in the early Soviet period was the Second Moscow Regional Conference of the All-Russian Union of Engineers which met from 18 to 21 October 1918. For the most part the conference concerned itself with bread-and-butter issues and had very little to say about the political situation, the development of the revolution or the outbreak of civil war. There was a protest about the effects of 'Red Terror' on engineers and calls for a speedy release of arrested engineers, but this was rather exceptional.[128] There was also a reference in a keynote speech by M. G. Evreinov on behalf of the Executive Committee which claimed the engineers put moral values above material ones, a clear echo of the traditional intelligentsia values, by now perhaps losing real meaning and beginning to degenerate into ritual ideological incantation.[129] For the rest, work conditions and related issues dominated attention. While it would be wrong to interpret this as sympathy for the Bolsheviks, in an active sense it did betoken a real step in that direction when compared with the first such conference to be held after the October revolution. Held from 4 to 6 January 1918, this conference of the Moscow Regional organisation of the Union of Engineers reflected much more political hostility to the Bolsheviks. The fact that it was held at exactly the same time as the Constituent Assembly was meeting and being dispersed in Petrograd helps to explain the higher political temperature. Indeed, one of the delegates, named Ratner, was killed in the course of a demonstration in support of the Constituent Assembly. A main task of the January conference had been to formulate a response to the Bolshevik's experiments in industrial organisation. From all sides there came vigorous condemnation of the 'social anarchy' that was said to be destroying the industrial economy, and members of the union were called upon to withdraw their support from all control and supervisory bodies encroaching on the proper supervisory functions of engineers. Such bodies were to be boycotted by members of the union and engineers who disobeyed were themselves to be boycotted.[130] This was, in effect, a declaration of war against the Bolsheviks and an open trial of strength that the engineers lost, in that this militant mood had been toned down to relatively mildly worded protests about the terror at the October conference. And yet the engineers' militance did not meet with complete defeat in that, at the instigation of Lenin himself and over the heads of vehement protests from the egalitarian left of the party, soon to be branded with the description 'left-wing childishness', the Soviet government moved towards a policy of reconciliation with the scientific, technical, military and managerial élite in the hope that a significant proportion of them could be persuaded to put their much-needed skills at the service of the new state. This opening up towards 'specialists' inaugurated a policy that lasted until the late 1920s, by which time Stalin considered the war was ripe to replace the remnants of the old technical élite by people who had been trained in Soviet educational institutions.

The centrepiece of this policy was to increase material incentives and rewards for specialists beyond the levels of skilled workers and beyond those of the highest state functionaries, including Lenin. In addition, very scarce resources were made available for scientific research even in the darkest moments of the civil war. A proliferation of small institutes working on shoestring budgets began to make their appearance. The physicist A. I. Ioffe, for instance, noted that the first steps to organise the radiological institute, which he came to head, were taken in September 1918 by Grinberg and Kristi, Education Ministry functionaries dealing with science.[131] In January 1919 a conference of one hundred physicists from all over Soviet Russia was held in Petrograd.[132] Many of those who staffed the new institutions were formally underqualified and very young. Some even went directly into research before completing their undergraduate courses. 'The physics and technology faculty', Ioffe tells us, 'was jokingly referred to as the kindergarten, but the experiment justified itself.'[133] The story was repeated in many similar institutions. The extent of research was such that the Supreme Council of the National Economy was even able to put out an impressive list of more than 150 pages of scientific work in progress in 1918–19. Theoretical and practical work of great breadth was being undertaken ranging from producing motorcycle sidecars and trailers to comparing different fuels in aircraft engines.[134] The academic report of Moscow University for the period 1917–19, submitted to the Education Ministry, shows an equally wide range of activity in the scientific and medical faculties. Some of the publications, for instance T. I. Iudin's work on the clinical and psychological effects of hunger, based on observations in German prisoner-of-war camps, took on a morbid appropriateness given the circumstances of the time. None the less, a remarkable amount of scientific publication was recorded for this period. Conversely, the account makes no reference to any publications emanating from the historical/philosophical and law faculties.[135] The Academy of Sciences was also able to pursue its activities even though the wartime shortages leading to the afflictions of cold and hunger took their toll. None the less, 'from 1917 to 1927 the Academy of Sciences retained the essential features it had inherited from the pre-revolutionary epoch'.[136] Encouragement of material support for scientific and technical activities quickly began to reap dividends similar to those who have seen in connection with the engineers. Hostility was softened into criticism combined with constructive work. Patriotism, geared to the task of rebuilding the completely ruined national economy of Russia, for the benefit for everyone and not simply the Bolsheviks, became increasingly important themes for the scientific and technical intelligentsia. The scientific Utopianism of the new government also added another dimension that began to attract Russian engineers who, like their colleagues in other times and other places, began to believe more and more in technological solutions to human and social problems. Saint Simonian dreams began to emerge and even seemed to have found a government devoted to their realisation. A non-party engineer, I. P. Bardin, recounted in his memoirs how his pre-revolutionary dreams of turning Russia into 'a fairy-tale country of technical marvels, where everything was mechanised, blast-furnaces ran like clockwork and people in mines did not have to fear anything unexpected' began to appear to be a step nearer reality.[137] Setting aside more complex reflections, Bardin probably spoke for many engineers when he said that, for him, the fundamental question was 'do the interests of Soviet power coincide with my aspirations as an engineer?'[138] Many, apart from Bardin, came to answer this question in the affirmative and it ran like a leitmotif through the 1920s, to take on a new lease of life with the peak of Utopianism that coincided with the first years of the first five-year plan (1928–30). Increasingly, technical and social reconstruction as a national task began to attract non-party Russian patriots such as Ustrialov and Bardin, to replace hostility and indifference to the Bolsheviks with active support, albeit often hedged around with implicit or explicit conditions. Among the first steps in this direction was the Soviet government's encouragement and subsidising of the Academy of Sciences Commission for the Study of Scientific Productive Forces (KEPS).[139] This type of co-operation was extended in late 1918 to bring scientists and engineers into the Scentific-Technical Section of the Supreme Council of the National Economy.[140] In addition to material concessions, the Bolsheviks also operated their two-pronged policy of winning over as many neutrals as possible and dominating the institutional and organisational life of the scientists and engineers. The process of assimilation of the engineers, for instance, was speeded up by the use of administrative methods to circumvent the leadership of the old union by downgrading its status to that of an association and setting up a new national organisation linked to the Soviet trade union movement. Like other branches of the movement, the purpose of the new organisation was not to defend the interests of members against the state but to act as an agent of the state in diffusing its ideals and policies down to the grass roots. The result, as Kalinin expressed it at the first national conference of the new organisation in December 1922, was that the slow transformation of 'the intelligentsia masses' into 'defenders of the revolution and, in some cases, revolutionary activists' was taking place on an ever-increasing scale. The fact that the trade union leader Tomsky was the other chief speaker shows how far organisational leadership had fallen out of the hands of engineers themselves and into the ever-expanding mesh of state supervision.[141]

Materially and institutionally the situation of the artistic intelligentsia was very different from that of the scientists and engineers. There was considerably more support for the revolution from the former, at least after a somewhat shaky start, and their affiliation to the revolution came to be closely linked to access to the not inconsiderable state patronage available, patronage for which they competed against a small, but growing, number of thoroughly Bolshevik – or proletarian as they often styled themselves – intellectuals. From early on the proletarian group seriously questioned the party's policy of supporting and encouraging any non-Bolshevik intellectuals no matter how sympathetic to the revolution they might be. In this respect they shared the underlying principles of the party left, which had opposed the turn towards technical specialists in rather similar terms. Such concessions appeared to these leftists to be a partial defeat in the class struggle, which they wanted to see carried on without compromise. Thus, non-party artists were seen as a Trojan horse of the bourgeois enemy. For the time being, however, the 'proletarian' forces were so weak that, as in the technical sphere, the party leadership had little alternative to a policy of limited concession and some encouragement aimed at converting more of the artistic intelligentsia to Bolshevik values.

Institutionally, the life of the artistic sympathisers with Bolshevism was a little more clear-cut in that one organisation, the Education Ministry, dominated the material lives of this group. Many of the channels of patronage had their source in the Education Ministry. Whether it was a matter of giving a lecture or workshop for Proletkul't, becoming an art school lecturer, or a museum curator, executing a bust or even participating in an architectural competition, or simply decorating streets and squares for revolutionary festivals, it was the Education Ministry that, through its many subdivisions, was likely to be paying the piper. Perhaps the most prominent branch of the ministry in this respect was its Fine Arts section (known as IZO from its Russian name), which quickly became the engine room of avant-garde art in Soviet Russia. Through the patronage of the Education Minister, A. V. Lunacharsky, the organisation came to be dominated by adherents of the futurist school and its constructivist and suprematist successors. D. P. Shterenberg was at the head of IZO with Vladimir Tatlin in charge of its Moscow branch. Kasimir Malevich and Vassili Kandinsky were also involved. Its close association with one particular school guaranteed fierce opposition from all the rest, on right and left, and critics were not slow in coming forward. The left attacked Lunacharsky for putting IZO in the hands of bourgeois aesthetes; the right attacked him for giving exclusive support to the avant-garde. Analagous arguments arose over music, drama, literature and education.[142] Thus, the arts was a microcosm of the general political problem facing the Bolshevik leadership, which was attacked from the right and by an increasingly strident left within the party itself.

The relationship between the party and leading writers and artists is one of the best-known aspects of the political and intellectual history of the period thanks to a series of monographs, biographies and memoirs devoted to the question. A brief examination of the reactions of certain central figures and the evolution of their ideas about the revolution will therefore be sufficient for present purposes, namely to elucidate the attitudes of this group, to indicate the complexity and ambiguity of their outlook and to differentiate them from other sections of the intelligentsia. It is also perhaps worth reiterating at this point that the word 'sympathiser' is being used in a very restricted sense to describe such people. In general, the people in this category, though often as hostile as anybody else to the Bolshevik seizure of power in its early stages, came round to participate actively in various Soviet-sponsored political and sometimes propagandistic enterprises. Thus, they tended to give more support to the government in the civil war than the neutral intelligentsia who often sympathised with the centre-liberal, Kadet outlook. Where the latter gave practical support to the Bolsheviks for nationalistic and patriotic reasons, the former, the 'sympathisers', tended to retain stronger echoes of radical populism and frequently participated in Soviet activities in order to satisfy their still-strong impulses to serve the people. By and large, while not blind to the black side of the revolution, these people hoped that the promise of the revolution might yet assert itself and, in any case, they had even less sympathy for the Russian and European bourgeoisie, the old ruling class and the tsarist system than they had for the Bolsheviks.

Perhaps the most prominent and, in many ways, typical member of this group was Russian's best-known living writer at that time, Maksim Gorky. Gorky had been a close associate of Lenin long before the revolution and had been close to leading members of the party. He had also differed with Lenin over certain fundamental principles and had been close to Bogdanov and Lunacharsky in the philosophical and artistic disputes of the 1907–12 period. The party school set up by these three to raise the educational and cultural level of the working-class members of the party was based near Gorky's home on the island of Capri.[143] Relations between Lenin and Gorky, though smoothed out somewhat in the intervening years, became extremely acrimonious in the revolutionary year of 1917. Gorky was able to fund an independent radical newspaper, *Novaia zhizn'* (*New Life*), which became increasingly critical of Lenin's tendency to streamroller democratic procedures, particularly as he intensified his drive towards an armed uprising. It was in *Novaia zhizn'* that Lenin's two most prominent critics from within the Bolshevik central committee, Kamenev and Zinoviev, published their arguments against Lenin's course of action just one week before the October insurrection and at a time when preparations for it should have been in full swing. Thus Gorky's outlook of sympathy for the liberating promise of radical social-democracy tempered by scepticism concerning the viability of Lenin's tactics for realising that promise had been established long before the revolution itself took place.

In the revolutionary years Gorky's outlook became dominated by the fear that Russian culture and the intelligentsia that embodied it were too fragile to withstand the waves of violence and pitiless cruelty welling up from what he had called the lower depths of society. Like many other *intelligenty* he believed that civilised values were in danger of being destroyed by barbarism from below. Writing of his impression of the July uprising, Gorky expressed his horror at the course the revolution appeared to be taking. Instead of mob violence, 'the slow flame of culture' was needed to cleanse Russia of 'its inbred slavery'. Unlike others, however, he accused the intelligentsia of abandoning its duty and of being in part responsible for this state of affairs:

I am sure that if the part of the intelligentsia which, fearing responsibility and avoiding danger, has hidden somewhere and is idle while taking delight in criticising what is going on; if this intelligentsia, from the first days of freedom, had tried to introduce other guiding principles into the chaos of aroused instincts, if it had attempted to arouse feelings of a different order – none of us would have experienced the multitude of those abominations which we are now experiencing.[144]

The substance of his bitter criticism of Lenin was that he was playing recklessly on these chaotic instincts. 'These sectarians and fanatics are gradually arousing the instincts and hopes of the ignorant masses – vain and unrealisable under present conditions',[145] he wrote in December. At the same time, however, his belief in the future remained an important source of hope: 'in order to become people capable of action we must believe that these frenzied days smeared with filth and blood are the great days of the birth of a new Russia'.[146]

For Gorky, the force capable of bringing about this rebirth was the conscious, genuinely socialist intelligentsia that would guide and educate the masses into the new values. His most characteristic work of the period was to use his influence to protect as many intellectuals as he could who had fallen foul of the Cheka and other agents of the Bolshevik dictatorship. He achieved this in three ways: direct intervention, not infrequently with Lenin himself; through organising state patronage to provide a little income for those suffering extreme hardship; and through setting up pressure groups to extract concessions from the authorities. Though valuable, his work in these areas was barely able to scratch the surface and often aroused hostility to him where he failed rather than gratitude where he succeeded. He has been reproached for allowing one of Russia's leading poets, Nikolai Gumilev, who was implicated in the Tagantsev conspiracy in 1921, to be executed 'before Gorky had got around to doing anything'.[147] None the less, nobody was able to achieve as much as Gorky in this respect and a wide range of intellectuals were helped.

As the situation changed and the civil war began to develop, so Gorky's attitude began to evolve. Where his socialist principles had led him into conflict with Lenin in 1917, so they led him to recognise Soviet power as the only hope, once the political situation began to polarise. A *rapprochement* between himself and the Bolsheviks began to develop, based on a shared opposition to counter-revolution. By the end of 1918, he was to be found sharing a platform with Lunacharsky, Zinoviev and others in order to appeal to intelligentsia and white-collar workers to resist foreign intervention. He had, he said, always defended the working class and supported the resolution passed that called for the intelligentsia to unite with the proletariat in urging Britain and the United States to keep their hands off Russia.[148] This did not mean that he gave unqualified support to the Soviet authorities. He continued to press them for material concessions for the intelligentsia and, as mentioned above, fought for intellectual freedom throughout these years. His aim, in which he failed utterly, was to set up publishing facilities free of government and party intervention. In December 1920 he, together with Kropotkin, protested to the Eighth Congress of Soviets about the closing down of the few remaining private publishers. Kropotkin phrased his objections in terms of general principles and the need for freedom, while Gorky limited himself to pointing out that the State Publishing House was very inefficient and could not meet demand. It was even failing to supply school text books in adequate quantities. None the less, his opposition to party and government encroachment in this field had been consistent.[149]

Gorky's position in these years has often been misunderstood. Some have seen him as an apologist for the regime from this early date, prefiguring his last years when he apparently performed the same function for Stalin in the 1930s. And yet many of his writings of this period, particularly his journalism, remain suppressed in the Soviet Union even though he is an officially approved writer. The key to this paradox is that his vehement opposition to the Leninists, expressed in 1917, was, indeed, tempered as the choice between either Lenin or the counter-revolution presented itself more starkly. But at the same time, he never abandoned his underlying belief that socialism could only be built on the basis of decent and humane values, embodied in the intelligentsia, rather than on the cruelty of the ordinary people whose natural goodness had been perverted by centuries of tyranny, serfdom and wage-slavery. Thus his pessimism and his optimism, his support for and his criticisms of Bolshevism, his attempts to defend intellectuals of many different persuasions through providing food rations or a little paid employment and his efforts to set up a publishing house controlled by writers rather than officials, all rose from this root. His tactics changed as he was forced to retreat in all these areas but he does provide an interesting example of a radical intellectual whose response to Bolshevism was critical but had to be tempered as a result of the absence of a viable alternative. In 1922, for example, he continued to argue that only Soviet power was capable of invigorating the inert masses. But even so, he expressed disagreement with the attitude of the Soviet authorities to the intelligentsia. It should not attack them, because, Gorky said, only by nurturing people of talent could the government achieve its objectives. It was wrong to squander rare talent and, instead, honest people who really believed in the 'good of the people' (*blago naroda*) ought, since they shared the same aims, to be able to agree with, rather than shoot, one another.[150]

At first sight, it appears odd that the most enthusiastic supporters of the revolution should have come from groups much more distant from Bolshevism than Gorky. However, closer examination suggests that the enthusiasm for the revolution shown by these writers and artists was of a very different order from that characteristic of Bolshevik activists themselves. What they tended to see in the revolution was an opportunity to further their own literary and artistic interests and enthusiasms. In very few cases did any of them have any more than an inkling of the ideas of Marx and of the deeper political aims and objectives of the new leaders. Rather they projected their own ideas onto the revolution. From the Bolshevik point of view there was always a good deal of criticism for allowing so much influence to these groups and, like the specialists in other fields, their survival was dependent on patronage in very high places. Relations between various schools within them was also marked by the competition for patronage from virtually the only remaining source: Narkompros.

These groups have attracted more attention than any other part of the intellectual and cultural scene in these years and it is not necessary to repeat this work here.[151] In the majority of cases the interest in them arises from the fact that they embodied the artistic revolution and the sense of exhilaration to be found, despite the practical difficulties of the civil war period, among many intellectuals sympathetic to the revolution. In many ways they seem to exemplify the liberating aspects of the revolution. According to this view, it was the change of atmosphere in the revolution associated with the rise of Stalin that destroyed this creative outburst. However, the very foundations on which the new movements were built also have to be taken into consideration because, in many respects, they were already a halfway house to political control from their very origin.

As we have already seen, the instinct of almost all artists after the February revolution was to be very distrustful of any initiative that smacked of state encroachment on artistic freedom. As a result, the Provisional Government made little impact on artistic and cultural life, which remained highly spontaneous throughout its life. However, after October the situation eventually changed to the extent that many members of the avant-garde were prepared to take advantage of the new conditions in order to carry out, and even, in not a few cases, to impose their own revolution in the name of the party and of the new government. The claim of the avant-garde to represent the same values as the Bolsheviks was very unconvincing, particularly to Bolsheviks, and they were frequently reminded that the party, not the artists, would decide policy. Warnings against their overenthusiasm were increasingly frequent. In many cases they were criticised for themselves narrowing down the field of what was considered acceptable in art and trying to establish their own orthodoxy. The relative pluralism of the war communism period was defended by Lenin, Lunacharsky and others against the attempted hegemony that many artists, particularly those of the self-styled left, themselves wished to impose.

It has to be borne in mind in assessing this period that, in the first place, by attempting to colonise parts of the state apparatus to achieve their own ambitions the avant-garde had themselves opened up the way to more active state involvement in the area. Secondly, their sometimes irresponsible and eccentric use of their position provided an excellent excuse, and perhaps even reason, for the party to intervene even further in order to control them. It was not difficult for the authorities to undermine them on the grounds that their works were unintelligible to the ordinary person and that, in their outlook and personal behaviour, they showed themselves to be bourgeois decadents rather than proletarian artists. The accommodating label of 'futurists' was applied to many of them and became the chief term of artistic abuse in party policy documents at this time. Even Proletkul't was branded with being infiltrated by futurists. Some of the more extreme positions held by some of the artistic avant-garde, especially the cultural iconoclasm favoured by those who wanted the artistic revolution to begin with a clear and complete break with the art of the past, were exploited by the party and applied indiscriminately to groups such as Proletkul't to provide a fig-leaf of respectability for policies motivated by quite different objectives.[152]

A brief example may help to show how these stages worked in the field of art. Much attention has been given, rightly, to the leading Soviet art school of the 1920s, Vkhutemas (Higher State Artistic and Technical Studios), which pioneered many innovations in pure and applied arts. As such, it is often seen as a good example of artistic tolerance, particularly since it was not dominated by any one faction. However, such an interpretation overlooks the fact that it was set up in 1920 to replace the broader and more autonomous network of the State Free Art Studios, themselves set up by the abolition in 1918 of the Stroganov School of Applied Art and the Moscow School of Painting, Sculpture and Architecture. The State Free Art Studios allowed 'within their walls the free existence of all defined artistic trends, the studios give every student the opportunity of developing his individual skills in whatever direction he wishes'.[153]

While Vkhutemas retained, at least for a while, something of this atmosphere, such wide-ranging autonomy was no longer on the agenda. The goal of Vkhutemas was to link art and production, not to provide an enclave for artistic freedom. Thus, the founding of Vkhutemas was itself part of the process of greater organisation and central control that was in evidence in many spheres of intellectual life once the civil war came to an end.[154]

The relation between artistic sympathisers with the revolution and the party was, then, far from straightforward. The intellectuals who 'accepted' the revolution tended to do so from the point of view of their own conception of the revolution, not from a desire to accept Bolshevik guidance. If anything, such respect for the Bolsheviks as they could muster tended to be because they believed that the new leadership was, in some way or other, the authentic voice of the people, a belief the Bolsheviks, not unnaturally, assiduously cultivated. Rather than accept party supervision they, as has not infrequently been pointed out, thought of themselves as the guides of the party. They hoped that the authorities would recognise them in this role and hand the field over to them. The party thought otherwise. There can be no greater contrast between these artists and those, of quite different calibre, outlook and experience, who were behind the founding of the Association of Artists of Revolutionary Russia, which was set up by a few proletarian artists who had been present at a furious debate between the futurists and their detractors in 1922. In response they decided to set up their own organisation and go along to the authorities and ask them how they should develop revolutionary art. It was suggested that the best thing for them to do would be to set up their easels in factories and to portray the proletarian way of life. They were happy to oblige.[155] The avant-garde lived on a totally different plane.

The party had, none the less, been happy to go along with them for a variety of reasons. The most obvious was that the avant-garde had been more prepared to go along with the party in the very early days when more established artists had shunned the new authorities. In addition, the avant-garde considered itself anti-bourgeois and was imbued with the rhetoric of revolution, even though what they meant by it was very different from what the party understood by the term. There were other important reasons for party toleration of the avant-garde. Lunacharsky, and many of the intelligentsia Bolsheviks, retained a respect for the arts and for culture even when they did not agree with certain schools and tendencies. For instance, while party leaders often criticised futurist domination of artistic life in these years, and asserted that futurism was emphatically not the party line in art, they did not suggest that the futurists should be silenced. There was general agreement in these circles that culture should be preserved. Lenin's view, shared by others in the leadership, veered towards making established cultural values available to the ordinary people. This also opened up the way to employing many otherwise unacceptable intellectuals on harmless but useful projects, such as Gorky's World Literature series, and the preservation of museums and monuments. Another reason was that there were various practical needs that called for collaboration with artists in the same way that education needed collaboration with teachers and so on. The party needed artists to produce propaganda and many of the best-known names from the avant-garde were employed on this. Increasingly, the restoration of industry and the ambitious plans for the future required the participation of artists and architects. One of the main aims of Vkhutemas was that it should 'prepare highly qualified master artists for industry as well as instructors and directors of professional and technical education'.[156] Finally, respect for culture and the arts was very quickly incorporated into Soviet Russia's international image-building, particularly since a lot of the attention of the outside world from the early years was focused on the plight of intellectuals in the country.

While no individual fully typifies the processes under way in this period, a glance at the career of one person helps to show how they affected the concrete experiences of intellectuals. Many individuals could be chosen for this purpose – Blok, Belyi, Maiakovsky, Lissitsky, Malevich, Tatlin. These are all people who, in a special way, capture something of this early revolutionary moment. One person who is less frequently thought of in this context, to the detriment of an understanding of his work as a whole, is Marc Chagall. At first sight his experience during the war seems atypical in that this was a time of great creativity and recognition for him, as for others of the avant-garde, which, as we have already noted, was something of an exception in this respect. In Chagall's case, this was connected with his great love for Bella Rosenfeld, whom he married in 1915, and the birth of his daughter Ida in 1916. He painted numerous works and was represented in several of the major wartime exhibitions. He was invited to send twenty-five works to the 'Year 1915' exhibition. Sixty-three were displayed in the Dobychina Gallery in April 1916 and four paintings and sixty-nine drawings in November and

December 1917. Forty-five of his works were on display at the 'Jack of Diamonds' exhibition in November 1916.[157] Even so, Chagall commented that, in the wake of the German victories, 'My painting lost its edge.'[158] Although he was stimulated by the events of the revolution he was not a participant. 'The actors and painters', he recalled, 'have gathered in the Mikhailovsky Theatre. They mean to found a Ministry of the Arts. I attend as an onlooker. Suddenly, I hear my own name proposed for minister by the young artists. I leave Petrograd and return to Vitebsk. I still prefer my home town to being a minister.'[159] The difficulty of conditions in Petrograd had also, no doubt, contributed to his decision to return to Vitebsk. Some months after his return, in August 1918, Lunacharsky appointed him to be Commissar for Art in the Vitebsk province. According to his letter of appointment his duties were 'to organise art schools, museums, exhibitions, lectures on art, and all other artistic ventures within the limits of the city and region of Vitebsk'.[160] For two and a half years he threw himself into his organisational work. In October 1918 he decorated the streets of the city for the celebration of the first anniversary of the revolution.

And on October 25th, my multicoloured animals swung all over the town, swollen with revolution. The workers marched up singing the International. When I saw them smile, I was sure they understood me. The leaders, the Communists, seemed less gratified. Why is the cow green and why is the horse flying through the sky, why? What's the connection with Marx and Lenin?[161]

These were the questions that undermined his career as a Commissar and, after a painful conflict in which his appointees and apparent friends, including Malevich, Lissitsky and Puni, turned on him 'when I was off on one of my usual expeditions to get bread, paints and money for them',[162] he was forced to leave his beloved home town. For the remainder of his time in revolutionary Russia he fulfilled a number of commissions, which he was hard pressed to get payment for, and spent a short period working at a colony for orphans near the village in the Moscow region where he, Bella and Ida were living. Characteristically, even this was a source of great pleasure to him.

I taught those poor little things art. Barefoot, lightly clad, each shouted louder than the other, and cries of 'Comrade Chagall! . . .' rang out on all sides. Only their eyes could not or would not smile. I loved them. They drew pictures. They flung themselves at paints like wild beasts at meat. . . . What has become of you, my dears? When I remember you my heart aches.[163]

However, conditions became increasingly difficult and payments for his work were either unforthcoming or inadequate and he decided to return once more to Western Europe, leaving in the summer of 1922, hoping that 'perhaps Europe will love me and, with her, my Russia'.[164]

Among the forces that had driven him out of Russia were the new economic circumstances, as a result of which the state patronage he had enjoyed during the civil war had dried up. Artists no longer received grants. The state no longer had any money to buy his paintings. Nor did anyone else in Russia. The transition to NEP and to economic accounting and profitability blew a chill wind of market forces through the intellectual life of the country and brought chaos to many individuals and institutions. Such state support as there was began to be channelled more frequently to members of the realist school and less frequently to any of the avant-garde.

But above all, Chagall's flirtation with the revolution in these years reminds us that one of the fundamental forces distinguishing those, like himself, who worked actively with the Bolsheviks from those who remained neutral or were hostile was that Chagall saw in the revolution, despite all its faults, a step forward in the life of ordinary people. He was not terrified and appalled by the 'dark people as Andreev was, rather he loved them and tried to bring his art closer to them. Populism should take its place alongside the whimsicality, optimism, false naïvety and Jewishness always associated with Chagall. It remained with him long after. In the mid 1930s his triptych *Revolution*, depicting an acrobatic Lenin standing on one hand in the middle of a carnival, referred back to the joy Chagall had felt in the heroic years. His painting *White Crucifixion* of 1936, inspired by the worsening plight of Jews in Germany, has, as a symbol of hope, a rag-taggle Red Army composed of the *narod* appearing in the background as liberators.

From this point of view, the enthusiasm of many other intellectuals for the revolution takes on a different perspective. The sympathy many of them showed has often been taken to mean that they were, at least in part, close to the party or, according to some, dupes of the Communists. One of the most intensely argued cases is that of Aleksandr Blok. Usually, the debate revolves around his attitude to

Bolshevism. *Émigrés* and Western scholars try to show that he was not really a revolutionary, while Soviet critics try to show that he was practically a Bolshevik. The debate around him is particularly acute because his poem 'The Twelve' is the greatest work of art of the revolutionary period. In reality, the poem, and Blok's enthusiasm for revolution that goes back to 1905, are not an endorsement of Bolshevism in all its aspects, but rather a symbol of hope that, in the end, the ordinary *narod* will triumph and benefit from the revolution.[165]

Belyi's reaction to the revolution was rather similar. 'The cultural life of contemporary Russia', he wrote, 'is a mixture of contradictions and extremes . . . the death and resurrection, the destruction and birth of a new culture – all this is in collision; there are no norms.'[166] A new Russia was, he said, being born and undergoing an ordeal by fire. For him, one of the most prominent features of the cultural life of this terrible but also stimulating experience was the enthusiasm for learning that it unleashed.

> In Russia I became accustomed to the collective work of discussion groups, to immersion in problems of culture, consciousness, meaning; to problems of literary style and rhythm. . . . Sometimes I did not feel like a lecturer but the conductor of the consciousness of those who attended, the organiser of the chaos of the soulful sounds of the most difficult orchestra.[167]

Belyi even went so far as to compare the Russian circles favourably with their equivalent in Berlin, to which he had come after his exile. In the latter, he claimed, the favourite topics included fees and the flavour of ice cream.[168] Khodasevich confirms the enthusiasm of Russian intellectual life in his memoirs of the period, in which he recalls, from his experience as a lecturer in Proletkul't studios, 'the splendid qualities of the Russian worker audience, above all its genuine aspiration to knowledge and intellectual honesty'.[169] In 1921 he was persuaded to give some lectures on Pushkin to an audience composed of, mostly female, postal workers in Petrograd. Despite having been reluctant to get involved he confessed that 'I even began to experience some pleasure in this occupation.'[170] Despite practical difficulties, the life of the spirit went on. In Belyi's words 'the absence of paper is not a sign of the absence of cultural thought'.[171] Both Belyi and Khodasevich pointed out that, in many cases, this activity went on despite rather than because of the new authorities. Crude attempts to apply class principles led to the termination of the work of both of them in Proletkul't. Khodasevich recalls that an earlier set of lectures, also on Pushkin, in 1918 'went very well, but it was precisely this that displeased the top leadership of Proletkul't'. From their point of view the cadres of the new proletarian literature should be learning Pushkin's technical skills without getting involved in his 'creativity or personality'.[172] For Belyi, although acrimonious debates were engaging the leaders of the new movement, 'the poets from the proletariat were persistently, modestly, and conscientiously studying the muse of Pushkin, Tiutchev, Gogol' reverential receivers of the gift of the eternal culture of art'.[173] For both Belyi and Khodasevich, intellectual contact with ordinary people had been a rewarding and even stimulating experience. It was this, rather than adoption of orthodox revolutionary principles, that brought many intellectuals like them to see some value in what was happening in these years.

For these non-party intellectual activists, then, their work was not so much an endorsement of Bolshevism but rather an expression of hope that the revolution would bring about the liberation of the ordinary people. They were not Bolsheviks, they and the party knew this, but they believed that the revolution had opened up new ways to bridge the gulf between the intellectuals and the *narod*, between the educated and uneducated. In many ways they were a third force, being neither opponents of the Bolsheviks nor party members. As such their association with the Soviet government had many intrinsic limitations and contradictions that began to appear very quickly after the revolution, and would no doubt have continued to do so whether or not Stalin had eventually won out in the inner party struggle. Long before this happened, by the end of 1922, even the spectrum of those prepared to work with the authorities had been thinned out. Blok had died. Chagall, Belyi and Khodasevich had either left the country or been expelled. Even within the party the range of the permissible was narrowing significantly in these years and it is to this process that the next two chapters are devoted.

3 The Bolsheviks and Cultural Life during the Civil War

Contrary to the general impression, the Soviet government did not use methods of wholesale oppression until it was faced with the task of wrestling with half the world without and counter-revolutionary terror within.

N. Berdiaev, *Dream and Reality*

The ambiguous pluralism that characterised the life of the intelligentsia during the first three or four years of the revolution can also be found among those of its members in and close to the party at this time. In part, the root of the ambiguity and complexity is the same in that the desperate conditions of civil war deflected the attention of the powerful into more pressing questions of survival. This left something of a vacuum in which those who took cultural questions seriously were able to try out their schemes. As a result, the Bolshevik approach to questions of education and culture also showed a degree of pluralism which, like that of the wider intellectual society, was steadily and ineluctably eroded from a very early stage as battles for control within and between cultural policy-making institutions were fought, won and lost by protagonists. Thus, although cultural questions had a very low priority in the party in these years, developments were taking place that played a major role in moulding the shape of party policy towards cultural issues in later years. These developments were focused on three institutions: The Proletarian Cultural-Educational Association (Proletkul't), the Ministry of Education (Narkompros) and the Central Committee of the Communist Party, in particular its Agitation and Propaganda Department (Agitpropotdel) and its predecessors. The balance between them changed very substantially in the years 1917–22, the initiative swinging away from Proletkul't and increasingly towards the Central Committee. In these years at least, Proletkul't and Narkompros were directly descended from elements in the pre-revolutionary intelligentsia while the Agitprop functionaries who became involved, such as V. I. Nevsky and Ia. Iakovlev, had not had close links with this group prior to the revolution. Partly as a result of this, as an examination of the three groups reveals, they embodied wide differences of attitude about the essence, objective and methods of cultural revolution.

NARKOMPROS

Of the three institutions Narkompros has attracted the most scholarly attention and it is unnecessary to repeat this in detail.[1] All accounts are agreed that Lunacharsky, at the head of Narkompros, represented a conciliatory line in relations with the old intelligentsia. He based his policy on the pragmatic need to avoid a split with the group that embodied Russia's cultural expertise – artistic, scientific and technological – a split that, he believed, would seriously damage the revolution's prospects of survival. In addition, he had a great respect for the cultural élite as the cream of any society, with the right to be protected even at the expense of less-gifted members of that society.[2] He was also optimistic that, once they realised its real meaning, the intelligentsia would come over to the service of the revolution. Thus his period in office, from 1917 to the spring of 1929, was marked by continued efforts to win over rather than destroy the established intelligentsia. At the same time, he was fighting a continuous rearguard action and was forced from very early on to give up position after position in the face of more boldly confrontationist forces in the party and in his ministry. These forces wanted to break the old intelligentsia as quickly as possible and replace it with a new socialist intelligentsia, the roots of which would lie in the working class rather than the gentry and middle class, as was the case with the existing intelligentsia. Concentration on the role and attitudes of Lunacharsky has led to an underestimation of these tendencies moving away from conciliation. From very early in the revolution all the advances were being made by Lunacharsky's opponents. From as early as 1918 his so-called soft line on culture was being eroded and undermined in a process of increasingly militant 'proletarianisation' of cultural and intellectual life. The speed of erosion varied but the process itself was never halted or reversed. At best it was slowed down.

The divisions within Narkompros make it difficult to say that the ministry stood for a united approach to the question of cultural revolution. While Lunacharsky was undoubtedly the dominant personality in the ministry, it is not so easy to assess how much influence he had in decision making. As with all leading party and state figures in these years, the demands on his time and attention were so great that careful consideration of all areas within his responsibility was impossible, and many areas were only nominally supervised by him, with lesser figures providing the main administrative drive and continuity. Lunacharsky's chief interest meant that much of his attention was devoted to liaison with the old intelligentsia while other areas were left substantially in other hands. This administrative overloading, even chaos, affected Narkompros particularly acutely in these years. On the one hand it was a large ministry with tentacles reaching down to every village school with which contact could be maintained in the prevailing conditions. On the other, its work was peripheral to the vital short-term problems of defeating the counter-revolution and securing Soviet power. These factors combined to leave a certain amount of leeway for pragmatism in the work of Narkompros. It was too complex an organism, both in terms of its widespread administration and of the delicacy of the educational activity with which it dealt, to be brought under centralised control. Here, as elsewhere, the Soviet government depended on a minimum of goodwill from non-Bolshevisks in order for the institution to function at all. The difference of opinion among Bolsheviks them-selves as to how best to nurture this goodwill and develop a more amenable revolutionary consciousness were fully represented within Narkompros. As a result, Narkompros resembled a coalition of the various views within the party rather than a unified example of a single set of principles. In short, it was a rather ramshackle bureau-cratic empire, the importance of which lay in the fact that it was the centre of a vast network of state patronage of education, the arts and high culture. In this respect it had a virtual monopoly, in that all other major sources of patronage – wealthy gentry and industrialists, a cultured middle-class audience and readership and so on – had lost all influence by comparison. As a result, groups competing for state patronage needed friends in Narkompros and parts of the empire were colonised by different factions, some at national level, others on a regional or local basis. At all these levels Narkompros was channelling funds to groups engaged in deadly rivalry with one another. At one extreme, funds were provided for a project to translate all the classics of the world literature into Russian, an enterprise that relied on the efforts of many of the old intelligentsia; while at the other extreme, it funded futurists who declared their intention to destroy all pre-existing culture to enable the new one to be created on a *tabula rasa*. An examination of the principles of leading figures in Narkompros, of its decision making in key areas, of the impact of its policies and of the outlook of its beneficiaries will bear out this analysis.

Throughout his career Lunacharsky's outlook was founded on two assumptions. The first was that progress and the human achievement reached their highest point in the intellectual and spiritual spheres, pushed onwards by the work of towering geniuses but also leaving a role for lesser figures and for the collective action of ordinary people. The second was that Marxism was the current highest point of that process and the Russian revolution an epoch-making step in human history. Many people believed one or the other of these propositions Lunacharsky's distinctiveness arose from the fact that he was one of very few who combined both. From this arose his dual nature. He shared the high valuation of intellectual life with the rest of the intelligentsia but also shared the complete Bolshevik commitment to revolution. His enemies in the intelligentsia criticised him for his attachment to revolution as carried out by the Bolsheviks, while his revolutionary enemies attacked him on account of his lingering sympathy for intellectual life in general. His friends prized his achievement of maintaining a balance between the two.

The most sustained exposition of these principles came in his two-volume work *Religion and Socialism*, published between the 1905 revolution and World War One. The fundamental feature of man's religious quest, Lunacharsky argued, was the breaking through from one level of consciousness to the next, each transition moving man further from the subjection to nature represented by animism, which attributed divine powers to natural forces, to an ever greater mastery over nature and subjection to no natural force or supernatural being. Marxism, scientific socialism, was the highest point of this quest. He followed Marx and Feuerbach in assuming that it was not God who created man but man who created God. The final stage, Lunacharsky argued, was for man to rid himself of the false God he worshipped and create the real one: man himself in the fullness of his powers and attributes. This tendency, shared by a number of other Marxists in this period, was, not surprisingly, called God-building. In 1909 Lenin led a charge against these ideas and Lunacharsky, ever the compromiser, played them down thereafter. But there is no reason to believe that Lunacharsky abandoned them. Indeed, they appeared in modified form in his speeches, articles and literary works of the 1920s and are consistent with his activities at Narkompros.[3]

The combination of these two principles continued to give Lunach-

arsky's outlook a personal coloration. For him, the task of revolution
and the task of cultural development were synonymous. As a recent
study of his career has pointed out, Lunacharsky understood the
revolution to mean the 'intelligentification' of society, the raising of
the cultural level of the masses to that of the élite.[4] It followed from
this that the established intelligentsia had to be preserved in order
for it to hand on its accumulated knowledge and expertise to the
masses. As it succeeded in doing this, and the cultural level of the
masses rose in consequence, so the gap between intelligentsia and
people would be effaced and the two would become
indistinguishable – a vision going back in many respects to Lunacharsky's God-building days, as the tone of one of his statements about
this shows:

> In the future the masses will be transformed into the intelligentsia,
> and this will be the death of the present intelligentsia, but an
> extraordinarily joyous death, for it will signify the final victory of
> the proletariat. Then a classless society will be created, then the
> moral equality of all humanity will be achieved, and then the
> intelligentsia will not be needed.[5]

Even for Lunacharsky, conciliation of the intelligentsia was intended
to lead to its death, though for him this death was far in the future
and 'extraordinarily joyous'.

For the most radical elements in the party this was unacceptable.
They were more inclined to the short, sharp shock. Lunacharsky's
battle against them went back to the early days of the revolution. In
1918, in a pamphlet devoted to 'The Cultural Tasks of the Working
Class' Lunacharsky was at pains to point out the universality of
human culture and the fragility of cultural values, which could be
severely damaged by thoughtless action. It was necessary, Lunacharsky argued, for cultural values to be preserved in order for them
to be of use to the proletariat, who would develop them in accordance
with their own needs and interests. In Lunacharsky's words 'The
culture of the new class is a new variant, an organic metamorphosis
of the single universal culture.'[6]

The only other figure of national stature associated with Narkompros at this time was Nadezhda Krupskaia. She had long been
interested in education and had, indeed, according to her memoirs,
first met her future husband, Lenin, at a study circle meeting. Her
ideas about education can perhaps best be described as liberal-

progressive and reformist. She was much impressed by American educational ideas, particularly those of John Dewey. The essence of her outlook was based on the assumption that mastery of knowledge and learning was necessary for true liberation of the individual. She differed from her sources in the obvious respect that, for her, a Marxist content was an essential element. For Krupskaia, this meant that in order fully to emancipate the individual it was necessary to place an understanding of the labour process at the heart of the educational system. This would entail some practical links between schools and productive enterprises but, equally important, the analysis of society and the teaching of intellectual principles would also be related to their place in the labour process.

Before the February revolution the kind of work she envisaged, focusing particularly on factory workers as the chief potential recipients, could only be carried on under very constrained circumstances. After February, however, conditions changed to such an extent that much larger-scale operations could be undertaken and, as already mentioned, after her return from Switzerland with her husband, she threw herself into organising worker education, mainly in the Vyborg district of Petrograd.

The remaining influential personnel of Narkompros were, for the most part, also members of the traditional intelligentsia, although there was a significant leaven of workers, which tended to become more marked by the end of the civil war. Among the intelligentsia figures in Narkompros, one of the major forces in shaping policy towards high culture in general and higher education in particular was the historian M. N. Pokrovsky. Pokrovsky's association with Lunacharsky went back to the post-1905 period when Pokrovsky was an active collaborator in the party schools of Capri and Bologna.[7] He was also a member of the 'Bogdanovite' *Vpered* group in these years, though by 1917 there was little trace left of his flirtation with these heresies. His attitude towards the higher-education establishment, to which he had for a time belonged, was one of almost unbridled contempt. In his view, the old professoriat was a nest of counter-revolutionaries and liberal hypocrites who would be best swept away if they refused to accept the new political authorities. Pokrovsky was particularly vehement in his hostility to religion, which he understood purely and simply as a smokescreen to confuse the formation of class consciousness among the workers. Any hint of concessions to the church in its educational function in these years could be guaranteed to bring forth a torrent of venomous polemic from Pokrovsky. It is much easier to discern what Pokrovsky opposed about the existing culture of Russia, than to see what he wanted to put in its place.[8]

The trio of Lunacharsky, Krupskaia and Pokrovsky remained at the centre of Narkompros until the end of the 1920s. Krupskaia was named Deputy Commisar in 1918 but, with characteristic modesty, quickly turned down the title, although she continued to exercise equivalent functions, specialising in adult education. Pokrovsky, less sensitive to the incompatibility of socialist morality and high-level bureaucratic appointment, took over the office of Deputy Commisar for Education until 1932. A variety of lesser figures, including M. Reisner, Otto Shmidt, E. A. Litkens and Ludmila Menzhinskaia within Narkompros, and Iu. Larin and Ia. Iakovlev, whose primary responsibilities lay outside the Commissariat, also made an impact on certain areas of educational policy in the period up to 1921.

The first major policy issues that Narkompros had to face in the educational field show the nature of its approach very well. Having taken over the ministry, the new administrators had to decide how best they could adapt the existing educational system to the new needs, as they perceived them. This meant transforming the school system and getting a grip on the universities. Policy making and its attempted implementation in both these areas are illustrative of the way Narkompros was beginning to work.[9]

The main discussion of how to develop an approach to the school system took place in the State Commission for Education in a series of meetings in the summer of 1918, in the course of which new educational principles were thrashed out. Debate centred around the setting up of so-called Unified Labour Schools. The first major discussion took place on 20 July. The chief item of business was the presentation of a set of proposals by the veteran revolutionary P. N. Lepeshinsky for establishing Unified Labour Schools. The new type of school should, he argued, be based on new principles. In the forefront of these should be labour, by which he meant the collective efforts of mankind to establish its mastery over nature. This would provide a framework for the all-round, harmonious, socialist development of the child. Schools would be open to all, without discrimination as to social origin or gender. They would embrace the values of internationalism. Religion would be excluded because it was 'a means of enslaving the individual in the interests of the class state'. In terms of organisation the schools should have a large degree of independence. 'The people themselves will build the new schools.'

They would be self-governing, cater for their own needs and be responsible for 'organising mental [*umstvennykh*] forms of labour'. Co-ordination would be built up from below, with some unspecified form of moderation of differences. Finally, the schools would not be divided up into classes by age but according to equality of ability. Learning would, implicitly, be largely self-motivated as it was proposed that three or four teachers per school (though the optimum size of school was not mentioned) should be sufficient, and teaching would be carried on through 'lively discussions'. Lepeshinsky's ideas were a distillation of the extremely fertile socialist, populist and anarchist pedagogical ideas of the previous half-century, drawn from sources all over Europe. He was seconded by V. M. Pozner, a colleague of Lepeshinsky in the Moscow department of Narkompros. He added very little that made the proposal more acceptable. Indeed, his major contribution was the suggestion that, with the agreement of doctors, the schools should operate seven days a week throughout the entire year.[10]

The last point gave just that air of cloud-cuckoo that sometimes besets would-be reformers in education ministries, even those far different from that of revolutionary Russia. It provided an excellent opportunity for those opposed to Lepeshinsky's ideas to subject them to general ridicule. Krupskaia was the first to attack. The task of government, she said, was to put forward concrete, specific proposals, not to deal in general principles. She then went on to discuss general principles. The danger was that schools of the type proposed would be cut off from the rest of the life of society. There should be a stronger element of productive labour. The health and welfare of teachers and pupils required breaks in the school year.[11] Most of the other speakers were unequivocal in their criticism of the impracticability of the ideas. Pokrovsky eventually joined in saying that to decree Labour Schools was as unrealistic as establishing socialism by decree. What was needed was some way of relating the proposals to the school system that actually existed.[12]

Pozner, judging from his reply, was quite stung by the tone of the discussion which, he asserted, not without justification, had been carried on in an argumentative spirit rather than a collaborative and collective one.[13] When all was said and done, he concluded, the proposals at least pointed to the future while the objectors envisaged the necessity of following after events. 'This', he concluded, 'is a position of pedagogic opportunism.'[14] In opposition to Pokrovsky's objection, he pointed out that slogans and decrees had an important function in showing the way ahead just as the Declaration of the Rights of Man had done. The rest of the Commission was unimpressed and Pokrovsky's motion, that more specific proposals should be brought to the next meeting, was accepted. An attempt to have the revised proposals published and to bring people from the localities into the discussions was rejected.[15] Thus after four and a quarter hours of discussion, the meeting was ended.

The behind-the-scenes negotiations that then took place must have been stormy. No revised draft was ready for the next meeting on 27 July and the issue was postponed to 8 August. In fact, the next meeting appears to have taken place on 17 August.[16]

This meeting was presented with not one but two drafts, one emanating from Moscow, reflecting Lepeshinsky's views, and one from Petrograd, reflecting the views of his critics. The appearance of two substantially different drafts is unambiguous evidence of the inability to find common ground, and the remaining procedures were geared to achieving victory for one of the two drafts. The advantage of Moscow was that it appeared to have more grass-roots support, if its 'unanimous' (according to its supporters)[17] acceptance by the First All-Russian Congress on Education (a meeting of militants rather than a representatives' conference of practising teachers) is anything to go by. The advantage of Petrograd was that the draft had the support of the leading figures in the ministry. Given this line-up of forces the debate moved towards its inevitable conclusion.

The next, also inconclusive, round of discussions took place on 17 and 19 August. This time Lunacharsky was present. He opened the meeting by proposing acceptance of the Petrograd declaration because it was rooted in the existing situation in the school system. The Moscow declaration, he argued, went further and put forward 'a more revolutionary plan' which would be 'more difficult to realise'. It would destroy 'that bridge which much be thrown across between thousands of old schools and our radical projects'.[18] Pozner replied, saying that the type of school envisaged, which he referred to as the 'commune school' (*shkola-kommuna*), would be 'a cell of the future society'.[19] The possibility of compromise between these two positions was slight and the arguments added little of substance. Lunacharsky said that to include pupils in school administration was 'a completely unnecessary game with democratism' and Menzhinskaia compared the proposed schools, in their isolation from the outside world, with monasteries.[20] The meeting was postponed after three hours and resumed two days later. Again discussion went round in circles. One contributor, Krivtsov, objected to the Moscow draft on the grounds that education should liberate from labour and convert man from being slave of the machine into its master (though this was surely one of the objectives of the Moscow draft). 'The Petrograd declaration', he concluded, in rather foreboding terms, 'comes from children of the proletariat, but the Moscow one from those of the intelligentsia.'[21] In the end, the proposal was handed to another commission with a brief to report back on 24 August. Not surprisingly, it failed to meet this deadline. Instead, the final act was played out on 12 September, more than a week after the new school year should have commenced. This final meeting was significant if only on account of the unusually large number of people – twenty-nine – who took part, many of whom had had nothing to do with the earlier stages of the discussion. The reason for this soon became clear as, with very little preliminary debate, the meeting moved to a decisive vote of 19:10 in favour of the Petrograd declaration. The main supporters of the Petrograd draft throughout the discussions, Lunacharsky, Pokrovsky, the Menzhinskaia sisters and Krivtsov were joined by a variety of influential party, state and artistic personalities, including Bonch–Bruevich, Enukidze, Tatlin, Briusov, Preobrazhensky and Mitskevich–Kapsukas. Ul'ianova supported the Moscow draft. Of the two leading Proletkul't figures involved, one, Lebedev–Poliansky, supported Petrograd, the other, F. I. Kalinin, supported Moscow.[22] The vote brought a storm of protest from the leaders of the defeated group who argued that since their proposals had been adopted by the All-Russian Congress on Education but rejected by Narkompros it showed up differences between the Commissariat and the localities and threw current work into complete disarray.[23] This last futile protest led to nothing. The meeting concluded by appointing an editing commission to put the finishing touches to the victorious proposal before its presentation to Sovnarkom. In accordance with the common Bolshevik practice, the three commission members were drawn from the defeated minority and included both Pozner and Lepeshinsky. Although they were able to append a statement of their principles to the document, the practical proposals were all derived from the Petrograd draft, which was formally approved by the Central Executive Committee (VTsIK) on 30 September.[24] The postponed school year began on 1 October and hundreds of thousands of pupils returned after their unexpectedly long vacation, no doubt completely unaware of the dramatic events surrounding their future. It is not at all clear what impact all this had on their schooling. Given the chaotic conditions of the time and the weakness of the Bolshevisk within the schools – the major argument used by proponents of the Petrograd draft – one may be forgiven for thinking that it made very little difference.

What the debate does show, however, is the style of work that was developing in Narkompros. Where Lepeshinsky and Pozner appear to have expected positive criticism and some trace of idealism and long-term forward thinking about the essence of what a Soviet school should be, they found hostile, bureaucratic opposition, the packing of committees to ensure victory for the opinion of the powerful, a refusal to bring lower ranks into the discussion and a tendency towards opportunism. From the point of view of the majority position, the outcome was a victory for realism and common sense rather than for excessive experimentation. However, it was Pozner himself who, in the course of the debate, had claimed that his proposals successfully avoided the dangers of being drawn into timid accommodation with existing forms of schooling on one hand and of being drawn into anarchy on the other.[25] There was no easy way to determine where this line should be drawn and the Education Ministry was only one of the many pioneering Soviet institutions that were being riven by arguments of this kind. In another major area of concern, higher education, a similar dispute was taking place, although the subjects of reform, the universities themselves, proved to be more durable defenders of the status quo than the schools. Here experimentation had even less scope within Narkompros and a strategy of siege and harassment began to develop after direct frontal assault had not produced the desired results.

The summer of 1918 was an extremely busy one for those in Narkompros dealing with the traditional education system. At the same time as the ministry had woken up to the fact that the first new school year since the October revolution was about to begin and that nothing had been done to reform the system, it was also decided that, in the short space of time remaining before they reopened, the universities should be brought more into line with socialist principles, although, as in other cultural fields, there was no clear conception of what those principles were. For the time being, Narkompros was prepared to content itself with adding more responsibility for adult, working-class and political education, opening institutions up to women students on an equal basis, making provision for election and periodic re-election of professors and giving more opportunities for students to participate in university government. As with many

Narkompros measures of this period, its objectives were a mixture of worthy principle and more mundane political manoeuvring. On the face of it, the reforms were not too divorced from what the liberals who dominated the academic establishment professed as their own principles. But, at the same time, each of the proposed reforms was a calculated move by the ministry to undermine the authority of that establishment, whom they unequivocally denounced as remnants of the old order who must be brought under tighter supervision. Narkompros's attempt to implement its principles brought out the inextricable intertwining of its two objectives. The main element of its proposals was to separate the research, teaching and popular education functions and concentrate them in separate institutions within each university. Provision was also to be made for replacing tenure with a system of periodic election of professors, seven- and ten-year intervals being most frequently mentioned. In common with attacks on university tenure in other contexts, proponents of its abolition waved the spectre of the inert professor who had produced nothing since obtaining his privileged post. Opponents, not unreasonably, tended to suspect that the purpose of election was actually to increase political interference in the universities rather than to burn dead wood. This suspicion was fuelled by the linking of this proposal with a widening of the governing institutions of the university to include radical elements within and 'social institutions' without, namely party, Soviet and state bodies.

Narkompros launched its package at a hastily convened conference of higher-education institutions held in July. The ministry representatives appear to have had a very rough ride. On the third day they were able to get the delegates to agree to the setting up of university departments devoted to the study of socialism, on the grounds that 'an atmosphere of complete freedom of scholarly teaching and of laying out of views and ideas of all tendencies must reign within universities'.[26] Once again the proposal combined a liberal disguise for what could also be seen as a crude political manoeuvre. It is, however, a mark of the difficulties Narkompros faced that it was relatively happy with such minor successes. For the most part it seems to have been subject to a barrage of criticism from the academics. The leading exception to this was the eminent Moscow biologist K. A. Timiriazev whose views on the proposed reforms were published in a pamphlet at this time. The matrix of his acceptance of the reform plans was one of belief in the necessity of democratisation of the university system on liberal grounds. The main features of the reform – making education free, dividing up its functions and so on – were welcomed as sensible. His only complaints tended to be about the language used. Opening universities to what the document described as 'people of both sexes' meant, he pointed out, that only hermaphrodites would qualify.[27] Apart from Timiriazev, who was not himself present at the conference,[28] there was very little support and the fragmentary archive account shows there was a barrage of criticism from the floor directed at the platform. However, there was not a complete breakdown of relations. Instead, a preparatory commission, evenly divided between nominees of the ministry and of the professors, with some students on each side, was set up to prepare a second and more representative conference. This opened in September, once again, by accident or design, leaving very little time before the commencement of the new academic year. If the July conference had been a setback for the ministry, September was a complete disaster.

Attendance at the conference was heavily weighted towards academics from Petrograd and Moscow, which is not surprising given the prevailing conditions and rapidity with which the conference was called. There were 193 academics (74 professors and 119 tutors) from a variety of universities and institutes in these two cities, including two from the Theological Academy in Petrograd. There were also representatives of the universities of Nizhny, Perm, Kazan and Saratov and other provincial higher-education establishments such as the Kazan Theological Academy and Voronezh Agricultural Institute.[29] The Narkompros delegation included its leading figures and comprised Lunacharsky, Pokrovsky, Reisner, Riazanov, Kalinin, Lebedev–Poliansky, Iu. Tan, Pozner and the Bonch-Bruevich's.[30] This turnout of the ministry's biggest guns failed to persuade the conference. One delegate appeared to speak for the whole assembly of academics when he argued that universities had to be handled with care because they were 'institutions dear to the heart of the Russian' which, like a 'benefactor' (*blagovenie*) or 'elder', had, over many years, 'spread their good deeds through the Russian land'. They had, he continued, been sources of the highest hopes and the most treasured memories of many generations.[31]

The conference rarely operated at this level of generalisation. Most of its activity was in the form of a line-by-line discussion of Narkompros's proposals, which were pretty thoroughly savaged. The most symbolic alteration was the reinsertion of the word 'autonomous' in the proposed definition of the Russian university.[32] In all cases the universities refused to accept the full proposals for reorganisation put before them, though they did accept some redivision of functions, election of faculty meetings and regrouping of institutions. They also allowed limited student representation in university administration, providing it did not exceed one-quarter of the faculty meeting.[33]

This unfavourable outcome, from the point of view of Narkompros, seems to have been unexpected. Perhaps those who had prepared the plan thought that what to them must have looked like its very moderate and restrained terms, which even allowed each university to have its own press, might find favour with the academic world or at least with its more radical younger members. However, professorial power was barely dented by this onslaught. In fact, when elections for professors were eventually held it tended to be the radicals, if anybody, who lost their chairs.[34] The calling of a general conference had succeeded only in drawing together all the opposition forces in one place at one time. Clearly a new approach had to be devised if the ministry's objectives were to be achieved.

New tactics were not slow to emerge. At the 21 September meeting of the State Education Commission, the first to be held after the acrimonious and time-consuming issue of the Unified Labour School had been resolved, the main item was what to do about higher education. Reisner summarised the outcome of the two conferences. The approach through agreement had, he said, been preferred to reform from above in the hope that the professors would be prepared to enter into dialogue over the proposals. The failure of this hope meant that two unacceptable options existed: either accepting the universities as they were or pushing ahead with the proposals regardless. The academic establishment stood in the way of the latter; the former could not be countenanced given the old-fashioned nature of the universities. To resolve this he proposed a kind of salami tactics of getting around the opposition by implementing the proposals step by step. The first priority, he argued, was to change the membership of the professorial establishment in order to break up 'its caste character' and undermine its position of privilege.[35] Pokrovsky added that the more business-like outlook of professors in higher technical education had made them easier to deal with than the universities, and that the two chief objectives should be to raise the productivity of research and teaching and to aim for universities in which the proletariat would be the dominant force.[36] The objectives of gradual implementation of the reform and rapid proletarianisation dominated Narkompros tactics in the ensuing period.

In practice, the first example of salami tactics had preceded the September conference when, on 6 August, Sovnarkom decreed that the universities should be open to all aged over sixteen without payment and without regard to sex or formal qualifications. After the September conference this approach to reform became the norm. The ill-fated insistence on election of professors, the first item in Reisner's agenda, was the next major element to be implemented. According to the higher-education department's report for 1918, which confirms the main lines of the approach described above, the provision for elections was 'one of the most important reforms of the higher schools'.[37] Despite the fact that at the conferences of July and September the reform project had been opposed by 'a significant part' of the student body, the next objective was to ensure that one-quarter of the ruling bodies of universities should come from among the students.[38] This approach was sustained throughout 1919 and a series of decrees implemented parts of the reform project. In November 1918 the higher-education collegium of Narkompros proposed that the personnel of the newly created faculty of social science at Moscow University should include A. A. Bogdanov, N. I. Bukharin, R. Iu. Vipper, V. P. Volgin, V. N. Il'in, I. A. Pokrovsky, M. N. Pokrovsky, S. I. Prokopovich, M. A. Reisner and D. B. Riazanov among its twenty-eight members,[39] which indicates the degree of compromise with non-party figures they had in mind at this time. Perhaps the most important reform of this period was the institution of Workers' Faculties (*Rabfaky*) which was decreed on 19 September 1919. Typically, this gave the universities just two weeks to set up such faculties, the aim of which, according to the final version signed by Pokrovsky, was 'the preparation of workers and peasants for higher education in the shortest possible time'. They were intended to be full and equal parts of higher-education establishments.[40]

This phase has been described as one of 'piecemeal reform'[41] but it should be emphasised that it was not so much the reforms that were piecemeal as their implementation. The objectives of the 1918 project remained firmly in the minds of the higher-education policy planners in Narkompros. The principles laid down in its discussions at this time remained in force, and they saw themselves as carrying out a consistent plan stage by stage. The restraining factor was the degree of resistance put up by the universities, and this was being echoed all the time. The most impatient elements of Narkompros were not happy with this rate of progress. A minor incident of

November 1918 illustrates this. Narkompros had been taken to task in the newspaper *Izvestiia TsIK* because it was responsible for Moscow University, which was said, in the article, to be in a filthy condition and to be cold. Pokrovsky brought a draft reply for discussion by the higher-education collegium held on 29 November, the day after the article had appeared. It was cold, he said, because firewood allocated to Narkompros was being confiscated at railway stations by other institutions. The poor state of the University was because the students had not cleaned up the lecture theatres. He commented further on the incident at the meeting to the effect that it might rebound to their favour if they were able to show to the higher authorities that their hands were tied in dealing with the universities. 'It is necessary', he said, 'to take rapid measures against that "autonomy" of the universities which exists at present and which serves only as a cover for sabotage.'[42] He was supported by Fedorovsky who said that they were indeed in difficulties as a result of the 'policy of conciliation'. Not only was there sabotage but also genuine opposition, which could not be tolerated. At the same time, he argued, the material position of professors and teachers should be improved so that 'existing sympathy or, in the most extreme cases, loyalty in relation to our measures will be safeguarded'.[43] The meeting accepted a proposal from Artem'ev that the five months' grace left to the professors by the Sovnarkom decree on elections of 1 October should be annulled so that they could no longer engage in their 'in several cases, destructive' work. They also agreed to increase rations for academics.[44] Thus, even such a small issue could reveal the depth of the volcano within Narkompros, which was, for the time being, restrained with increasing difficulty. Only judgement about the appropriate moment to increase the tempo of change divided the policy makers. By 1921, when the next conference on higher education was called, the atmosphere was totally different and the academics were called in to an apparently carefully selected meeting which voted in the revised reform proposals of that period without being given any opportunity to prevent their adoption.[45]

It is also significant, and points to something of a vacuum in Bolshevik plans, that the reforms were organisational. With the exception of religion, which was severely constrained rather than totally eliminated from Russian education at this time, there was very little specific, detailed attention given to reform of the curriculum. In so far as it was dealt with, it tended to be in terms of vague principles such as 'proletarianisation', or, as Otto Shmidt tried to do with increasing intensity, making higher education more 'practical' and less 'academic',[46] or decreeing 'labour schools' without defining what they might teach, let alone what books and similar resources they might use. It may be that the problem of curriculum content arose from the fact that the only serious attempts to define what a proletarian education should consist of in the fullest sense were being carried on under the increasingly suspect auspices of Proletkul't. Before turning to examine its efforts in this period, one other area of Narkompros activity, its dealings with writers and artists, the creative intelligentsia, has to be considered because it shows a rather different shape from that discernable in its dealings with institutionalised education.

The main point of difference in the area of policy towards the creative élite is that there was a good deal more scope for self-generated activity outside the direct control of Narkompros. For the time being, members of this group with a penchant for politicking were able to secure mini-empires of their own. In part this arose because the authorities did not possess the desire, the power or the knowledge to impose serious control on the content of art. From their point of view, particularly given the poor initial response of creative intellectuals to the October revolution, it was more satisfactory for them to back certain individuals and give them control, particularly over such patronage as there was available, and guide cultural activity in this relatively indirect way. The main difficulty that arose from this approach, from the party's point of view, was that the choice between 'Red' and 'expert' was particularly painful. Soviet artistic life was riven by many factions, but one of the deepest divides was between established artists and writers of confirmed talent and ability on the one hand, and devoted supporters of the government's ideals on the other. This is not to say that each group was well defined and internally cohesive, far from it. Within this larger division many smaller factions were busy competing with one another, a particularly serious business given the acute privation and scarcity of resources they experienced in the first four or five years of the revolution. The outcome, never entirely eliminated from Soviet intellectual life in the formative years, was a Darwinian struggle for survival in which the only winners were those elements within the party who identified the existing intelligentsia as incorrigibly bourgeois and were happy to see its members themselves driving each other out of artistic life or into exile. By and large, leading Soviet figures who were themselves of intelligentsia background, such as

Lunacharsky, Bukharin, Trotsky and Lenin, were more aware of the damage this caused to the socialist project than were those from the less highly educated majority of tsarist Russian society. Among the latter the achievements of the revolution had built up an intoxicating belief in proletarian invincibility and a kind of moral superiority based on the rightness of their cause. In short there developed an as yet restrained sense of proletarian chauvinism.

Narkompros was not governed by any overarching vision of what cultural revolution could or should be. In fact, those having such a vision found life very difficult in the ministry. Instead it was governed by a practical approach to problems based on gaining leverage, in the cultural institutions, by steady erosion of resistance. There was no clear idea of how control would be used even if it were achieved. Policies built up on a pragmatic basis. Visionaries and idealists were distrusted. It was clear that, although they were being tolerated for the time being at least, there would in future be less and less room for radical experiment. The history of Proletkul't in these years shows this process in operation.

PROLETKUL'T

Where Narkompros was strong on organisational reform and weak on the principles of cultural revolution, Proletkul't (the Proletarian Cultural-Educational Association) was the reverse. Its members devoted a great deal of effort to filling the concept of 'proletarian culture' with appropriate content. In the early revolutionary years a loose network of cultural groups of many different kinds, engaging in a kaleidoscopic variety of activities came under the aegis of Proletkul't. Its activities involved tens, even hundreds, of thousands of people on a regular basis. And yet in 1920 these activities were severely curtailed by a decree of the Central Committee instigated by Lenin himself. The ostensible reason for the censure was that Proletkul't had developed an iconoclastic attitude towards the cultures of the past and was being increasingly influenced by 'futurism' in this respect. It was also criticised for attempting to be independent of party and state control as it tried to keep its nominal supervisory body – Narkompros – at arm's length at the same time as the relative independence of Narkompros itself was being encroached on by the Central Committee. A closer look at the history of Proletkul't in these years confirms that it was, indeed, heavily involved in trying to develop an authentic proletarian culture, though without any overall marked tendency to destroy cultures of the past. Its open aspirations to independence, which had been challenged by the party as far back as 1918, appear to have been much more significant in bringing about its virtual demise in 1920.

Suspicion of Proletkul't in the highest places was not allayed by the fact that its central inspiration A. A. Bogdanov (1873–1928), had, in the wake of the 1905 revolution, been a rival of Lenin for the leadership of the Bolshevik faction. Perhaps the threat Bogdanov posed to Lenin at this time was more apparent than real because his whole cast of mind pulled him away from the vicious infighting, of which Lenin was such a master, and towards a wider and more cerebral approach to the question of revolution. It was on account of his intellectual boldness and philosophical writings that he was esteemed by intelligentsia radicals associated with the Bolsheviks. Bogdanov's writings were about the nature of perception and its implications for Marxist philosophy rather than the vigorous and penetrating analyses of the agrarian question and class relations in Russia that Lenin was producing at this time. None the less, Bogdanov's writings filled a newly perceived gap in Russian Marxist thinking. The intellectual and spiritual renaissance of the early twentieth century, which put an increasing emphasis on individualism and idealism, had caught Marxists unawares. They were wrapped in the rather drab-looking positivist dogmas of Plekhanov and were being outdistances, so they thought, by the new principles. Many of them, notably Lenin, dug into the already prepared trenches of positivist Marxism and took aim squarely at Bogdanov. When this proved insufficient, Lenin eventually produced the devastating barrage of *Materialism and Empiriocriticism* (1909) in which Bogdanov was referred to as a 'jester' and attempts to find 'a "new" view in philosophy' were said to be 'vain' and to show 'poverty of mind'.[47]

It was in this atmosphere of intellectual 'searching', as it was called, that the ideas of Bogdanov developed and matured. The basic conceptions on which Proletkul't was founded can be traced in Bogdanov's pre-war writings. The central feature of his outlook was that cultural revolution, understood as the revolution as it was reflected within the minds and daily life of all those involved in the process, was a vital component of revolution. Its dismissal to the periphery of revolutionary thinking was not only undesirable, it was also severely damaging to the potential outcome of the revolution. Thus Bogdanov's distinctiveness lay in the fact that he took the question of cultural revolution seriously, as an essential element, whereas for other Bolsheviks and Marxists it was an afterthought. The chief focus of his activities in the period from 1907 to 1914 was the elaboration of the idea of proletarian cultural revolution and the attempt to create institutions devoted to this question. It may be that Bogdanov had stumbled accidentally into this area, in the sense that his defeat in the inner-party struggle drove him into less conventionally political activities, but there can be no doubt that this 'diversion' brought Bogdanov into an area of activity to which he was temperamentally suited and fully attuned intellectually.

The most developed account of Bogdanov's ideas at this time on cultural aspects of the revolution can be found in the extended pamphlet *The Cultural Tasks of Our Time*, published in Moscow in 1911.[48] In it Bogdanov defined what he meant by culture; elaborated on aspects of its function in past societies; emphasised its significance for future socialist society; suggested how it might be developed; proposed an institution to train its bearers; and meditated on the relationship between the working class and culture. This was a rather ambitious programme to fulfil in ninety pages, which serves to remind us that, stimulating though they may be, Bogdanov's writings tended to be sketchy, superficial and allusive. Culture, he wrote, was 'the entire sum of the material and non-material acquisitions made by man in the labour process and which elevate and enrich his life, giving him power over nature and over himself.'[49] Spiritual culture, he argued, had both an organising function and a disorganising one. The former could be seen in many classical and medieval works of mythology, scripture and epic, which were in fact 'encyclopaedias of life' for their respective peoples. Some encapsulated specific scientific and production oriented knowledge about, for instance, agriculture. Music and dance developed as 'the language of the emotions'.[50] A corollary of this organising function was that, in the period of their development, all cultural systems had a disorganising function with respect to what preceded them. Bogdanov referred here to urban-bourgeois and Catholic cultures – the latter comprising what he called 'a mighty cultural phenomenon' – which had gone through a period in which they had brought about the destruction of existing social institutions.[51] As a focus for the growth of socialist culture Bogdanov suggested the production of an encyclopaedia and the founding of a Proletarian University. The former was inspired by the model of Diderot in pre-revolutionary France. Bogdanov understood the *Encylopédie* to be an attempt by the rising French bourgeoisie to prepare its cultural revolution.[52] The Proletarian University would break free from the traditional university, despite retaining its name, and develop without emphasis on specialisation and without the authoritarian structures of the old institution. It would not be an instrument for the transfer of knowledge from one head to another, but would prepare people for the massive task of transformation that lay in front of the Russian working class.[53] Both of these ideas had been floated by Bogdanov before. The effect of earlier criticisms of his views can be seen in his defence of his attitude to working-class culture. Revolutionaries who praised the working class should also, he argued, show confidence in its own creative ability and not simply try to present it with absolute truths.[54] For those who missed the allusion, Lenin and Plekhanov were identified as the targets of this comment. He also criticised those who considered time spent on cultural matters to be a waste of energy. For Bogdanov, it was one of the areas in which strength and energy grew and developed; it was, in effect, an investment not a spending of energy.[55] Finally, the idea that proletarian art should deal only with proletarian life, the habits and struggle of the working class, and that everything that lay outside those boundaries was of secondary importance, was described by Bogdanov as 'extremely mistaken and naïve'.[56] Significantly, Bogdanov was already defending himself against the two kinds of opposition that dogged his post-revolutionary career, that of dogmatists and of proletarian chauvinists.

By 1912, then, the basic foundation of Bogdanov's ideas had been laid. Many of the themes went back into his early career as a revolutionary, while others were of a more recent development. He cut his teeth as a revolutionary and propagandist among the workers and political exiles of Tula in the mid 1890s when he claimed that he abandoned his populist orientation and took a definitively Marxist direction, at least as far as the argument over whether Russia could avoid the capitalist stage of development was concerned. Bogdanov claimed that it was the chance arrival of Lenin's writings on Struve that brought this about in early 1896.[57] Be that as it may, Bogdanov, like many others, broke with populist doctrine but not with what might be called the populist impulse of service to the people, which remained an essential element of his character from his early medical education – a classic way to serve the people for many intellectuals – through to his ultimately fatal blood-transfusion experiments of the 1920s. This impulse was often expressed in his work as an educator and propagandist. In the Tula years he gave illegal lectures to workers of the town, many of them from the state armaments factory located there. S. A. Sokolov, a former attender at one of these, recalls being taken, with appropriate precautions, to one such lecture by an acquaintance. Bogdanov was, he wrote, a young man 'with a pleasant face and expressive, intelligent eyes'.[58] Significantly, Sokolov remembers that in answer to his question about factors affecting the productivity of labour, Bogdanov emphasised that in addition to the health and strength of the worker and the technical means at his disposal, the most important element was 'what one might call the *intelligentnost'* of the worker' – meaning, approximately, his degree of self-awareness and consciousness – 'as a result of which the previously enumerated characteristics are brought together and give the highest productivity to his labour'.[59]

Other key elements of Bogdanov's ideas, notably his rigid, positivist, materialist interpretation of life in which metaphysics and authoritarianism were seen as 'fetishes' analogous to the 'commodity fetishism' described by Marx[60] and the assumption that the role of the intellectual was to help the worker to become an independent actor in the revolutionary process, can also be found in his Tula years.[61] Thus it was deeply engraved in Bogdanov's outlook that the intellectual was the servant of the worker in the revolutionary movement and that the intellectual's role was to bring out the intelligentsia-like qualities (*intelligentnost'*) of the workers themselves. One can see here a great similarity with Lunacharsky's idea that the task of the revolution was to bring about 'the extraordinarily joyous death' of the intelligentsia through fusing it with the working class and breaking down the distinction between them.[62] It is not improbable that Lunacharsky derived this notion from Bogdanov since they were close associates in the years following the 1905 revolution, not least because Lunacharsky was married to Bogdanov's sister until 1922.

The chief enterprise that Bogdanov, Lunacharsky and others embarked on in those difficult years for the revolutionaries was a series of schools to educate workers from the grass roots that were set up in Capri and Bologna in 1909 and 1910.[63] The practical results of these schools were minimal for a variety of reasons. First, the number of recruits to them was small. Secondly, they were infiltrated by tsarist agents and the few returning students were mostly arrested very quickly. Thirdly, bitter faction fighting, particularly with the Leninists in Paris, cast a pall over the exercise. None the less, the schools are revealing of the plans and hopes that the organisers had, and of some of the assumptions they made about the nature of cultural revolution. There are also some interesting sidelights on the reaction of the students to the rather rigid curriculum the organisers had in mind for them. It is with these considerations in view that the following examination of the work of the Capri and Bologna schools is presented.[64]

While details of the fragmentary material about the schools are sometimes inconsistent, there is sufficient evidence to be able to say that the chief function was to produce propagandists for the social-democratic idea who would also have some rudimentary practical administrative and organisational skills. Indeed the Capri school called itself a 'propagandist agitational school'. The idea was that pupils would become the focus of legal and illegal work, building up a party network and passing on their knowledge and skills. All the draft plans and surviving course programmes show that the greater part of the activity of the school was devoted to propagandistic material. All the sources agree that the work of the school included three groups of lectures: 'Party Theory', which consisted largely of a survey of the history of trade unions, labour movements and revolutions in modern Europe and Russia plus one or two themes such as the question of nationalities; the 'Philosophy of Proletarian Struggle', devoted to the questions of ideology, world-views and socialist culture; and a concluding section on the 'Current Moment'.[65] The printed version adds a fourth section at the beginning entitled 'Party-Organisational Work' dealing mainly with practical problems of organising a party cell such as small- and large-scale activities, legal channels such as clubs and study circles, organising libraries, establishing links with publishers and, finally, handling the finances.[66] Attention was not evenly divided between the four major themes. The section on 'Party Theory' occupied the greatest amount of attention and within that there were blocks of thirty lectures each on political economy (presumably the economic theory of Marx) and on the history and theory of the labour movement and social democracy in Russia. By comparison, the section on the 'Philosophy of Proletarian Struggle' as a whole came to only twenty-three lectures,[67] and that on the 'Contemporary Moment' to only five lectures.[68] Thus there can be little doubt concerning the main direction of the attention of the school. The few materials from teachers and students at the school confirms this. There is a *Workers' Catechism* giving simplified and pat answers to knotty problems of the social-democratic faith.[69] A student exercise book and lecture notes show a certain over-

simplification of issues, for instance that idealist philosophy is insepa-
rable from the bourgeois idea, and that religious beliefs are contrary
to science. The notes on the 'History of England' (*sic*) divide
development up into neat pre-packaged stages.[70] Anonymous lecturer's notes at the school give a similar impression. A lecture on the
theme 'Agitation is Art' unpromisingly informed its listeners 'Tolstoy
said that art is a means to infect the masses with the sympathies of
the artist. From this it follows that every true agitator is an artist and
every true artist is an agitator.'[71]

From the point of view of cultural revolution the most interesting
section was that on the 'Philosophy of Proletarian Struggle'. Bogdanov
gave five lectures that appeared to concentrate on promoting his
views on the dangers of authoritarian thinking as expressed in his
book *The Fall of the Great Fetish* (*Padenie velikogo fetishizma*).
Gorky and Lunacharsky gave lectures on art and literature. Clearly,
these would have reflected the God-building ideas they both held at
this time.[72] This is hinted at in another anonymous note for a lecture
in which religion and philosophy are said to be 'in essence one and
the same' in that they deal 'with knowledge of the unending spirit
(God)', with truth and with the absolute as distinct from the 'finite
spirit (Man)'.[73]

It was in this area that some of the sharpest clashes with the
Leninists came about, and a comparison with the programme of
Lenin's rival school in Longjumeau is illustrative. The main bulk of
the course here consisted of forty-nine lectures and four revision
classes, all given by Lenin, divided up into political economy, the
agrarian question and the theory and practice of Russian socialism.
None of the remaining thirteen lecturers gave more than twelve
lectures and most gave substantially less. Almost all were on the
theory, practice and history of European socialism and the labour
movement. Lunacharsky was to give four lectures on 'The History
of Literature and Art' but, it was laconically noted, these were not
given.[74] Thus one can see an important difference between the two
approaches, that of Capri and that of Longjumeau, in the attention
given to philosophy as such. Although philosophy was a lesser theme
at Capri it was, none the less, taken seriously. The Leninists ignored
anything but the immediate theory and practice of the class struggle.
This difference of emphasis is to be found at the heart of divisions
between the Bogdanovites and the Leninists after 1917 as well.

A final, and perhaps prophetic, aspect of the school is the reaction
of the subjects of the exercise, the twenty-seven students themselves.[75]

The pace of work at the Capri school was very intense. In addition to formal lectures there were daily practical sessions on speech-making, underground printing, and even a mock election campaign in which the lecturers and students played the role of representatives of various political parties, Gorky becoming a Black Hundred for the occasion.[76] Some of the liveliest and most interesting activities took place outside the formal teaching framework. Polemics between different party factions were only allowed in non-teaching hours. The students mixed with Gorky's house-guests and engaged in lively discussions on literature and politics at these receptions, in the course of which 'as well as tea, no small quantity of good, imported wine was drunk'.[77] German Lopatin was living on the island and entertained the students with reminiscences of his meetings with Marx.[78] On the more sombre side the students were well aware of the dispute with Lenin, which clearly cast a shadow over proceedings from the very beginning. Five of the students obeyed Lenin's summons to go, in mid-course, to Paris where he set up a rival school. Others went along later, stopping on the way to enjoy a guided tour of the sights of Rome led by Lunacharsky. On arrival in Paris some of them apparently preferred to visit a museum rather than go to a meeting arranged with Lenin. Kosarev, who tended to the Bogdanov line at this time, confessed that he was less certain of his position after meeting Lenin than he had been before, even though Lenin made it abundantly clear that such things as student participation in running the school, which had been such an important part of life in Capri, would have no place in his school since it would allow heresies in. The school would be firmly under the control of the Central Committee,[79] exactly the policy Lenin later elaborated to control Bogdanov's post-revolutionary efforts in Proletkul't. With respect to the effect of his experiences on Capri, Kosarev concluded that, although the returning students were quickly arrested, they did become important organisers for the party from the February revolution on, and he personally benefited in that, although he could read before he went, the knowledge he possessed had been picked up by chance and Capri gave him the opportunity to make it more systematic.[80]

Kosarev was not the only one to be ready for the opportunities that arose in the wake of the overthrow of tsarism. In the cultural sphere, as elsewhere in Russian society, a great upsurge of activity and self-organisation came about and it was in this atmosphere that Proletkul't began to crystallise. Even at its peak, Proletkul't was a loose and informal organisation, so it is not surprising that its early history is lost in the wave of locally generated enthusiasms and projects. Workers educational and cultural groups, set up by political parties, trade unions, factory committees, local soviets and independent groups of like-minded people, began to form. The new opportunities for political expression called for people to produce posters, decorate streets, design celebratory festivals, produce cartoons and caricatures for the rapidly expanding political press. Evidence of the extent of participation in such enterprises is fragmentary. What there is suggests that there were many enthusiastic leaders of such groups but a rather sparse band of followers. Throughout the February to October period various bodies made appeals to bring these scattered organisations together. Preoccupation with more pressing issues probably accounts for the limited response to such efforts. At around the same time, on the very eve of the October revolution, the founding meeting of Proletkul't was taking place. Its official title was the First Petrograd Conference of Proletarian Cultural-Educational Organisations held from 16–19 October under the auspices of the Central Soviet of Petrograd Factory Committees.[81] This meeting, like its smaller-scale predecessors, appears to have been notable chiefly for exposing the variety of approaches to the problems of nurturing proletarian culture that came out in the debates. Its effects were probably dissipated in the upheaval that was about to break out anew the following week. In any case, no formal, organisational structures on a national scale came from this meeting. For the following months, the business of building proletarian culture remained as localised and random as it had been since February. It was only in the late summer of 1918 that a national Proletkul't organisation came into existence.

None the less, for Bogdanov it looked as though 1917 would provide the opportunity to put his ideas into practice on a hitherto undreamed of scale. In these years of burgeoning growth of Proletkul't he was very active in propagating his ideas. There were two areas in which he made a distinctive contribution at this time. These were proletarian science and the proletarian university. His views on science exemplify his approach to some of the most fundamental problems of cultural revolution. Using the word science in its wide Russian sense to include many areas of scholarship and systematic study, he argued that science had a class character. This did not derive from the fact that science defended particular class interests. Indeed, he went on, any science, such as vulgar political economy, that had this as its objective was not worthy of the name. Its class character arose out of the origins, point of view, working methods and statements of particular sciences, including abstract ones such as logic or mathematics. 'The nature of science consists in the fact that it is the organised experience of people and serves as a means for the organisation of the life of society.'[82] It followed from this that, in bourgeois society, science served the ends of the bourgeoisie in consolidating its position over the previously dominant classes and in defending its rule over the labouring classes. It was possible, he thought, to show how science had, in the past, served the organisational/productive needs of the hegemonic class. A series of examples of this, from astronomy to the development of the clock, pepper Bogdanov's writings at this time.[83] But the fact that science defended the bourgeois system of production was the main root of its limitations, he continued, because it could attain, under the conditions prevailing within that social order, the highest forms of organisation, because these had to be based on comradely or collective co-operation. These values contradicted the fundamental values of bourgeois society, which is rooted in individualism and competition. It is part of the historic task of proletarian science, Bogdanov concluded, to reorganise society on the basis of these new values and thereby enable science and human society to reach their full potential.[84] In order to embark on this path the proletariat, 'needs to transform to itself all the scientific heritage of the bourgeois world'. The historic task of proletarian science was to create 'in the realm of science something new, which the bourgeois world is not only unable to create, but which it is incapable of even putting on the agenda'.[85] Just what these marvels might be Bogdanov did not specify. Like most aspects of the future proletarian culture, they could only be created once the process was underway. Clearly it would correspond to the unleashing of the productive forces that Marx and his followers believed would be the consequences of socialist revolution. Bogdanov was essentially making an analogy with this process in the field of culture, but there is nothing of any substance on what proletarian science would be.

For the time being, the task was not to define the future culture but to establish the preconditions for its development. For Bogdanov, this entailed the acquisition and transformation of bourgeois culture by the proletariat and then the development of the creative aspects of proletarian culture. In addition to enumerating the values that would infuse this new culture, this initial task included the founding of institutions within which the new culture could develop. Obviously,

Proletkul't itself was, in Bogdanov's eyes, such an institution. In addition, Bogdanov wished to see his vision of the Proletarian University realised. In this sphere, too, general principles were more prevalent than specific content. In general terms, Bogdanov defined the basic unit of the Proletarian University as one 'where people of science would be united with people of labour who sought knowledge'. Teachers and taught would co-operate on a basis of equality. The academic and the practical would be closely linked. Very basic preliminary courses, starting with literacy, and an introduction to laws of the natural world and to the study of society, were to form the first stage, after which the student would go on to more advanced study. Specialisation would be avoided as it would limit the creativity of the individual. Instead, the three main groups of subjects – technical, economic and cultural – would be closely linked to one another. In a statement that could serve to describe much of his theorising at this time, Bogdanov described this outline as 'a very general plan'. Greater specificity, he concluded, would be worked out as they went along.[86]

At the heart of Bogdanov's ideas, then, lay a vision of the creative potential of proletarian revolution. It would open the way to a reordering of human knowledge and to its massive development in directions that could only be dimly foreshadowed. The proletariat would lead this process because it was the bearer of socialist values. Its position in society led it to be collective and co-operative in its outlook and these values, necessarily absent from bourgeois culture, were essential if humanity was to fulfil its creative potential.[87] The principles of the past, the authoritarianism of feudal society and the individualism of bourgeois society would give way to the new value of comradeship in socialist society and a new epoch would open in all aspects of creativity.[88]

It was extremely important, in Bogdanov's view, that the initiative should be taken by the workers themselves. Influence from outside might pollute the purity of the new culture. The culture of the past was certainly not to be thrown away. There is no evidence whatsoever that Bogdanov, or the leadership of Proletkul't, was iconoclastic in this crude sense. It is a constant theme of his writing that the culture of the past had to be acquired and transformed, not destroyed. The accusation constantly levelled at Bogdanov, that he was vandalising the cultural heritage, has no basis in fact. It appears to have arisen out of polemical struggles around Proletkul't which were stimulated by a desire to limit its autonomy, not over disagreement with its principles.[89] Given the diffuse nature of the organisation, it was not difficult to find proponents of violent overthrow of the past within its membership, particularly those influenced by futurists for whom this was something of an article of faith. But it is interesting to note that the quotation most frequently used against Proletkul't in this respect, from a poem that advocated, among other equally destructive acts, the 'burning of Raphael', was held up by Bogdanov himself as an example of a completely undesirable attitude to the past. In fact he associated it with one of the most damaging influences he had identified in the revolution, that of militarism and war. In the early months of 1918 he had been writing, rather pessimistically, that what was happening in Russia was a soldiers' revolution not a workers' revolution and it was coming to bear the imprint of militarism, most notably the monster of authoritarianism was beginning to exert itself once again.[90] The desire to burn Raphael and destroy museums was, he said, the outlook of the soldier not the worker. The soldier might and must, he said, bombard Rheims Cathedral, but why should the poet choose what he called this 'Hindenburgian' form? The proletarian must never forget that it was co-operation between intellectual generations and the sacrifices of the past that had made present-day opportunities possible.[91]

There were, of course, risks involved in exposing the proletariat to the cultures of the past, but the task of assimilating all that was great and beautiful in the treasure-house of art was, he said, one of 'the two grandiose tasks standing before the proletariat in the sphere of art'.[92] To explain and justify what he meant Bogdanov used two examples. First, the proletarian must approach the cultural heritage as the free-thinker approaches religion, in order to understand it without submitting to its power. The free-thinker does not look at religion from the point of view of faith but sees it from the outside. In such a spirit the proletarian will not submit to the culture of the past but turn it into a means of constructing the new life and into a weapon against the old society itself. To clinch his argument, Bogdanov used, as his second example, the work of Karl Marx himself. Most of Marx's work, he argued, was derived from bourgeois sources such as British government documents and the writings of petty-bourgeois economists and critics of capitalism such as Sismondi, Proudhon, Balzac and many others. Out of this material Marx was able to mount an attack on the past and build a vision of the future.[93] All Bogdanov's views on the cultural heritage are consistent with these principles and no one has been able to find any examples of him encouraging the destruction of the art, science and culture of the past rather than its acquisition and transformation. By and large, the movement itself appears to have shared his views on this.

While Bogdanov was undoubtedly the major figure in Proletkul't, it is far from the case that the organisation as a whole was uniformly subject to his influence. Among the most active leaders his ideas were clearly paramount, but beyond them a variety of principles can be traced. Thus one can identify within the organisation a core of 'Bogdanovites', some critics of Bogdanov at leadership level and a grass-roots membership containing vociferous militants who were quite capable of going their own way and did not hesitate to press their ideas on the leadership.

The central Proletkul't organisations were, however, firmly in the hands of the Bogdanovites even though, presumably for tactical reasons resulting from long-standing hostility between himself and Lenin, Bogdanov kept in the background. The nominal leadership was in the hands of his associates from the time of the Capri school. P. Lebedev–Poliansky and F. Kalinin, brother of the future President of the Soviet Union, Mikhail Kalinin. Bogdanov was not even a member of the Presidium of the First All-Russian Conference,[94] though he was a member of Proletkul't's Central Committee subsequently and of the editorial board of its journal. His main institutional responsibility was as head of the organisation's science section. However, the majority of the active leadership undoubtedly took their cue from him. The ideas put forward by them in this period are, in the main, indistinguishable from those of Bogdanov himself. They tended to act as a group to defend the basic shared ideals of Proletkul't from the attacks of those who were more militant, and from those closer to the party leadership who were suspicious of Proletkul't's emphasis on independence and autonomy. In the forefront of the latter was Lunacharsky and Krupskaia, both of whom were to have participated in the First All-Russian Conference of Proletkul't in September 1918, though Pokrovsky had to stand in for Lunacharsky who was called away at short notice and, ironically, it was Bogdanov who took over Lunacharsky's designated topic 'Art and the Proletariat'.[95] Unity was the order of the day at the conference and there was little sign of the tension that was to break out later between Proletkul't and Narkompros. Pokrovsky referred to the ministry as the younger brother of Proletkul't, the latter being defined by him as 'local organisations' that were complementary to the ministry.[96] Krupskaia talked on principles of socialist education and, perhaps significantly, the customary resolution on the topic was not put to the conference, on the suggestion of the Organising Bureau, because 'life had not yet provided sufficient incontrovertible evidence' for a satisfactory resolution to be put forward.[97]

Perhaps in the hope of maintaining relations with its 'little brother', Proletkul't gave space to Krupskaia and Lunacharsky in its journals and at its conferences. In many respects the content of their views was not so different. For instance, an article by Krupskaia in *Proletarskaia Kul'tura* (*Proletarian Culture*) on the role of workers' clubs was rather innocuous,[98] but at times the leaders of the ministry might make an emphasis different from that of Proletkul't. For instance, Lunacharsky's theses on 'The Proletariat and Art' in an earlier issue laid stress on the 'universality of human culture' which cut awkwardly in comparison with Proletkul't's emphasis on the class nature of culture.[99] However, this was rather minor compared with what was to come. In the April–May issue of 1919, Lunacharsky attempted to limit Proletkul't's sphere of activity to running its studios. At the same time he did defend it against some of its powerful critics in Moscow who wished to take over its main Moscow operation, but it was clear that institutional infighting was becoming much more acute.[100]

One of the sources of this pressure was coming from below. The First All-Russian Conference had shown, in the interventions of some representatives of the provinces, a much cruder and more aggressive 'proletarian' approach to cultural questions. In the debate on 'Revolution and the Cultural Tasks of the Proletariat' one delegate called for the overthrow of bourgeois culture, not its assimilation.[101] Others called for a more unified and dictatorial assault on cultural questions including the establishment of 'a cultural-educational dictatorship'.[102] There was a call to disregard 'bourgeois writers of genius such as Tolstoy and Dostoevsky' because 'their psychology is alien to us' in that they preached 'patience, humility and love for all of humanity', whereas in a revolution what is needed is 'the song of the storm-petrel' to strengthen revolutionary resolve 'in the moment of irreconcilable tensions of battle'.[103] Interventions of this kind can be found in the record of the discussions throughout the conference, though it is not possible to say how representative they were. None the less, they were vociferous and the leadership had to spend a good deal of effort refuting them.

It was clear, then, from the very beginning that Proletkul't's life would not be an easy one. There was suspicion of it at the very highest levels of the party on account of the history of factionalism of its leading figures. Bogdanov had never returned to the party after his expulsion in June 1909. Proletkul't was based around a vague conception of proletarian culture that fell between the 'conciliatory' line of Lunacharsky and the out-and-out proletarian chauvinist line of some of the grass-roots activists. It professed to believe in facilitating pure proletarian revolution, but was largely led by intellec-tuals, though there was, admittedly, a significant sprinkling of worker-intellectuals of whom Kalinin was the most prominent. It also had to fight for its own place in the chaotic institutional jungle of overlapping cultural-propagandistic organisations set up by party and state bodies, at central and local level. In addition, many local soviets, factories and trade unions created their own cultural organisations which might or might not wish to co-operate with Proletkul't. Last but not least, unlike its rivals in this field, Proletkul't had no independent source of income and every rouble it spent or distributed to its local branches came to it from Narkompros. An examination of its institutional history in this period confirms these complications.

A major theme of Proletkul't's nominal Chairman, Lebedev–Poliansky, in the first speech at the First All-Russian Conference was the organisation's search for a secure institutional identity. Relations with Narkompros were, of course, uppermost in his mind, but at this point relations were relatively harmonious. The work of the two organisations was to be co-ordinated, but 'by co-ordination . . . we have in mind not the principle of subordination of the lower institution to the higher but friendly, free collaboration'.[104] In response to vigorous questioning from the floor by B. D. Kapner of the Moscow Metalworkers' Union, who claimed that having 'parallel institutions' was 'abnormal',[105] Lebedev–Poliansky was able to quote Lunach-arsky's own approval of 'complete freedom' for proletarian organis-ations such as Proletkul't and of the independence of proletarian cultural organisations of an artistic-scientific-creative type such as Proletkul't should be'.[106] With respect to local Departments of Popular Education, however, Lebedev–Poliansky called for strict demarcation between them and Proletkul't as they were 'different types of organisation, created on the principle of a definite division of labour in the struggle for the future culture'.[107] Its claim to independence was also emphasised by P. Kerzhentsev in the first issue of the journal *Proletarskaia Kul'tura*. In his view, Proletkul't's task was not primarily to educate workers, or to teach artistic skills and produce professional writers, actors, artists and so on, but to bring together working-class activists who wanted to create the new culture. Its task was to create for the proletariat the conditions in which 'all who wished to develop their creative instinct in the field of science, literature, theatre, the school and so on could find the fullest possibilities to create freely and to work in a friendly, comradely environment'.[108] This was its distinctive feature and the foundation of its claim to independence for 'No other organisation devotes itself to these tasks'.[109]

It is not easy to judge the extent to which Proletkul't actually achieved the identity its leaders had in mind for it. Most of the available information refers to its leadership and its activities in Moscow and Petrograd while much of its membership was spread throughout the provinces, as it quickly developed into a mass organisation, having some 80,000 people actively associated with it in 1919.[110] Given the conditions of the time, it would appear that, even under ideal circumstances, the degree of central control that could be exerted would be slight. If one adds to this the fact that one of the most deep-rooted principles of its leadership was opposition to authoritarianism, it becomes clearer that the motivation to centralisation was also weak. Indeed, one of the characteristics that was said, at the discussion on Proletkul't's role at the First All-Russian Conference, to distinguish it from state institutions such as Narkompros, was the fact that Proletkul't 'would not issue decrees',[111] as this would infringe its chief purpose in life which was to nurture 'the cultural independence of the proletariat'.[112] 'Proletarian culture could only be worked out through the process of independence at grass-roots level, among the broad worker masses'.[113] Proletkul'ts were to be 'laboratories of proletarian culture' according to Ignatov,[114] while, for Lebedev–Poliansky, Proletkul't supplemented the work of Narkompros 'like a laboratory in a well-equipped factory in which strenuous, arduous creative work would take place which aimed at improving the organisation of production'.[115] Unlike the Ministry, which had to deal with the mass of the population, the peasantry, the urban poor and so on and not just the proletarian class, Proletkul't could concentrate on a 'strict class point of view' and, without the distraction of dealing with the petty-bourgeoisie, on providing 'the proletariat with the maximum possibility for pure class creative work'.[116] Thus, in every respect, Proletkul't's aim was to assist local autonomy. This in itself was bound to weaken and diminish the role of the central leadership and, indeed, introduced a contradiction in the whole enterprise to the extent that, despite encouraging local creativity, the leadership saw itself as a protector of the essence of the enterprise and as arbiter of the creativity that they were aiming to release. The conflict between these two aspects was never resolved. So, in addition to its problems with overlapping responsibilities with powerful, central and local state and party organisations, the Proletkul't leadership was aiming to devolve as much responsibility as it could to local initiative.

The central leadership, then, did not aim at, nor could it have achieved in the conditions of the time, tight control over all aspects of the organisation. Its work was largely devoted to guidance in the application of the movement's principles in the light of everyday practice; liaising with, arbitrating between and nurturing, with such material resources as it could command, the local Proletkul'ts, and defending their creative autonomy from challenges at the local level; and, finally, creating a permanent, central, national (even international in aspiration) core with a well-defined, secure and autonomous identity and institutions, including its own journal. At all these levels it met with many frustrations and some very severe reverses in its first three years of existence.

One of the most pressing problems, from the point of view of putting its principles into practice, was defining the degree of proletarian purity the organisation should preserve in its activities. The militants who took a hard line on this wished to exclude anyone who was not a worker. Apart from making the position of many of the organisation's intelligentsia leaders potentially tenuous, this also led to practical difficulties such as the lack of expertise among such people to carry out the task of adapting and transforming Soviet culture. Bogdanov had always considered the participation of sympathetic intellectuals a key part of the process of handing over existing culture to the under-educated working class, and the issue of using intelligentsia specialists in its local activities never aroused a great deal of controversy. If appropriate proletarians were not available, then, by all means, non-proletarians should be used. Active intelligentsia sympathisers with the Bolsheviks such as Briusov took part in Proletkul't and, in Briusov's case, could be well paid for their participation. In December 1919, for instance, he received payments of 5000 and 20,000 roubles from Proletkul't for a series of lectures and other work on Russian literature. By comparison, at that time Proletkul't's highest officials received salaries of about 3500 roubles per month.[117] Clearly, Proletkul't was prepared to pay its specialists relatively well. Others who participated in local Proletkul't activities in these years included Belyi and Khodasevich. Participation of such people is clear evidence that Proletkul't was not pursuing a path of class apartheid or cultural iconoclasm as some of its critics have persistently asserted. Although it was wary of the participation of such people, they were accepted as a necessary element in the process of proletarianising culture. The slightly more knotty problem of peasant participation in Proletkul't activities arose early on. The Central Committee decided on 4 March 1919 that it had no objection in principle to peasants receiving Proletkul't subsidies.[118] The participation of peasants sometimes led to friction at lower levels from the more proletarian chauvinist elements, but the leadership did not reflect this occasional hostility.

Much more of the leadership's time was taken up, in these years, liaising with the local Proletkul'ts than on any other aspect of the organisation. Indeed, the local Proletkult's and their activities, mostly consisting of 'studios', were the heart of the organisation. Figures for the distribution of its funds show where the main interests of the organisation lay. In the second half of 1919 it had a budget of 35 million roubles with 8.6 million going to the centre and 26.3 million to local organisations of which Petrograd (8 million), Moscow (4 million) and the Moscow region (5 million) took the lion's share, with the remainder (9.3 million) presumably being distributed throughout the provinces.[119] How funds were divided up between different sections is more difficult to determine, but some approximations can be made. Figures in the Narkompros archive for Proletkul'ts budget in 1918 give the total expenditure as 2.7 million roubles divided between the major categories as follows: theatre, 483,500; cinema, 106,000; music and singing, 40,600; fine art, 218,000; clubs, 335,150; literature, 494,100; libraries, 331,200; schools, 306,000; extramural, 306,000; miscellaneous, 72,400; calling a conference, 40,000.[120] It should be borne in mind that Proletkul't was only set up on a national basis in September 1918, hence these figures do not refer to a full year. They are, however, sufficient to form an impression of priorities and costs between the various departments. The budget figures also show that Proletkul't was involved in a wide range of activities. At the grass roots, amateur theatricals, factory choirs, folk instrument ensembles, reading rooms, lectures and short courses on practical and theoretical topics flourished, though only a small minority of the population took part. By and large, these activities seem little different from adult and worker education initiatives common in western Europe and North America in the pre-war period and were an extension of the activities chronicled by Kleinbort in pre-war Russia.

None the less, these activities put a series of demands on the meagre resources of the Proletkul't leadership which it could hardly cope with. From the very beginning it was forced to turn down requests for advisers and lecturers to be sent to the provinces to give assistance and explain the organisation's policies. Occasionally lecturers were seconded but demands on the personnel at the top were enormous in the early days. The requests, too, could be rather haphazard. For instance, in February 1919 they were asked to send a delegate at two hours' notice to address the second national conference of post and telegraph workers.[121] Requests for money were also frequent and were often beyond its resources. In the early days it was not uncommon for those that could not be fulfilled to be handed on to Moscow Proletkul't in the hope that they might have some spare capacity.[122] This pointed to one of the main difficulties of central Proletkul't, namely that it was little more than a co-ordinating committee that had only a small number of personnel of its own and was at one remove from the actual activities of the organisation, compared to local Proletkul'ts such as that in Moscow which had more personnel, premises and finance for its day-to-day activities. Indeed, an early attempt by Ignatov to set up a Proletkul't club in association with the Soviet of Khamovnichesky district in Moscow in October 1918 caused a serious dispute between the central leadership, in the person of Ignatov, and Moscow Proletkul't. While the dispute was ostensibly about the demarcation of overlapping responsibilities, there was a sub-theme of differing approaches to Proletkul't work that dragged on much longer than the argument about the Khamovnichesky club.[123] In this case the central leadership defended the club's independence from the local Proletkul't organis-ation. In disputes arising in the provinces that came to its attention, the central Proletkul't tended to urge local Proletkul'ts to assert their intellectual independence of the local soviet. For instance, in April 1919 a request for guidance from Saratov Proletkul't in connection with its relations with the local *ispolkom* (soviet executive committee) brought the response that Proletkul't was free of local control in the creative sphere but political control lay with the *ispolkom*.[124] Disputes also arose between different parts of Proletkul't in the same locality. The most serious was between Petrograd Proletkul't and the Petrograd Proletkul't Theatre. Bogdanov was seconded to Petrograd to conduct an inquiry. He presented his conclusions to the Central Committee meeting of 12 August 1919, placing the blame squarely and unequivocally on Petrograd Proletkul't for its administrative high-handedness against the normally independent theatre, which, as a result, had been transferred to direct subordination to the Central Committee.[125] Clearly, relations between the component parts of Proletkul't had not settled down and the differences, reflecting the *ad hoc* ground-upwards development of the organisation in 1917 and 1918 prior to the establishment of the central leadership, continued to cause friction. The central organisation had only tenuous relations with its two most powerful local organisations, which felt themselves strong enough to assert their independence. There was no clear way in which the central leadership could bring anything more effective than moral pressure to bear on its wayward followers since it was itself beholden to Narkompros for its funds. Direct lobbying between Moscow and Petrograd Proletkul't and Narkompros could defend their allocation and allow the ministry to sow dissention within the ranks of its troublesome offshoot.

If internal relations within Proletkul't showed the anarchic character common in the fledgling post-revolutionary institutions, its relation with the outside world, particularly its 'younger brother', Narkompros, showed even greater tension. In terms of its administrative power, Proletkul't was a minnow in a sea infested with sharks, of which the most threatening were Narkompros and, increasingly, the Central Committee of the party and its various departments.

The early phrases about complementarity between the work of Narkompros and Proletkul't[126] gave way to increasing suspicion. From 1918 to early 1920, the relationship between the two had a strong undercurrent of antipathy but this did not break out into open conflict of a serious kind. Before the setting up of national Proletkul't the main local organisations, in Moscow and Petrograd, worked closely under the aegis of Narkompros, describing themselves as being attached to the ministry. The posters advertising the founding conference of national Proletkul't for instance, described the group authorising the conference as the 'Department of Proletarian Culture attached to [*pri*] the People's Commissariat of Education.'[127] The establishment of a national Proletkul't marked a step away from subordination to Narkompros, but there was anxiety on both sides about defining this role. For the first year and a half the frequent frictions remained manageable, even though scarcely a month went by without some point of conflict. These could be the trivial day-to-day difficulties of any bureaucracy. For instance, in December 1919

Narkompros held up approval of fees Proletkul't had agreed to pay to Bogdanov, claiming that they would need special approval by Sovnarkom,[128] and in December 1918 it queried a request for cloth from the Klin Proletkul't for use by its theatre section.[129] Such problems could be routine or they could, given the pattern of frequency of such abrasions, indicate something more significant. In the sphere of organisational overlap the issues were potentially a little more threatening to Proletkul't, ranging from a proposal of Narkompros in November 1918 that it should set up its own Proletkul't section in its local organisations,[130] which would implicitly restrict Proletkul't's freedom of action in the provinces, to a proposal in January that the Narkompros literary department should set up 'workers' studios'[131] which would tread on the exclusive preserve of Proletkul't.

Within Proletkul't too, the differences that had been smoothed over at the First All-Russian Conference of Proletkul't tended to break out afresh, particularly under pressure from below where there was considerable resentment among Proletkul't militants at what they considered the lack of revolutionary energy of Narkompros, which was, it was frequently alleged, too much under the control of 'non-Marxists'. None the less, at the first delegate conference of Proletkul't, held in January 1919 and attended by a range of representatives from provincial branches of Proletkul't, a long wrangle over the question of subordination to Narkompros broke out. The leadership, which was no less wary of Narkompros than the members but tended to be tactically more cautious, had difficulty in getting its position across and Lebedev–Poliansky even resigned (temporarily) as a result. As at the First National Conference there was considerable criticism of Narkompros, but also doubt about the wisdom of having parallel cultural organisations in a situation of critical lack of resources.[132] Officially, however, the Proletkul't leadership attempted to hold fast to Bogdanov's vision of the organisation as the institution bringing together the politically conscious vanguard of the proletariat and its active non-proletarian sympathisers in 'laboratories of proletarian culture'.

In the event it was not Narkompros that brought about the most damaging blow suffered by Proletkul't in this period but the party Central Committee itself, and in particular its Orgburo. This set a pattern that was to be repeated a year later, with fatal consequences for the Bogdanovite vision. The issue at stake was that of the Proletarian University. Bogdanov's ideas on this had developed since his description of its general principles to the First All-Russian Conference. An article by him published in *Proletarskaia kul'tura* embellished the programme with further details, though the basic principles remained as they had been outlined previously.[133] Students were selected and came together in Moscow and the University began to function in Spring 1919. Almost immediately it was hit by a savage blow.

At the time it opened in March 1919, the President of the Proletarian University, N. V. Rogozinsky, who was attached to the Extramural Department of Narkompros and was consistently unsympathetic to Bogdanov's plans for the University, had submitted to the party Central Committee plans for it to be merged with the Central School of Soviet and Party Work, allegedly without any consultation with staff or students of the Proletarian University.[134] Needless to say this insensitivity to the people involved, which is far from unique in the annals of education administration, caused great indignation. However, the opposition was to no avail and the Proletarian University was ordered to be closed. Ostensibly, the decision had been taken by the Extramural Department of Narkompros on 23 July.[135] This action had been signalled by an article in *Izvestiia* on 17 July that criticised the principle of a Proletarian University. The real force behind it, however, was an unpublished decision of the party Central Committee which ordered it to be merged with the Central Party School. In the words of Bogdanov, at the meeting of the Proletkul't Central Committee of the 12 August, 'On the basis of a resolution of the Central Committee of the Communist Party the Proletarian University has been closed'.[136] An Orgburo order implementing this decision was produced on the 2 August. According to this the remaining students were to be transferred to political work at the front.[137]

The terms of these resolutions suggested that the closure was temporary and did not represent a definitive decision against the principle of the Proletarian University, rather that to set it up at the current moment was 'untimely'.[138] Comments by Bukharin, published in *Proletarskaia kul'tura*, backed up this impression. The merger with the Central Party School, which had been approved in principle by the party Central Committee on 3 July, did not according to Bukharin, represent a rejection of the idea of a Proletarian University, which 'on the contrary was considered to be useful and necessary', but rather was a result 'only of the difficult situation in the Soviet Republic'. The question of its re-establishment, he said, could be considered 'after the liquidation of the current military complications'.[139] Bogdanov grasped at this straw and Proletkul't proposed that it should be revived at the first opportunity.[140] For the time being, although its students were dispersed, no action was taken to liquidate the property of the Proletarian University. This was not attempted until April 1921.[141] Bogdanov did attempt to revive the Proletarian University in May 1920 but did not make any headway, not least because of the attack by Poland.[142] Even so, it is clear that even if circumstances had been considerably more favourable, Bogdanov's chances would have remained very slim indeed, and the argument that the decisions about the Proletarian University in 1919 and 1920 were determined by external conditions shows every sign of being merely tactical. After all, there was just as much demand for the students of the Central Party School to be redeployed to the front but this establishment was allowed to continue to operate.

The closure of the Proletarian University, and in particular the prominent role played in this by the Central Committee, points to the growing direct involvement of the party leadership in cultural questions. The growing intensity of the campaign against the Bogdanovites in Proletkul't, which developed after the closure of the Proletarian University, suggests that a much deeper process than simply response to difficult conditions was taking place. Before turning to examine the years 1920–2, when the party leadership began to turn more directly to intervention in cultural and educational affairs, it is worth making a brief examination of the party's embryonic attempts to act in this field in 1918 and 1919. The attempt to set up a Socialist Academy and to organise the penetration of higher-education teaching by Marxists was one aspect of this, but also important, and less well known, is the founding of the Central School for Soviet and Party Work and its evolution into the Sverdlov University.

PARTY EDUCATION: THE SVERDLOV UNIVERSITY

Where Narkompros had organisational plans but lacked a clear vision of the role of culture in the transition to socialism, and Proletkul't lacked organisational strength but was motivated from the centre by Bogdanov's vision, the party leadership, which became increasingly drawn into cultural and educational policy, lacked both vision and organisation in this sphere during the civil war years. To turn from Narkompros and Proletkul't to the initial attempts of the Central Committee to set up its own educational apparatus is to move from a world in which, for all their differences, the leading characters – Lunacharsky, Pokrovsky, Krupskaia and Bogdanov – agreed on the importance of culture and its values and to enter a completely different world with different priorities and values. For the party leadership the long-term questions of cultural transformation, which were of great importance to the radical *intelligenty* of Narkompros and Proletkul't, were submerged by the tidal wave of immediate problems and crises that their rapidly improvised solutions had to address. Direct involvement in cultural and educational questions developed from the need to find suitable administrators and propagandists for the new system. The absence of a large, educated and highly conscious working class to take over the administration of the new state, and the actue shortage of people who had more than the crudest idea of what the Bolshevik enterprise was intended to be in the medium and long term, posed acute problems for the leadership. In the civil war years, when the leadership was preoccupied with the even more pressing problem of organising a shattered economy and defeating the Whites, cultural-educational questions had a low priority, except in so far as there existed immediate gaps to be plugged. None the less, approaches to these issues began to emerge that, far from being re-evaluated in the light of victory in the civil war, had a decisive bearing on the future policy of the party towards cultural transformation. This theme is the main subject of the next chapter but, for the sake of completing the picture of cultural life during the civil war and preparing the ground for subsequent discussion, an account of the main features of these early measures is given here.

The people involved in developing party education of this kind have received much less attention than those involved in Narkompros and Proletkul't. This is not surprising given the rather superficial nature of their ideas and the simplicity, not to say crudity, of their educational practices, which were reduced essentially to propaganda. Thus, the intellectual atmosphere is quite different. An examination of the activities of the most important institution in this area at this time, the Sverdlov University, and of the ideas and career of its founding rector, V. I. Nevsky (1876–1937), shows this contrast very sharply.

Although he was a graduate of Kharkov University, Nevsky does not appear to have frequented the intelligentsia milieu in the pre-revolutionary years. In 1917, he made his mark as an activist in the Petrograd Bolshevik Committee, urging aggressive action in July, but being more cautious in October. There is no evidence that he was at all involved in cultural and intellectual affairs. He was primarily an organiser and party zealot with no observable inclination to ideas and the life of the intellect. It is thus something of a surprise to find him emerging as a key figure in the organisation of the intellectual life of the party and, ultimately, of the country. In this he is typical of the reliable party militants, grouped around the Central Committee of the party, who began to play a key role in bringing intellectual life under greater party control and in working out a policy in this sphere. As with others of this breed, Nevsky's career includes participation in a wide range of institutions and commissions geared towards these objectives. The posts he held were so diverse that it is hard to pinpoint where he was based in formal terms. He was appointed to committees on behalf of the Central Committee, the Organisation Bureau of the Party and the Executive Committee of the Soviet. Distinction between these central institutions was very blurred at this time and it is more important to realise that Nevsky was part of a tiny group of trusted party leaders who supervised activities in many areas. His career spanned the State Publishing House (Gosizdat), the Commission of Inquiry into Narkompros (1920), which he headed, the Political Education Section of Narkompros (Glavpolitprosvet) and the Lenin Library, of which he was a Director from 1925 to 1933. He wrote a number of pamphlets and articles, mostly in party propaganda and agitation publications, specialising in party theory on philosophy and science in general and in attacking Bogdanov's ideas in particular. He was commissioned to write an attack on Bogdanov included in the first post-revolutionary edition of Lenin's *Materialism and Empiriocriticism*, published in 1920. This turn towards theory was presumably grounded in the fact that he had studied science at postgraduate level and there were very few equally qualified people in higher party circles at this time who could engage in polemic of this kind. His first step, however, was not into theory but into organising practical party agitprop activities, most notably as Rector of the Sverdlov University from 1919–21.

A glance at his publications in this period shows why Nevsky's work in this area has been consistently overlooked.[143] His aim was to introduce the largely ignorant population of Soviet Russia to the political principles of the leadership. In particular, he stressed the importance of getting books and printed materials into the countryside. In a speech to a conference of the newspaper and magazine publishing organisation 'Tsentropechat', he proposed the setting up in many rural areas of a Peasants' House that would be affiliated with the local party schools that the 9th Party Congress had decided to set up. The idea was very close to that of the 'reading huts' that sprang up in these years, and both were essentially an extension into the countryside of the idea of the Workers' Club, the latter already supported by Krupskaia and also actively promoted by Proletkul't.[144] These institutions were intended to become rural centres, and almost churches, of the new scientific and rational system. He also wrote about similar work in the cities. In a handbook for workers in urban libraries, Nevsky, and his co-author N. Khersonskaia, outlined the kind of tasks the librarian was expected to perform. These included pointing out the most reliable books on a whole range of questions that the visitors to the library might raise, including political, professional, religious, sexual and leisure problems. The good librarian would encourage discussion and arrange meetings on prominent issues of the locality. The practice of under-lining (in pencil) the key passages in books was also recommended as part of the librarian's task. It was also expected that the librarian would deal with the sexual and emotional problems of local people.[145] Clearly, Nevsky's focus in such works was on narrow, immediate, practical and propagandistic questions. The point was not the creation of a new culture but the transfer of the correct values from those who possessed them to those who did not.

His more scientific and philosophical works were no more promi-sing. Bourgeois scientific philosophy he argued, tried to undermine the proletariat and its materialist philosophy by, as Vernadsky supposedly did, concluding that modern science was incompatible with materialism. Behind this was, according to Nevsky, the philosophy of Thomas Aquinas and, ultimately, belief in God.[146] The assumption that bourgeois thought could be reduced to idealism and religion was also predominant in another article of the time in which thought was either religious or healthy. 'The philosophy of dead reaction – that is what we can call all the writings of bourgeois philosophers of our time.'[147] The crudity and energy of Nevsky's writings on this theme make him a worthy successor to the Lenin of *Materialism and Empiriocriticism*.

Despite, or perhaps more accurately because of, his intellectual limitations Nevsky has to be taken seriously as an example of the kind of approach to cultural questions that was finding support at the heart of the party. His work at the Sverdlov University at this time shows the same principles at work. The syllabus, to put no finer point on it, was geared to the propagandisation of the students so that they in turn could pass on their half-digested knowledge to others. Each of the two years of the long course introduced in 1920 comprised nearly 1500 hours of lectures, made up of approximately 300–400 hours of natural science; 400 hours of history; 450 hours of economics; 100 hours of law; 150 hours of a foreign language.[148] Cyclostyled notes suggest that cramming was the main purpose of the exercise. Assigned reading included Engels's *Anti-Duhring*; Hilferding; Bogdanov's *Short Course in Economic Science*; Kautsky's *The Economic Doctrines of Karl Marx* and *The Agrarian Question*; Trachtenberg's *Money*; Lenin's *The Development of Capitalism in Russia* and *Imperialism*; and Bukharin's *Imperialism and the World Economy*.[149] The overall impression is that it was more akin to a seminary devoted to the study of dogma rather than a university pursuing new ideas.

Figures for the June 1921 intake of 347 candidates to the second-year course show the student body to be largely male (84.2 per cent); aged 20–5 (64.7 per cent); Russian (67.6 per cent); having only elementary education (59.4 per cent); and of working-class origin (55.0 per cent). All belonged to the party, though only 35.7 per cent had been members at the time of the October revolution.[150] The basic formal entrance qualification appears to have been literacy[151] though it did have a *rabfak* attached.[152] Most of the recruits were political activists in the party (61.2 per cent), the soviets (45.9 per cent), trade unions (32.8 per cent) and the press (43.0 per cent).[153] It was their work in these areas that made them candidates for the school. On completion of their course most of the graduates were assigned to work in areas of party and state administration defined by the Central Committee according to its immediate needs. In 1919, for instance, according to a Central Committee minute, of 1100 completing initial course work 650 were mobilised. Most of the remainder were commandeered by various government bodies. Nevsky was allowed to select fifty to stay on for further study.[154] Curiously, it would appear that, though their education was very theoretical, many of the tasks to which they were assigned were practical, though as party activists the two spheres were probably less distinct than might otherwise be the case, in that they would be, as it were, community leaders in a practical and intellectual sense.

In addition to the long courses, a series of short courses of 10–14 days and upwards were also given.[155] These catered for lower level agitational-propaganda needs. It was in order to respond to these needs that the school had been set up in the first place. It is difficult to give a precise account of its origin as this is lost in the flurry of disorganised, unrecorded and improvised activities of the revolutionary government in its earliest days. A renewed effort appears to have been made in early 1919 by Sverdlov to co-ordinate and develop practices that had emerged in the course of the previous year and to set up what was initially referred to as 'The School of Soviet Work attached to VTsIK' (the Executive Committee of the Soviet).[156] The death of Sverdlov, in the middle of preparations for its opening on 1 June 1919, provided it with a suitable patron saint and it became known as the Sverdlov University. It was also transferred, at least partially, to the authority of the party. Its early months seem to have been rather disorganised. Its first students were recruited unsystematically and application enquiries were still coming in from the provinces some weeks after it was supposed to have started operation. Commissariats and other party and state bodies were asked, in February, to give an outline of contributions to the course and to nominate lecturers to its staff. In the fashion of the time they were given one week to come up with proposals.[157]

When it finally began to operate the University was still subject to many difficulties. The practical problem of heating, finance, the condition of the buildings and a serious shortage of books all made their mark. As if that was not enough, lecturers frequently failed to show up to give their lectures. Bukharin missed one of three he was due to give. Piatakov missed five out of ten, Vladimirsky eleven of nineteen. Even Nevsky, already its head, missed six out of fifteen.[158] It is hard to know what the 1500 people attached to the University in 1919[159] would have made of these pioneering steps. In any case they did not have much time to complain, as its initial courses were of short duration and by October its 1100 graduates were being dispersed through the military and state apparatus as mentioned above. The Central Committee assignments came through only two days before their courses were due to end.[160]

As with other institutions in the field, it was only in the period 1920–2 that a more systematic and organised policy was applied. A new effort in this direction stemmed from an Orgburo resolution of 24 April 1920, which definitely closed the door to the still-lingering hopes of Proletkul't that a Proletarian University might be established. Instead, the Orgburo decreed that 'all forces and means of the Proletarian University are to be handed over to the Sverdlov Communist University'. The Orgburo approved the Sverdlov University's plans for a two-year course, but also called on it to take 'decisive measures to broaden the short course to the maximum degree'.[161] Later in the year the Orgburo also tried to press it to expand its intake, but the university authorities demurred, citing the continuing shortages and, especially, the strain this would put on the living conditions of students, who were already in danger of suffering from an epidemic.[162]

The transfer of the remaining resources of the Proletarian University to the Sverdlov University serves to remind us that the latter was, in a literal as well as metaphorical sense, the heir of the former. Indeed, the Sverdlov University was an implementation of at least part of what Bogdanov had envisaged. The Capri School had devoted a great deal of its attention to equipping party militants with the practical skills they required. Such is the dialectical process that Bogdanov should be credited with part of the responsibility for the idea and content of the party school. It was in response to this idea that Lenin had set up his rival school in 1909 and, ten years later, it was at least partly as a response to Bogdanov's Proletarian University that the Sverdlov University was set up. The similarity between the two institutions should not, however, be over-stressed. There was one outstanding difference. It was essential to Bogdanov's vision that the task of cultural transformation should be seen in its largest and most imaginative dimensions. The Proletarian University was to be an instrument by which a new class would freely create a totally new culture and set of values. The administrators of the Sverdlov University had no comparable ambitions. For them, the institution was intended to transfer knowledge and skills for much more immediate and pragmatic purposes. It was not intended to create new values but to transfer doctrine from the relatively limited circles who possessed it to the wider population who did not. In a sense, this has remained an essential element in Soviet political education and culture ever since. Even the 'new' Soviet man was not a step into the unknown so much as an attempt to achieve a pre-existing blueprint. Lenin's lack of enthusiasm for 'new' ideas in *Materialism and Empiriocriticsm* foreshadowed this in part, and was to be in evidence again in these years when he uttered the remarkable statement in October 1921 that 'the time when it was necessary to draw the political outlines of great tasks has passed' and instead it was time rather 'to put them into practice'.[163] This had been foreshadowed earlier in the year when he had said 'What we need is more factual knowledge and fewer debates on ostensible communist principles.'[164] For many, even in the party, the 'political outlines of great tasks' remained sketchy in the extreme.

The Sverdlov University serves, then, to show us that a third force was beginning to assert itself in Soviet intellectual life, a force that was ominously short on imagination and breadth but very well supplied with loyalty to the party. The Sverdlov University was a faltering first step towards controlling intellectual life through institutional means rather than through capturing the commanding intellectual heights. Power in intellectual life had begun to flow into the hands of the Nevsky's of the post-revolutionary world and away from the Bogdanov's, Lunacharsky's and even the Krupskaia's. Instead, half-educated people were being filled with pre-packaged, crude dogma to bolster their already apparent revolutionary conviction and energy. The combination was to prove an increasingly influential one throughout the 1920s and institutions such as Sverdlov University became breeding grounds for proletarian chauvinism. After all, their chief task was to provide skilled working-class replacements for 'bourgeois' intellectuals and to carry out proletarian revolution in the field of culture. The old intelligentsia had already begun to fight a rearguard action and, although it was not yet apparent, even its representatives inside the party, most notably Trotsky and Bukharin, were to fall victim to it. The Sverdlovtsy were an excellent breeding ground for 'Stalinism' in culture, and it is no accident that Stalin used the Sverdlov University as a forum of some of his major forays into the world of theory.

A final reflection thrown up by the Sverdlov University is that it was itself an institution shaped by the fundamental forces of the revolution. It came into being at the interface between the increasing institutional power of the party and its rather feeble active support among the population. In a sense it was a quintessentially Leninist enterprise, in that its function and the function of its graduates was to instill socialist consciousness in the still-indifferent or hostile mass of the population for whom the revolution consisted largely of short-term considerations. If the construction of socialism was to succeed, it was necessary to win them over in a fuller sense to Marxism and to party ideology. As yet, the party leadership itself had not given much time and attention to this question, but, as the civil war drew to a victorious close, militants who had seen off tsarism and its whole train of foreign backers were returning from the front brimming with confidence and looking for new horizons to explore. For many, the most obvious remaining challenge lay in cultural revolution. The last remaining outpost of the bourgeoisie appeared to be its cultural hegemony. They were prepared to fight, and the party leadership began to grapple with the issue in a more direct and determined way.

4 Laying the Foundations of Cultural Power

When you have dealings with a professor you must be prepared in advance for the very worst.

F. Engels

There is a widespread tendency among historians to think of the 1920s in Russia as a period of toleration and cultural achievement. The decade has been called a 'golden age of Marxist thought'.[1] A 'soft' line on culture has been identified.[2] The period has been referred to as 'NEP in culture'.[3] Compared with what came after, the 1920s were more tolerant – it would have been hard for them to be less so – but compared with the civil war the picture is rather different. The foundations of cultural policy in the 1920s were laid down in 1920–2 and the major interventions in those years included the virtual closing down of Proletkul't; the ending of university autonomy; the forcible deportation of scores of intellectuals; the bankruptcy of numerous small-scale cultural institutions as a result of NEP taxation; the constraining of remaining private publishing; and the setting up of a constantly expanding censorship apparatus. Cultural and agitational/propaganda issues played a much more prominent role in Party Congress and Conference decisions in this period. It is clear that a revolution in cultural policy was taking place in these two years and the objective of this chapter is to try to throw some light on the processes behind it.

The chief factor underpinning these events was the steady encroachment in the cultural sphere of the party at the highest level. Where policy in the civil war years had been harsh and violent, it had also been arbitrary and, as has been seen, this allowed a number of improbable survivals in a few sheltered lagoons. Once the war was over, and cultural policy moved higher up the agenda, party policy became more systematic. It took the form, primarily, of setting up a number of bodies intended to enable the Central Committee to exercise a closer supervision over cultural policy (though not all these experiments were initially successful) and to give it the means to begin to implement its own ideals in this sphere. One of the most noteworthy features of these developments is that they mark a

142

decisive step away from what Lenin had termed on the morrow of
the October revolution 'allowing full creative freedom for the
masses' – which he had understood in the light of enabling them to
follow their instincts in the creation of social and political institutions
rather than in the realm of ideas – towards the capture of existing
leading cultural institutions and the creation of new controlling
institutions. In this sense these years mark a decisive stage in achieving
an October revolution in culture. Capture of cultural power from
above, rather than as a result of the triumph of socialist consciousness,
lay behind the events of this period. Bolshevik culture began to make
its impact through seizure and creation of institutions by a minority
who used them to impose their values on wider society. The route to
the new cultural hegemony was via the capture of the institutional
commanding heights of the new culture, not as a result of a process
of open conflict of ideas and evangelisation of the new values. As
with other aspects of the revolution, in the sphere of culture it was a
question of getting hold of the institutions first and using them to
shape consciousness according to the prescription of the élite, rather
than allowing new institutions to emerge that corresponded with the
consciousness of the population. Signs of this development were, of
course, present before 1920 but had not been as systematically
pursued as they were in these years.

   As yet there were limited factors impeding the full implementation
of this new approach, of which three are the most significant. In the
first place, it was still necessary to conciliate remnants of the skilled
professional and managerial groups of tsarist society in order to speed
up the recovery of the economy. This implicitly left some small space
for a degree of cultural toleration. Associated with this was the need
to learn cultural skills from sympathetic non-Bolsheviks, soon to be
referred to as 'fellow-travellers' in the cultural sphere. Secondly, the
new authorities were still raw and incompetent and it proved to be
more difficult than some of them had imagined to put the new
principles of cultural control into practice. As a result, some of the
more hot-headed schemes were failures, discrediting, for the time
being, those associated with them. Both of these factors point to a
fundamental feature of Soviet life at this time, namely the continuing
weakness of party and state and a continuing need to compromise
substantially. At the same time, in areas to which the authorities
gave priority, they could bring sufficient concentrated force to bear
to destroy their opponents. The third factor limiting cultural policy
at this time was a lack of agreement within the leadership as to what

that policy should be. In broad terms they were divided between former members of the intelligentsia who, while disagreeing about a great deal, shared a belief that cultural policy required care, caution and patience – Lenin, Trotsky, Bukharin, Lunacharsky and Krupskaia all agreed on this at least – and an increasingly strident, confident and aggressive group of 'proletarians' that had come into existence during the civil war and wished to preserve its ethos and principles into peacetime struggles on cultural 'fronts' carried on by 'armies' and 'squads' using 'artillery' and other 'weapons' to 'liquidate' the old culture and create the new in the same way that this had been done in other spheres during the civil war. Even the supposedly conciliatory Lunacharsky eventually talked of the cultural 'third front' in the title of a collection of his articles published in 1925. By and large, the proletarians emerged from lower levels of Russian society than the established *intelligenty* who dominated party policy-making and had come to prominence as energetic militants during the struggle against the Whites. The division between these two groups, ostensibly only one of the pace at which shared ideals of socialist culture should be realised, became a source of conflict throughout the 1920s with the initiative slowly, but apparently irreversibly, passing from the former to the latter. For the time being, however, the division, and in particular the influence of the former, put a brake on the wilder schemes of the latter. None the less, this did not prevent the laying of the foundations of a formidable apparatus of cultural control in the period from the end of 1920 to the end of 1922. For all their differences, participants in this debate were all Bolsheviks and had no truck with unnecessary toleration of what were deemed to be non-socialist values. All shared the opinion that the purpose of the party was to lead society firmly into the realm of socialism, in the cultural sphere as much as any other. Thus, for the time being, there were major areas of agreement between the two groups, especially when it came to the question of establishing the leading role of the party. In these years major steps were undertaken to ensure this in the cultural sphere. The first body to feel the impact of this mood was the institution that appeared most threatening, in the long run, to party hegemony, the institution that from the very beginning had asserted the importance of its independence from the party and had tried, to the best of its ability, to defend its autonomy from party and state. Ironically, it was also the institution that appeared to share most closely the party's ideals with respect to culture. Far from protecting it, this, combined with its claim to autonomy, made it all the more dangerous. For this reason, the party leadership decided as its first priority to bring Proletkul't under its control, while impeccably bourgeois institutions such as the Academy of Sciences and, to a lesser extent, some universities retained a degree of independence for a longer period.

THE MUTILATION OF PROLETKUL'T

On 1 December 1920 *Pravda* published a letter 'On the Proletkul'ts' which comprised the text of a resolution of the Central Committee of the Bolshevik Party followed by an explanatory gloss. In effect, though not in name, Proletkul't was suppressed. While the organisation lingered on through the 1920s and was not formally wound up until the decree on cultural organisations of 1932, from December 1920 onwards it was only a shadow of what it had been previously. Its grandiose vision was proscribed, its activities were curtailed and encroached on from all sides by local and national party, soviet and trade union organisations, and its leading personnel were purged. The chief head to roll was that of Bogdanov who played hardly any part in its subsequent activities. Lebedev-Poliansky was also removed and the decree represented a surgical strike against the Bogdanovites in the organisation. Pletnev replaced Lebedev-Poliansky as its head.

Ostensibly, the resolution was motivated by party impatience with the supposed iconoclasm and proletarian sectarianism said to have been displayed by Proletkul't, in particular among those of its supporters who were influenced by futurism. While such attitudes did exist within it, as Bogdanov himself was only too well aware, there are grounds for thinking that the real reasons for its virtual suppression lie elsewhere. The most obvious is that iconoclasm, proletarian sectarianism and even, to a degree, futurism continued to flourish – even to grow steadily throughout the 1920s – in Soviet culture, and no other action was taken at this time by the party to control them. Indeed, it seemed positively to encourage some of these attitudes. Secondly, it was the Bogdanovites not the 'iconoclasts' who were purged. Thirdly, some of the leadership who were less Bogdanovite, or at least remained Bogdanovite only *in pectore*, continued to remain influential figures in the development of party cultural policy in the 1920s and, with the exception that they kept quiet about the larger Bogdanovite vision, continued to follow much the same principles and act in a fashion very comparable to what they had been doing prior to the decree.

One does not have to look very far for an alternative explanation. A supposedly secondary reason for the action against Proletkul't was that it claimed a degree of autonomy in the field of culture. That the attack on its autonomy was a more plausible motive is suggested by a number of factors. First, it was those who most prized its independence who suffered. Secondly, of all its themes of the pre-decree period, the only one that was definitively undermined was that of autonomy, which was never raised again. (Some of its practical proposals, most notably the Proletarian University, had already been rejected, of course.) Thirdly, Lenin continued to suspect Bogdanov of factionalism. In addition, more circumstantial indications lead one to the same conclusion. Above all, the way the fate of Proletkul't fits into the wider context of related policies at this time may be significant. For instance, accounts were being settled with other aspects of 'left-wing childishness', under which accommodating banner Proletkul't could be included. It should also be remembered that, in the earliest formulation of its independence, Proletkul't had seen the political sphere as the party's preserve, the economic sphere as belonging to the trade unions and the cultural sphere as its own province. It is surely more than coincidence that the party was simultaneously destroying the independence of both of the others. This is not, of course, to say that there was a conspiracy afoot here, simply that in both areas similar forces were coming to bear. It also fits in with the other policies of cultural co-ordination mentioned at the beginning of this chapter. A closer examination of events leading up to the decree confirms the view that it was its claim to autonomy that was its most serious failing in the eyes of Lenin and the party leadership.

The decree did not fall on Proletkul't out of a blue sky. Indeed, 1920 saw it suffering an unremitting series of reverses of many kinds. In February its deputy leader, F. I. Kalinin, who was one of Bogdanov's protégés from the time of the Capri school and a prime example of the type of worker-intellectual Proletkul't was aiming to produce, fell victim to the typhus epidemic raging at that time. While its enemies could not be blamed for this blow, the rest of its reverses were inflicted in a more calculating fashion.

The political reverses Proletkul't suffered must have been doubly difficult to bear in that, as the civil war was moving rapidly to a victorious conclusion, particularly after the Polish invaders had been repelled and the Red Army had advanced towards Warsaw in August 1920, expectations of rapidly improving conditions for its work must have seized Proletkul't along with many other institutions. The apparently more favourable situation at the front removed one of the party's key ostensible reasons for having suspended the Proletarian University the previous year[4] and, not unnaturally since it remained of great importance to him, Bogdanov took the opportunity to try to revive it. However, the attack by Poland coincided with his initiative and, at the Proletkul't Central Committee meeting of 6 May, he proposed that, especially in view of the fact that the members of the Sverdlov University had been sent to the front, the matter should not be raised with the government until conditions were more favourable.[5] The projected low profile was not, however, low enough to escape the attention of the authorities, and Bogdanov's retreat on the issue had been occasioned less by the Poles than by the Orgburo, which two weeks previously had decreed that 'the opening of a Proletarian University is not allowed'.[6] This time no elaborate excuses about current difficulties and the hope that things might change for the better were appended to this stark decision. Instead, the resources of the Proletarian University were transfered to the Sverdlov University. The chances of resurrecting it after this appeared unlikely in the extreme.[7]

In addition, relations with Narkompros remained tortuous throughout 1920. Abrasions continued to multiply. Some of them were relatively petty, such as Narkompros's decision of May 1920 not to include Proletkul't personnel on its list of those to be supplied with groceries and other commodities, on the grounds that they were not Narkompros employees.[8] This could only have had an unsettling effect within Proletkul't and was a reminder that its proposed independence would have costs as well as benefits. At a more serious level, relations were worsening from early on in the year when Narkompros began to embark on plans of its own for a literary section which would have its own 'workers' studios', a preserve that Proletkul't considered to be, above all else, its own. Kalinin was deputed to point this out to the collegium of Narkompros. At the same time, Narkompros was proposing to set up a national conference of proletarian writers. This also posed a problem for Proletkul't. To refuse to participate would smack of factionalism, to take part would compromise its independence. For the time being it decided to keep a watchful eye on developments, without committing itself.[9]

Proletkul't was not the only source of protest at the nature of the new Narkompros literary department. A range of radicals raised their voices in protest, particularly at the apparent influence of traditional *intelligenty* in the organisation at the expense of those with a stronger orientation to the proletariat. There were also worries that they would exert too much power. Krupsakaia, for example expressed her fear that the nine members of the literary section would attempt to consolidate their own influence on literature and stifle new developments. They would, she said, 'only put brakes on the new literary trend'. Certainly some form of organisation was desirable, she continued, but 'let them have fewer powers. They must not take unions, associations, clubs and literary circles under their monopolistic control. All these organisations must have the right to find their own identity, the right to choose whatever literary direction they like.'[10] The terms of Krupskaia's criticism are strangely similar to the kind of comments that had frequently emerged from Proletkul't. As discussion proceeded on how to respond to the new institution, Proletkul't's position became increasingly hostile. The meeting of its Central Committee on 28 April pointed out that the literary section would be heavily dependent on the already existing academic section, which was, so it was claimed, staffed with non-Marxists. Similarly, it asserted that 'material questions were being resolved, for the most part, in favour of writers of bourgeois origin' and decided to recall its representatives and not refill their seats in the negotiations.[11] It is also more than coincidence that at this time Proletkul't appears to have stepped up its efforts to forge links with trade unions as a firmer platform for achieving contract with the proletariat. This had always been an aim, but such defenders as Proletkul't had at this time tended to come from the unions. On 15 October, for example, a meeting of the Moscow branch of the Metalworkers' Union passed a resolution supporting the independence of Proletkul't from Narkompros.[12] It is interesting to note that after the decree of December, Proletkul't lived even more under the wing of trade unions. However, in the crisis of 1920 support of organisations such as unions, which were themselves undergoing a similar policy of co-ordination, could be ambiguous.

Proletkul't's continuous rearguard action against Narkompros was not helped by the fact that there was a fifth column within its own ranks. At the 14 February meeting of Proletkul't's Central Committee, at which policy with respect to the literary department of Narkompros was formulated, two Proletkul't 'representatives', who appeared to have been close to the ministry's point of view, were reprimanded. Lebedev-Poliansky criticised the Central Committee member Dodonova, who was present at the meeting, for engaging in unauthorised talks with Lunacharsky which, he claimed, were 'against the rules, harmful to Proletkul't and confused the Central Committee's general policy of upholding the independence of the Proletkul't's'. The meeting resolved that all such contacts should require prior consultation with the Proletkul't Central Committee.[13] Dodonova's loyalty to Proletkul't appears, thereafter, to have held up and her lapse was put down to a misunderstanding. The same cannot be said of two other leading figures in the organisation, the poets M. P. Gerasimov and V. T. Kirillov. Gerasimov had been appointed to liaise between Narkompros and Proletkul't when the latter had been set up on a national scale in September 1919.[14] By 1920 he appeared to have Narkompros's interests closer to his heart and the 14 February meeting had cause to reprimand him for participating in the preparations for the conference of proletarian writers organised in the name of 'the Proletkul't of the Workers' section attached to the literary department' of Narkompros. Gerasimov's mandate was withdrawn and he was ordered to attend a meeting of the presidium of the Central Committee in order to give an explanation of his conduct.[15] He does not seem to have complied and relations remained very strained as the proposed conference approached. In May the Central Committee responded to an attack on Proletkul't made by Gerasimov at a meeting of the Collegium of the Literary Department of Narkompros by withdrawing Gerasimov's right to represent the Central Committee or to allow him to participate any further in it. A similar case against Kirillov was postponed for undisclosed reasons.[16] Clearly, both of them were in the process of burning their boats as far as Proletkul't was concerned and were, instead, throwing in their lot with Narkompros and the proletarian initiatives associated with it.

These events serve to remind us of the complexity of the issues surrounding the conflict between Proletkul't and its rivals. It was not a question of proletarian versus non-proletarian principles in the field of culture in which, supposedly, Proletkul't represented the former and Narkompros the latter. In reality, Proletkul't was coming under increasing pressure from non-Proletkul't proletarian writers and artists whose views on the nature of proletarian culture found their counterpart within Proletkul't. In terms of such views it would be extremely difficult to draw a distinction between those within and those outside the organisation. On the issues of 'sectarianism' (understood to mean the need for separate development of proletarian culture) and 'iconoclasm' (violent hostility to the bourgeois heritage) the non-Proletkul't groups were equally, and sometimes more, militant, certainly if compared to the Bogdanovites. It was, after all, Kirillov himself who had, in 1918, written the poem most often used (then and now) as evidence of *Proletkul't's* 'nihilism' in which he had urged 'the burning of Raphael in the name of our tomorrow' as well as the destruction of museums and the uprooting of artificial flowers of culture. As we have seen, this earned him a reprimand from Bogdanov who described such an attitude as 'Hindenburgian'.[17] The vital difference between these proletarians and Proletkul't lay not in their cultural outlook but in their preparedness to work closely with the party and not claim independence, a factor that heavily reinforces the judgement that Proletkul't's real sin in the eyes of the authorities was its claim to independence.[18]

Further support is given to this by an examination of Proletkul't's increasingly doomed efforts to protect itself in the summer and autumn of 1920, in the course of which it was forced to make many concessions in order to retrieve whatever it could from an increasingly difficult situation in which it had very few winning cards in its hand. Relations with party and state came to a head and Proletkul't continued to suffer a series of setbacks. Its reorganisation came closer to implementation in a form that would deprive it of its independence; its efforts to organise a national conference encountered difficulties. The rival Narkompros-supported proletarian writers' conference and associated union continued to meet a fairer wind than Proletkul't itself. The minutes of the presidium of the Central Committee of Proletkul't, its everyday executive body, show, despite being somewhat cryptic and evasive the more significant the issue involved, the prevalence of these issues at this time. On 16 September the head of Proletkul't's organisational department, V. V. Ignatov, felt it necessary to attempt to confirm who was actually running which parts of the organisation, so chaotic had it become with the death of Kalinin; the on/off expulsion of Gerasimov and Kirillov; party *komandirovka*'s (a technique coming into use more frequently in the party at this time to post troublemakers into new occupations or bring them under closer supervision on pain of penalties for breaking party discipline if any resistance were to be effected) which affected Lebedev–Poliansky himself at this time to the extent that he was called in to work more closely with the party Central Committee apparatus; plus the continuing fissiparousness of the lower levels of the organisation.[19] This review of Proletkul't's order of battle cannot have been very reassuring. By mid-October, as a result of untoward events at its conference discussed below, the presidium was discussing revised terms of the agreement between Proletkul't and Narkompros, which developed into a form described by 18 October as a 'Proposal for the unification of Proletkul't with Narkompros' (*Proekt instruktsii ob'edinenie Proletkul'ta s Narkomprosom*).[20] On 24 November, there was an even more cryptic reference to the merging of Moscow Proletkul't with the Moscow Soviet which, it was said, put into effect 'the position worked out by the commission of the Central Committee of the Politburo'.[21] Together with other behind-the-scenes activities, it is clear that, as was normal practice, the resolution was only brought to the Central Committee after the way had been cleared for it by the activities of the Orgburo and other sub-departments.

It is interesting to note that at this time, as well as making agreements with the unions such as that with the Sugar Workers' Union which set up Proletkul'ts in sugar factories (most of which were located in the Ukraine), Proletkul't was also disbursing sums in unprecedented amounts to the more distant provinces. Although an organisation bureau for the Ukraine, Caucasus and Crimea had been set up on 23 January 1920, it was only during the crisis that there is a record of allocations being made. For example, on 6 September 500,000 roubles was granted to a Comrade Erzinkian for use in the Caucasus and 200,000 roubles to Comrade Puchkov who was appointed Proletkul't plenipotentiary in Turkestan. Erzinkian was sent another 2.5 million roubles on 21 September for use in Georgia and Armenia. On 24 October 1.5 million roubles was allocated to organise Proletkul'ts in the Ukraine and Galicia and on 28 October, 22 million roubles was assigned to Proletkul'ts in the Caucasus–Don region, 8 million to the Caucasus and the East (presumably the fortunate Erzinkian, once more) and 500,000 roubles for use in Siberia.[22] While it is hard, given the peculiar monetary conditions of the time, to know what these sums represented in real terms, and given that it would, in post-civil war circumstances, be a natural step to take at this time, it is none the less important that these grants would have laid a foundation for a more widespread base of recipients of patronage to replace the troublesome metropolitan Proletkul'ts which were being shot away from underneath central Proletkul't.

Clearly, this seed-corn did not have time to be harvested before the storm broke. While most of the reorganisational activity had been concealed from direct view, it was clear, even to the outsider, that Proletkul't was in deep trouble. Its main public activity at this time was its attempt to call a national conference and, associated with this, to work out a policy to the independently organised conference of proletarian writers in which Gerasimov and Kirillov was involved. The two questions were interrelated in that Proletkul't decided to put the issue to its own conference planned for mid 1920 but postponed, as a result of the Polish attack, to September. If they had hoped through an early meeting to pre-empt the new organisation they were frustrated. To make matters worse, on 26 August they were forced once more to postpone both their national conference and their own 'Proletarian Writers' Conference' to October, ostensibly on account of difficulty in finding a place to meet.[23] Whether or not these practical problems were genuine or had some ulterior cause cannot be established. In any case, the new ministry-based organisation held its conference first in early May, causing no little confusion among delegates who were impatient at the spectacle of the two rival groups claiming the proletarian equivalent of the apostolic succession in these matters. A group of them went along to Proletkul't Central Committee to find out what they were supposed to do and were told not to attend the conference and put their energy into Proletkul't's own planned conferences. The Proletkul't Central Committee refused to grant any recognition to the First National Conference of Proletarian Poets.[24] In the meantime, another straw in the wind was the collapse in September of Proletkul't's attempt to set up an exhibition of artistic achievements of Proletkul't members on the grounds that insufficient exhibits had been received from the provinces.[25]

The national conference of Proletkul't finally met in the first half of October. On the surface, the atmosphere of the conference as it opened was one of confidence in Proletkul't's achievements and in its future. The participants, who numbered over 300, did not, as at the previous conference in 1918, come almost exclusively from Moscow and Petrograd. There were even two delegates from abroad, one of whom was Eden Paul.[26] Proletkul't frequently laid claim to international status, although in truth its international links were very insubstantial, with the possible exception of the Proletkul't set up in Turin in 1920, which included among its organisers a young Italian Marxist named Antonio Gramsci.[27] The only contact it had with foreigners appears to have taken the form of briefings on its work, conducted through its grandiosely titled International Bureau, for the benefit of delegations visiting Moscow for events such as the Second Comintern Congress in July and August 1920. With respect to its activities in Russia, it claimed to have 80,000 activists involved in studio work and to have 'grouped around itself', whatever that meant, 'more than half a million workers'.[28]

An impression of maturity and responsibility was also nurtured, the conference being said to have had a 'strictly business-like atmosphere'. In place, the account went on, of agonising over 'what is proletarian culture?' and 'who needs proletarian culture?', the meeting concerned itself with putting principles into practice. The theoretical issues discussed, it was claimed, were much narrower than at the first conference.

A number of themes emerged. In the first place it was decided that there had to be a degree of 'professionalism', meaning that creating proletarian culture could be a full-time occupation for some without such people necessarily cutting themselves off from the working classes. After all, it was said, who could occupy themselves 'with a violin after an eight hour shift at a lathe'. In any case, it was shrewdly pointed out, to say that separation from the workplace diminished working-class consciousness was to criticise implicitly all those workers who had taken up responsible positions in Soviet institutions. Despite a 'warm and prolonged exchange of opinions' the delegates decided 'almost unanimously' that professionalism was admissible. It also declared itself against dilution of its proletarian character. Its special function as a laboratory of proletarian culture meant that it had to tie itself closely to the avant-garde of the working class and only from this basis draw other groups to itself. It also attempted to emphasise its specialisation in creative work as opposed to more straightforward educational and propagandistic work, hoping in this way, no doubt, to differentiate its task from that of state and party bodies devoted to the latter activities. The absence of large-scale central institutions, the Proletarian University and proposed central 'Palace of Proletarian Culture', was pointed out by the conference.

However, this aspect of the conference's work, including Bogdanov's address on 'The Paths of Proletarian Creativity' in which he recapitulated some of his underlying themes without, it would appear, adding very much to them, had an air of unreality in that the time-bomb of the organisational question and of relations with Narkompros was steadily ticking away. It was detonated, perhaps unexpectedly, by Lunacharsky himself, who had been detailed by Lenin to bring the organisation to heel.[29] The quotations given show his speech at the conference to have been one of his most forthright defences of the independence of Proletkul't, at least in certain areas of its work. Proletkul't's task, he said, was the establishment 'of new forms of artistic creativity' and the nurturing 'of new proletarian talents'. This,

Lunacharsky went on, 'is not a task for the state apparatus but for a free organisation of Proletkul't's type. From this point of view Proletkul't should be independent.' He envisaged Proletkul't being, as he put it, the leading customer for what the state could offer. In order to protect its independence Proletkul't should be able to flow wherever it wanted to. In advancing the flag of proletarian culture it might, he concluded, find support in the form of Narkompros.[30]

It it hard to explain the timing of Lunacharsky's remarks. It is true that he personally had shown less hostility to Proletkul't than others, in fact he had made an outspoken defence, saying it should be 'completely independent' in a speech at Rostov on 31 August 1920.[31] But it was clear that Proletkul't was experiencing severe difficulties at this time. But then, and this may be the explanation, so was Narkompros which was itself facing reorganisation and the setting up of Glavpolitprosvet. This latter, while ostensibly a sub-department of Narkompros, also threatened to be a Trojan horse by which the Central Committee could intervene much more directly in its affairs. Indeed, it was an unidentified 'member of Glavpolitprosvet' at the conference who raised a protest against Lunacharsky's speech and ran off to the Party Central Committee to complain about it. Lunacharsky was carpeted by Lenin who insisted that the party must have authority over Proletkul't.[32] The Politburo took up the question on 9, 11 and 14 October (the Proletkul't conference was in session until 12 October). On 11 October Proletkul't representatives were invited to attend. According to Dodonova's memoirs, Lenin asked them pointedly if the party supervised not only politics but also economics and culture.[33] Clearly only one answer was possible. Lenin insisted that Proletkul't should immediately recognise this fundamental truth and demanded that the conference should pass a resolution embodying this. As a result of this the party fraction at the conference was instructed directly by the Party Central Committee to put forward a resolution on the 'entry of Proletkul't into Narkompros in the position of a department (*otdel*)'.[34] After a 'long and heated' debate the party fraction, 'in the name of party discipline', forced the resolution through. The resolution had uncompromising implications for both Narkompros and Proletkul't and graphically illustrates the role that the party leadership saw for itself in the educational and cultural field at this time. It referred to the decision of the Ninth Party Congress calling for 'the closest links' between Proletkul't and Narkompros. 'The creative work of Proletkul't', it went on, 'must be one of the constituent parts of the work of

Narkompros' which was itself described as 'the organ realising the dictatorship of the proletariat in the field of culture'. In political-educational work it should be a department of Narkompros, subordinate to the latter, following the direction 'dictated to Narkompros by the Russian Communist Party'. At local level the same degree of subordination was laid down. Local Proletkul'ts were to be subject to local Departments of Education, which were themselves said to be subject to the authority of Guberniia (Provincial) Party Committees. 'The Central Committee will issue directives to the party organs and Narkompros will create and maintain conditions enabling the proletariat to engage in the possibilities of free creative work within its institutions.'[35]

It would be hard to find a better illustration of the balance of cultural forces as it was developing by 1920. The uncompromising picture of 'free' proletarian creativity being pursued solely within the context of strict party supervision, exercised through Narkompros, shows a thoroughly different reality from 'the complete creative freedom for the masses' promised by Lenin on 26 October 1917. The forms of subordination laid out in the decree (whatever their actual application in the conditions of the time, notably the relative weakness of the state and party fully to implement policies mentioned earlier) shows the emergence of the leading role of the party in the field of culture had already begun to take forms, at least in the institutional field, that are often, incorrectly, thought to have emerged later, notably under Stalin. The pattern of subordination laid down has remained in force in theory as the basic model for the exercise of Soviet cultural authority. The degree of implementation of the model has changed radically at different times. Also, as yet, the party did not have a coherent vision of culture to implement in a consistent way. None the less, the framework of control was being constructed. The party instructed the state institution as to what it should do; the latter organised the implementation of those instructions. It was also indicative that, in this incident, it was two 'intelligentsia' Bolsheviks whose outlook was being overridden, not on intellectual grounds but through the manipulation of party resolutions, institutions and discipline by *apparatchiki* with a desire to throw their weight about. Though they had drifted apart, and were to do so even more, Lunacharsky and Bogdanov, brothers-in-law, veterans of the hopes aroused at Capri, sharing some of the pre-revolutionary intelligentsia's ideals of raising the educational and cultural level of the people, were being swept aside by party militants.

After this débâcle, Proletkul't made a few more twists and turns
to free itself but its hour had come and the affair led swiftly and
surely to the Central Committee resolution of December. If the
decree marked the end of the Bogdanovite hopes for creating
proletarian culture, Lunacharsky's vision was also under renewed
and unprecedently vigorous attack from the same quarter.

THE REORGANISATION OF NARKOMPROS

It has been mentioned above that the pattern of events observed in
Proletkul't had its equivalent at the same time in the history of trade
unions and, one might add, the party itself, within which a substantial
step towards a further tightening of discipline and centralisation of
authority was being implemented in the form of the ban on factions
and associated measures approved, in the rather dubious circumstances of the emergency surrounding the Kronstadt rebellion, at the
Tenth Party Congress in March 1921, just three months after the
decree on Proletkul't. This Congress also passed an important
resolution defining the role of Glavpolitprosvet in co-ordinating
propanganda inside and outside the party.[36] This tightening of
control had its equivalent in the cultural field with the attempted
reorganisation of Narkompros, the aim of which was to make it less
friendly than it was thought to be towards the class enemy; to make
it more assertive of proletarian and revolutionary values; to make
education more sensitive to the needs of the economy; and, the
inevitable corollary of these, to bring it under firmer central party
guidance as a guarantee of its new direction. Had one imagined a
textbook example to crystallise the balance of forces in the Soviet
cultural field at this time, one could not have come up with anything
more revealing than that of the successive assaults from above on
Narkompros.

If 1920 had been a year of reverses for Proletkul't, it was also a
crucial year for Narkompros. Two major commissions into its activities
were conducted. The first was under the auspices of the Executive
Committee of the Soviet (VTsIK) and headed by V. I. Nevsky; the
second essentially (after a number of internal dry runs) set up by the
Central Committee of the Party under its protégé E. A. Litkens
(1888–1922). Of the two the latter was much the more significant.
The Nevsky commission did not effect any really extensive or lasting
proposals. The Litkens commission, on the other hand, attempted a

complete restructuring of Narkompros's direction, functions, organis-ation and leading personnel.[37]

Litkens's proposal involved splitting the administration of Nar-kompros into two: an Academic Centre, which would oversee policy, and an Organisational Centre to deal with administrative routine. The departments of the Ministry would be divided and placed under three umbrellas: one for school education (Glavsotsvos), one for technical training and higher education, implicity in that order (Glavprofobr) and one for political education (Glavpolitprosvet). The first remained uninfluential within the ministry compared to the other two. In addition to the Commissar it was proposed there should be an Assistant Commissar (that is Litkens), the former maintaining overall supervision and heading the Academic Centre, while the latter would control the Organisational Centre and take administrative power, a reflection of what was occurring in many institutions at this time, including the party. Despite influential opposition from Lenin, who referred to the proposals as 'artificial' in a letter to Lunacharsky, and from Krupskaia, who described it as 'construction on the empty place of a commissariat' it was eventually implemented by the Soviet cabinet (Sovnarkom) in mid-February 1921. There were some changes. The Commissar was to retain overall control through heading the whole Ministry through its collegium. There were to be two deputy commissars, one for the Academic Centre (to which explicit responsibilities for the arts and high culture were added) and one for the Organisational Centre. Pokrovsky and Litkens respectively were to take up these positions. Finally, Gosizdat, the State Publishing House, was added as a fourth department. In essence, however, it can be seen that Litkens's proposals had been largely accepted.

The success of Litkens is even more pronounced with respect to the sub-text of the reform, which, as is often the case, was far more significant than the formal, visible structure of the changes. In the first place it would be difficult to find someone who exemplified better the self-confidence and lack of finesse that was a common characteristic of party militants, particularly of Litkens's generation, returning from the civil war. After defeating the massed remnants of tsarist Russia and its chain of Great Power supporters, what was a mere ministry and a few 'bourgeois' intellectuals? At the party meeting on education that he convened over the new year of 1920–1 (coinciding with the Eighth Congress of Soviets), Litkens argued explicitly that 'military practice has put forward completely new methods of approach to cultural-educational work among the masses. . . . Military practice has taught us how to plan work.'[38] Secondly, it is clear that Litkens's involvement in the reorganisation was promoted by the Central Committee, to which he turned for support at critical moments. The forces in the Central Committee that backed him appear to have been hostile to Lunacharsky personally[39] or at least were critical of the shelter he gave to high culture at the expense of the low-level technical education, which was desperately needed to rebuild Russia's shattered economy. What is unquestionable in this respect, however, is that the situation was forcing a much more overt and aggressive attitude towards cultural and educational policy on the part of the Central Committee. Where its attention had formerly been focused on military and security matters, longer-term questions were now surfacing. Major figures in the party, such as Preobrazhensky, who was attempting to plot a more active strategy for the revolution as a whole than that adopted in March 1921, which formed the basis of NEP, engaged in polemic with Lunacharsky, accusing him in particular of imitating 'a ruined aristocrat who refuses to mend the roof in order to purchase an expensive painting or a library'.[40] For a while Preobrazhensky even took over as head of Glavprofobr and announced a policy of shutting down higher education in favour of an expansion of technical education. 'Higher education', he continued, 'must be greatly diminished in favour of lower' with the latter moving to specialise in 'what was of pressing importance for industry and agriculture'.[41]

It appears that Lunacharsky himself could sense, as so often in his career (which would undoubtedly have been much shorter were it not so), this change of direction towards party intervention and even praise it, despite remaining unconvinced, by the principles of class war on which it was based. At the Tenth Party Congress (March 1921) he said that the Central Committee must 'conquer the whole educational apparatus'. It would, he went on, be wrong to differentiate party spheres of activity from those of the state: 'The Party must be everywhere, like the Biblical spirit of God.'[42] This interesting echo of Lunacharsky's God-building language was, in fact, a reflection of the way things were going in 1921. Party/state spheres were very difficult to distinguish and it was the informal relations between powerful individuals rather than formal relations between institutions that were significant at this time. Certainly, the reorganisation of Narkompros and constant appeals to party patrons by the protagonists are quite striking. It was even the case that the party Orgburo was mediating interdepartmental disputes within Narkompros in the wake of its reorganisation. On 11 April 1921, for example, after Preobrazhensky had appealed to it, the Orgburo informed the Narkompros collegium that all work among adolescents would be under the control of Glavprofobr.[43] Such interventions were not unprecedented but their frequency and significance were greatly increasing here as in other aspects of cultural policy discussed in this chapter.

THE CULTURAL APPARATUS TAKES SHAPE

The events surrounding Narkompros, and for that matter Proletkul't, illuminate the basis of, and conditions attached to, growing party involvement in cultural matters. Above all, there was a spirit of continuing with the revolution, understood as establishing the 'proletariat' and removing the 'bourgeoisie' as rapidly as possible. The well-being of the idealised, or yet to be nurtured, revolutionary proletariat, the authentic voice of which was enshrined within the party, particularly in its leading institutions, was the yardstick of all actions by the Soviet leadership. At this time, 'productionism' – the belief that since socialism was only able to exist, according to Marx, in a society based on abundance, the first task of the proletarian revolution was to build up the wealth of the country at all costs in order to lay the foundations for socialism and, ultimately, communism – appears to have held sway over almost all sections of the party leadership. The consequences of this in the field of culture were views, such as those of Preobrazhensky, that immediate economic requirements should dominate educational and cultural planning, of course, only as a 'temporary' measure while the emergency existed. It must not be ignored, however, that there really was a very deep crisis of the agrarian and industrial economy of Russia at this time. The conditions of acute privation in the cities did not come to a stop immediately the civil war was over. In the countryside, shortages, and eventually massive famine in 1922, also continued. Be that as it may, productionist ideas were not simply a response to this short-term situation but were a more deeply rooted ideological expression of the dilemma of the Soviet government as a Marxist government in a relatively underdeveloped, indeed continually under-developing up to 1921–2, society. It has remained an important feature of Soviet ideology to the present day. As far as culture was concerned, the general consequences drawn from this was that high culture and the arts in particular were luxuries the proletariat could well do without, at least in the meantime when more 'real' problems had to be faced. Culture was thought of as being instrumental. It had two functions. First, it would provide the manpower skills needed for the economy. Secondly, it would explain to the population what the Bolshevik project was all about, that is, it would be propagandist, replacing, in a sense, the compulsory Orthodox religious education conducted in all tsarist schools with scientific, atheist, class-based Marxist education to enlighten the masses with the truth as perceived by its new leaders. If one adds to this the revolutionary self-confidence built up during the civil war, which, more than anything else, appeared to vindicate the view that militant class struggle could be successful if only it were pursued with sufficient energy and vigour, then one has the makings of the potent force of proletarian chauvinism that was so prevalent in the party, particularly with respect to culture, throughout the 1920s and beyond. According to this way of thinking, the chief criterion for any action was 'does it serve the interests of the proletariat?' – as understood by party militants, the actual opinions of really existing workers being secondary – and if so, any scrupulousness about methods could smack of counter-revolution and treachery. It was a morality of desperate warfare, which had, indeed, been the crucible in which it had been formed, before being transferred, with all its intensity, to the class war within Russia.[44]

The implications of proletarian chauvinism for cultural policy (and subsequent discussion will be limited to this, even though the evolution of policy in numerous other areas seems to follow a similar direction) can be drawn out throughout this period and beyond. Where artistic, educational and cultural policy had initially been left to intelligentsia Bolsheviks such as Lunacharsky, Pokrovsky and Krupskaia, as the civil war progressed, more militant, and short-sighted ideas began to challenge them. Increasingly, the challenge of these new forces provided the dynamic for and set the agenda of discussion of cultural questions. They can be found deeply entrenched in the attacks of Proletkul't and Narkompros described above (or, more accurately, in the attacks on Bogdanov and Lunacharsky and their supporters within those organisations) and as a shaping factor in the development of other policies mentioned below. Continuing further, it could be argued that the cultural policies of the 1920s mark an irresistible changing of the balance of forces in culture in their direction. For the time being, however, they were held in check.

The chief element in holding them in check was the continuation in the Bolshevik leadership of an older generation that had been part and parcel of the pre-revolutionary intelligentsia (even though some of them would never have admitted it). For these still-influential Bolsheviks, cultural life had laws of development requiring more subtle methods than those of crude propaganda and militant class struggle associated with the proletarian chauvinists. Lenin's views had been encapsulated earlier when, in a well-known comment to Lunacharsky, he had warned him against letting some of his fine boys do irreparable damage to the cultural life and institutions the Soviet government had inherited, especially the Academy of Sciences. According to Lunacharsky's later reminiscences Lenin had warned 'If some brave fellow turns up in your establishment, jumps on to the Academy and breaks a lot of china, then you will have to pay dearly for it.'[45]

Similarly, the opposition to Litkens and Preobrazhensky from Krupskaia, Pokrovsky and Lunacharsky also shows how distrustful they were of the new militancy. The ideas of this group in the party will be discussed in more detail in the next chapter. For the moment it is only necessary to observe that policies actually pursued were usually a rather restrained version of those proposed by the militants who were already making important advances. The actual policies pursued at this time, then, represented a compromise between the two groups. It should, however, be emphasised once again that the differences between them are less about the nature of 'cultural revolution', which was almost universally understood in a crude, productionist way, as about the methods and pace at which it was to be implemented. The exceptions to this, such as Krupskaia and, from outside the party though close to it in essential respects, Bogdanov, had seen their influence at its peak in the earliest days after which it had undergone continuous decline. The party leaders who had no special interest or expertise in the cultural area were no longer content to leave cultural policy in other hands and began to assert themselves increasingly in the cultural sphere. It is in this sense that, although parts of it did not last very long, Litkens's reform of Narkompros cannot be counted as having only 'negligible' results.[46] As Sheila Fitzpatrick shows, certain aspects of Litkens's reform were undone particularly as a result of yet another commission, that of Larin. This commission, with a brief primarily to cut public expenditure, launched an attack on Narkompros, which supposedly cut the number on its payroll from 1.2 million to just over half a million.

None the less, Litkens's reforms mark a major step forward in direct party intervention in the field of culture and as such represent an important success. Fitzpatrick's view that Litkens and the Central Committee were primarily carrying out reforms as a short-term response to Lunacharsky's defence of Proletkul't autonomy and apparent violation of party discipline,[47] and that they set for themselves 'the goal of rational administration',[48] overlooks the longer-term processes occurring here and elsewhere which were encouraging the tentacles of the Central Committee to stretch out further and further at this time. Litkens, in fact, exemplifies a new breed of party entrepreneurs of culture. These people were not, in many cases, noted for their interest in such issues prior to 1919 and 1920, and, although not entirely in agreement with one another, came, in 1920–2, to establish control of almost all cultural institutions that still retained some degree of independence. By and large, these entrepreneurs were associated with the Central Committee, which was setting up its own cultural agencies, its press section and agitprop department at this time, as well as important, supposedly state, institutions like Glavpolitprosvet and the censorship apparatus based on Glavlit within which it had a decisive voice in areas where it had formerly been less intrusive. The leading figures in this area, in addition to Litkens who fell ill in early 1922 and played no further role in politics between then and his tragic death at the hands of Crimean bandits two months later, include Ia. A. Iakovlev, N. L. Mesheriakov, P. M. Kerzhentsev, A. V. Voronsky and V. Polonsky among others, who could justifiably claim to be the founders of the so-called 'NEP in culture'. To understand this phenomenon it is necessary to examine the career patterns of and the principles professed by this group which constitutes an entity dominated neither by 'intelligentsia' nor 'proletarians' in the party but fusing elements of both.

Party Entrepreneurs of Culture

The number of Bolsheviks, and they were not alone among the revolutionaries in this, who had been actively involved in cultural life and the cultural dimension of revolution before 1917 had been very small. It follows from this that, as its cultural responsibilities broadened, the new Soviet state had to cast its net wider and wider in its search for reliable cultural policy-makers and controllers. It is not surprising, then, that the figures emerging via the Central

Committee, of which they were either members or close protégés of members, had not shown particular interest, expertise or achievement in the cultural field – for all that some of them were very sensitive, intelligent and capable people – in the way that the figures in the centre of our study up to this point had been. The new arbiters had arrived at their posts of responsibility via quite different channels. Their commitment had been a long-standing one to the revolution and, usually, to the Bolshevik party which many of them had joined around 1905. Thus they tended to put political principles first and intellectual life in a subordinate position. Culture was a more direct instrument of revolutionary politics than was the case for Lunacharsky, Bogdanov, Krupskaia, Pokrovsky and so on. As the civil war came to an end, they were swept into the cultural field with one prime objective: to finish off the last remnants of the bourgeoisie and of the tsarist élite they had been fighting all their adult lives. Ironically, it was indeed the case that it was only the intelligentsia, understood both as technical and administrative experts and as creators of spiritual values and ideas which had brought them into conflict with tsarism, that had retained any influence. The most dominant groups of tsarist society – the landowners, the capitalists, the industrialists, the army leadership – had all been thoroughly uprooted. Universities had survived longer than the generals, writers were still publishing while major aristocratic families were wondering how long the family diamonds they had been able to salvage would sustain them in exile. As was mentioned above, it was a combination of their political powerlessness and their temporary usefulness to the Soviet government that had brought this unexpected situation to pass. The new brooms of the Central Committee were determined that this anomaly should be swept away.

In this respect they shared some principles with the Proletkul't left, from which some of them, like Kerzhentsev, had come. But they differed from it in important respects. First and foremost, they were all party loyalists of some standing. Indeed, their secondment to the cultural field was a secondary effect of their party loyalty in that the careers of most of them show cultural administration to be only one of a number of fields in which they operated. N. L. Meshcheriakov (1865–1942) had been an active revolutionary since 1885 and a Bolshevik organiser since 1906, apparently without having shown any interest in intellectual affairs prior to his emergence as head of the State Publishing House (Gosizdat) in 1920. Ia. A. Iakovlev (1896–1939), another key background figure in setting up the Central

Committee's cultural apparatus, does not appear to have shown any cultural expertise or special interest in this field. His work at Glavpolitprosvet and at the Agitprop section of the Central Committee gave way to work in agriculture, Rabkrin (the Worker Peasant Inspectorate) and the party Control Commission later on before he suffered the fate of so many Old Bolsheviks. A. K. Voronsky (1884–1943), head of Glavpolitprosvet and founding editor of the journal *Krasnaia nov'* (*Red Virgin Soil*), another key instrument in furthering the party's intervention in the cultural field, had also been an organiser and activist in the party underground and had worked in the provinces on behalf of the party after October. There is no record of him having any marked interest in cultural life. Ironically, there were other figures in the same mould within and close to the party leadership who had had some experience in work with the intelligentsia, but they were often deployed as much outside the cultural sphere as in it. V. V. Vorovksy (1872–1923) had been a party spokesman in literary disputes and criticism after the 1905 revolution. He headed Gosizdat briefly in 1920 but was drafted into diplomatic work on which he was engaged as a member of the Soviet delegation to the Lausanne Conference at the time of his assassination by an *émigré* monarchist in 1923. P. M. Kerzhentsev (1881–1940), who had been active in Proletkul't, had a varied career. He headed ROSTA, the first Soviet news agency, which also had propaganda functions for which it is best remembered today since Maiakovsky and others produced some striking posters for it during the civil war. He later had spells as Soviet ambassador in Stockholm and Rome in the 1920s as well as at Rabkrin. From 1928 on, however, his career focused on agitprop and culture, which he was hard put to distinguish from one another. Even the displaced President of Proletkul't, P. I. Lebedev–Poliansky (1881–1948), was quickly redeployed to be head of Glavlit (the censorship apparatus) from 1921 to 1931. Ironically, given his links with the Proletkul't, he was one of the few leading party figures to remain in the cultural sphere all his life. He was associated with the Communist Academy in the 1930s and ended his career as head of the Leningrad Institute of Literature and member of the Academy of Sciences in the 1940s. Even during his time at Proletkul't he maintained close links with the Central Committee and had been seconded to it at that time. V. P. Polonsky (1886–1932) is the only major exception among this group in that his career was almost entirely within the cultural field and he was a late-comer to the party, which he joined only in 1919, having at one time been a Menshevik.

During the civil war he headed the Literary and Publishing Department of the Political Administration of the Red Army (1918–20). In 1919 he founded the Dom Pechati (House of the Press) and headed it until 1923. From 1921 to 1929 he was editor of the journal *Pechat' i revoliutsiia* (*Press and Revolution*). From 1926 to 1931 he held the editorship for which he is most renowned, that of *Novyi Mir* (*New World*). Among his other responsibilities in this period he was Rector of the Briusov Institute of Literature and the Arts (1925), edited the literature, art and language section of the first edition of the *Great Soviet Encyclopaedia* and from 1929 until his death was Director of what is today known as the Pushkin Museum in Moscow. Thus the type of career of these party entrepreneurs of culture shows them, in most cases, to have been, not surprisingly, political activists and revolutionaries before they were cultural specialists. This comes out very strongly when one turns to look at the principles guiding their work in the critical years of 1920–2.

Establishing these principles is no easy task since some of those involved, notably Iakovlev, left very little record of their views. The general approach can, however, be gleaned from their journalistic writings (none of them having produced anything more substantial at this time, which is not at all surprising given the immense organisational and political tasks they were undertaking), some of which were reprinted in collections such as *Intelligentsiia i revoliutsiia* (*The Intelligentsia and the Revolution*) published in 1922. In general terms, the matrix into which their ideas fitted was not a new one for the Bolsheviks. It was composed of two familiar elements. The first was fervent criticism of the intelligentsia on the grounds that it was 'bourgeois' and therefore incorrigibly opposed to the people's revolution as it had taken place in 1917. Naturally, the popular revolution was equated with Bolshevism and Soviet power so that, in effect, the arguments were often polemical defences of Bolshevism rather than assessments of problems at a deeper level. Features of the intelligentsia were evaluated according to the degree of hostility they appeared to show towards Bolshevism. Elements suitable to Bolshevik purposes were praised, the remainder roundly condemned. If much of the material was negative in this sense the second feature was its corollary. As with most party commentators on the intelligentsia, with the major exceptions mentioned previously such as Lunacharsky, Krupskaia and Bogdanov, there was very little visualisation of what was to replace the old intelligentsia nor how what was of value in established high culture was to be identified, absorbed and developed. It was much easier, and more effective, to denounce the real or supposed iniquities of the putative class enemy than it was to face the deeper problems raised by this critique. Very little that was produced by these cultural administrators (in these years at least) could be thought of as a serious contribution to Marxist discussion of the social significance of intellectual and creative life.

This is not to say that some of the writers were not sensitive to culture and perceptive in some of their comments on it, rather that their *partiinost'* (devotion to the party) was the dominant characteristic. Above everything else this feature required them to polemicise with the *émigré* intelligentsia and, implicitly rather than explicitly at this time, also with its remaining supporters within Soviet Russia. The arguments frequently took a form that has become much more familiar since. A publication or an individual was selected for criticism, an account – often extremely tendentious though not invariably so – of his or her ideas was presented. The chosen target was then, often in the most crude and reductionist way, deemed to be 'typical' of the class enemy and the attack proceeded along predetermined lines. Viacheslav Polonsky and A. Voronsky, eventually to appear relatively erudite and intellectual leaders of Bolshevism, showed themselves to be very adept at this kind of writing. Polonsky, reviewing an *émigré* journal devoted to publishing information about the revolution and the revolutionary movement (*Arkhiv russkoi revoliutsii*), said of one of the contributors that he was not prepared to attack the revolution on principle but simply to complain that there was no hot water, that there were shortages and that his normal way of life had been disrupted. The lietmotif of his memoirs was said to be 'let all the world perish but let me have my cutlets'.[49] All the contributors dealt with were dismissed in equally summary fashion as his objective was to destroy the credibility of the *émigrés*, whom he called 'seekers after "objective" truth', the emphasis lying, as it so often did, in the use of quotation marks around key words. Voronsky gave another *émigré* journal, *Russkaia mysl'* (*Russian Thought*), the same treatment. In an article, graphically entitled, 'The Old Weak-mindedness' he pointed out that it had developed from an earlier journal of the same name founded in 1905 by 'rejects [*izgoi*] and renegades from Marxism'.[50] He used it to dismiss Russian liberalism as having moved on to 'open Black Hundredism. It has already grown hopelessly decrepit and torpid. It is a living corpse.'[51] The rapid development of this style of argument, sometimes thought of as 'Stalinist' but used in this case by a man who later stood against Stalin, a style of argument which was based on obloquy, misrepresentation, selective quotation, a refusal to accept any kind of good faith on the part of the subject of criticism, a firm conviction of self-righteousness and vulgarity of thought and language, did not bode well for Soviet culture, which was supposedly on the threshold of a period of toleration engineered by these same people.

It should be emphasised that not all the contributions were on the same level. Voronsky himself showed that he could function in another gear if he so chose in a review of Ivanov and Gershenzon's *A Correspondence from Two Corners*, a work that he welcomed as an indication, particularly on Gershenzon's part, that the intelligentsia was breaking with its traditional way of thinking and becoming more favourable to the revolution. The letters were, he wrote, 'brilliant and original'. They showed certain 'positive' characteristics. In particular the evolution from *Vekhi* (which Gershenzon, had, of course, edited) to calling for the destruction of modern culture was, Voronsky concluded, 'not such a bad path'.[52] Other contributions were also thoughtful, notably those by N. L. Meshcheriakov and Pokrovsky who had not descended to the level of crudity visible elsewhere, and were all the more effective for making relatively sound arguments rather than simply hurling half-truths and insults.

The basic points and outlook of all the authors was, none the less, the same. In particular, it was believed that the old intelligentsia was living through a 'harsh collapse and re-evaluation of its spiritual values. The old intelligentsia', it was assumed 'was dying.'[53] The purpose of the authors was to diagnose this process, hasten it along and guide it into acceptable channels. Every gesture of potential reconciliation was to be welcomed, hence the qualified praise for Gershenzon's apparent nihilism. Many of the most positive parts of the volume were taken up with praising the growing number of *émigrés* who were said to be readjusting their attitude to Soviet Russia. None the less, here too, selective misrepresentation was common, with a view, presumably, to giving the impression that the liberal and conservative emigration was beginning to accept the truth of the revolution. In fact, such reconciliation as there undoubtedly was tended to be based on the old principles of nationalism, even 'great power chauvinism'. Added to this was the belief (said, in this volume, quite incorrectly to have 'lived out its last days even among its most fanatical followers'[54]) that the adoption of NEP indicated that Russia was returning to 'normal' and that the revolution had come to an end and was being replaced by a kind of restoration in which the old intelligentsia would have a part to play in national reconstruction.

The characteristics of the new breed of arbiters of Bolshevik culture were thus clear. In the first place, defence of the party and its principles and immediate policies was in the forefront. In this they differed from Bogdanov, for whom party domination was a threat to cultural development, and, at least until he saw it as inevitable, from Lunacharsky, who attempted to preserve some vestiges of cultural autonomy. Within this general framework, however, they were prepared to show some sensitivity to other views, on the firm assumption that they were transitional to a fuller acceptance of revolutionary values. There appears to have been a firm conviction that a sizeable proportion of the old intelligentsia might be won over, but there was nothing other than vague generalisations about just what they would be won over to, other than 'the revolution' or 'the proletariat'. Thus the ideas of these people contain few complexities to detain us. In most cases, as one might expect, their works were the writings of political activists. The natural environment for the politically minded is, of course, in institutions of power and it is in this sphere that this group of people became much more influential than they were from their writings alone. In this period an array of institutions of cultural control, emanating from the very centre of power, came into existence. Some of the forms of control remained weak and tentative but they were of great importance for three reasons. First, they marked a very substantial step towards greater cultural direction and control by the party at its highest levels; secondly, they exerted an important shaping influence on cultural policy and the limits of cultural freedom in Soviet Russia; and, thirdly, some of them and, less frequently, some of the individuals involved, remained important in shaping Soviet culture for a generation. The influence of central control in the early 1920s has been much underestimated. The assumption that there was a loose form of toleration and drift in cultural policy, even a vacuum, until the mid to late 1920s is quite wrong.[55] The essential difference between the civil war and NEP periods in culture is not one of attack followed by relaxation; it is rather the replacement of arbitrariness by greater organisation. In many cases, institutions and individuals that had been tolerated during the civil war were now being controlled. By 1922, the only institution that had eluded Bolshevik control in any meaningful sense was the Academy of Sciences. The institutions guiding this more organised approach were focused on the Central

Committee. In particular, they were its departments of Agitation and Propaganda (founded in September 1920) and its Press Section (founded in autumn 1921). Beyond the immediate party apparatus but incorporated in it through interlocking membership of key members lay the censorship organisation, Glavlit (founded on 6 July 1922), the political education organisation, Glavpolitprosvet (founded, as we have seen, through Litkens in 1920), and the State Publishing House, Gosizdat (founded in December 1917), which came to exert importance influence on publishing even by private publishers who came to rely on it for subcontracts. Even *émigré* publishing houses began to have links with it. Gosizdat also had censorship functions prior to the hiving off of Glavlit as a separate entity. The organisation for censorship of the performing arts, Glavrepertkom, was established in February 1923.

Direct intervention in the cultural sphere by the Central Committee and its departments was becoming increasingly important, and the Committee was also the focus of a network of subsidiary institutions, the key members of which looked directly to the party leadership. It should none the less be emphasised that the relationship was not one of simple hierarchy and following of instructions from above, but, rather, an interplay in which people of strong views, attached to certain policy approaches and strategies for developing the revolution, sought powerful allies of similar mind. Thus, the cultural administrators sought patronage for their schemes among those whose attention was less focused on cultural affairs. We have already seen something of this in Litkens's relationship with Preobrazhensky. Here, as in other cases, exact tracing of patronage connections is fraught with difficulty since evidence is often conflicting and self-serving, while reliable archival information is almost totally absent. One can, however, point to certain similarities in policy, gleaned from speeches and articles, which indicate an important degree of like-mindedness. For the present, cultural interventions by the handful of leading figures in the Politiburo were by and large of this kind in that they were brief and somewhat peripheral to the main interests of the people concerned. In this respect, Lenin is a rather typical example. In between his various arbitrations such as that concerning Proletkul't and speeches to conferences of teachers and other cultural workers, Lenin did not pay very much attention to high or low culture. Indeed, he completely subsumed it under the imperative of productionism.[56] Thus Lenin tended to be a figure whom second-ranking activists, notably Lunacharsky at this time (though Lenin did also support Litkens on certain key points in the reorganisation of Narkompros, for example[57]), sought to win over to their specific policy objectives. Lenin was not yet a major instigator of cultural policy. By and large, the same was true for other party leaders whose real attention, like that of Lenin himself, was only in the throes of being turned towards cultural policy as a significant issue in its own right. Bukharin, Trotsky, even Zinoviev, did not really address their attention to this area until 1920–2 and their major contributions, particularly in the cases of Bukharin, Trotsky and Lenin, came after NEP had got under way and the most pressing economic, political and diplomatic issues had been stabilised, at least to the extent of providing a breathing space. Even Preobrazhensky, whose career at this time included running the higher-education department of Narkompros (Glavprofobr) was only there briefly and, even while he was in charge, was primarily interested in economic policy in general and opposing NEP in particular, from which, it was perhaps hoped, his educational responsibilities would distract him.

Thus, the game of seeking patrons, so prevalent in the literary squabbles of the late 1920s, was already establishing itself, though with one difference. Up until his stroke in 1921, Lenin was the trump card. His support could not be countered. His authority was unquestioned in the party. As his illness made his active participation in politics less and less frequent, so the mantle of his authority fell from his shoulders and did not find a new wearer of equivalent stature.

For the time being then, subject to their gaining successful patronage to protect themselves from opponents, the second-ranking leaders had considerable scope for their own initiative since the major figures were looking in other directions. This can be seen from an examination of the institutions and the activities in which they were involved.

The Emergence of Institutions of Cultural Control

In the front rank of these lies the new departments of the Central Committee set up to organise policy with respect to party educational and cultural matters, the Agitprop and Press Departments. The Agitprop (Agitation and Propaganda) Department was set up in September 1920, though by March 1921 it had only seventeen people on its staff.[58] In autumn 1921 a Press Sub-department was set up.

The relatively small initial size of these departments should not, however, lead us to overlook their significance, partly because they expanded steadily in size and area of competence and partly because at the same time an outer network of subsidiary institutions, linked to the inner core by interlocking of key members, was also building up and carrying partly influence into new territory. This was an important aspect of the new structure of Narkompros, for example, the sub-departments of which took on the function of ensuring the supremacy of party policy and objectives within the ministry. In some cases, it is difficult to know whether these institutions, at least in terms of their ruling committees, should be thought of as state bodies with a significant party influence or party bodies on mission to the secular arm, so to speak.

Contemporary Soviet scholars have no doubt that the chief function of Glavpolitprosvet (the political education section) was to ensure party hegemony in this sphere. In an article, the very title of which – 'Glavpolitprosvet, An Organ for State Communist Propaganda' – shows the intermingling of party and state by this time, the main emphasis was laid on the channels of subordination set up. Though vague on many details, some of which can be made up for from other sources, the author shows the degree of party control over the new institutions. According to this version of events, after preliminary discussion, the Central Committee on 25 October 1920 instructed the Orgburo to examine a proposal approved by Narkompros entitled 'Polozheniia o Glavpolitprosvete' (Proposal on Glavpolitprosvet) which resulted in a Politburo resolution 'drafted by V. I. Lenin' in which 'particular attention was devoted to dividing up responsibilities between Glavpolitprosvet and the party'.[59] The final decree was signed on 12 November 1920.[60] The personnel said to be associated with it, in addition to Krupskaia who (rather intermittently in practice) headed it and Lunacharsky, shows the extent of Central Committee interest. As well as the committee members (Litkens, L. G. Shapiro and V. I. Solov'ev), others (Iakovlev, V. N. Maksimovskii and Ia. G. Doletsky) were seconded to it.[61] Stress was also laid on its expansion in 1922 and the inclusion in its leading personnel of V. Meshcheriakov, M. S. Epshtein, Z. P. Krzhizhanovskaia, A. S. Kurskaia, L. P. Menzhinskaia, M. A. Smukhova, N. A. Ruzer-Nirova and others.[62] Glavpolitprosvet was also said to be closely supervised at this time by the Agitpropotdel, on whose behalf R. P. Katanian, V. G. Knorin, A. S. Bubnov, K. A. Popov and Iakovlev are said to have been active in Glavpolitprosvet.[63] The article also pointed out that the scope of Glavpolitprosvet was also widened to encompass, in addition to its original agitation, propaganda, teaching (*uchebno-programmnyi*) and organisational functions, departments for the arts (with subdivisions for theatre, fine arts, literature and photography/cinematography), Soviet party schools (*sic*), libraries, clubs, the military and a bureau for national minorities composed of separate national sections.[64] Thus, Glavpolitprosvet came to have interests and structural divisions very similar to those that had been developed by Proletkul't. It provides very clear evidence of the direction in which the Central Committee was thinking at this time and in particular – and there is no reason to doubt the Soviet source on this point at least – that it was taking a more direct interest in these areas. Though there is no definitive evidence available on this point it would seem reasonable to assume that the leaders of Glavpolitprosvet took their cue directly from the Central Committee and the Agitpropotdel rather than going through the relatively isolated collegium of Narkompros whose control over its own ministry appears to have become increasingly nominal and itself subject to more party interference.

Evidence from all other critical sections of cultural life confirms the impression of more extensive and systematic party intervention. For example, the field of publishing, the prime medium for intellectual exchange and discourse at a mass level, was also being brought under stricter and more systematically exercised control at this time. This took two main forms: the creation of Gosizdat (State Publishing House), which had far and away the lion's share of book and pamphlet publishing, and the creation of a censorship apparatus (Glavlit), supposedly under the authority of Narkompros but, like other of its sub-departments, showing every sign of being independent. Glavlit was rapidly joined by similar apparatuses for censorship of the performing arts (Glavrepertkom) including, after an interval, music. One of the first acts of the Soviet government after it came to power had, of course, been the closure of first right-wing, then liberal and then non-Bolshevik socialist and anarchist newspapers. There was no question of going back on this even though the question was raised during the transition to NEP. While the government jealously guarded its monopoly of the newspaper press, including the exclusion of foreign newspapers, it did allow certain concessions to non-party publishing which, for a brief period in the early 1920s, were broadened slightly. Private book and pamphlet publishing, which as we have seen continued through the civil war period, was allowed to survive a little longer. There was even a flourishing of private publishers taking advantage of NEP to reopen their former businesses or establish new ones under the new conditions. Few of them lasted any length of time in the hostile environment, though a handful of very valuable collections of essays and journals did appear, particularly in 1922. Evidence taken from these three areas – Gosizdat, Glavlit and private publishing – all tells the same story.

Though it was formally founded in December 1917, Gosizdat was set up in practice by a decree of the All-Russian Soviet Executive Committee dated 19 May 1919. Among the major participants in the project were Lunacharsky, Pokrovsky, Lebedev–Poliansky and Vorovsky. It was formed by amalgamating certain existing Soviet and party publishing operations in Moscow and Petrograd and later spread to the provinces. In addition to acting as a central state publisher handling the output of the central government and its attached ministries it was also given the function, according to its statutes, of 'regulating and supervising' the 'publishing activities of all scholarly and literary societies and equally of all other publishers'.[65] It was able to achieve this through the state monopoly of paper, decreed a few days later by Sovnarkom on 27 May 1919[66] and by the abolition of charges for new books, which were to be distributed free. Naturally, this removed any economic incentive to publish and, during war communism, private publishing was a philanthropic activity. Only in the case of second-hand bookshops such as that of Osorgin described in Chapter 2, could one charge for books.[67] A consequence of this was, naturally, that private book distribution channels did not exist either, so at this level, too, the state exerted its influence. The private publishers appear to have circulated books locally to small circles, probably attached to surviving independent intellectual institutions such as the universities. Thus, it is clear that the authorities were already establishing a formidable apparatus of control over intellectual discourse, all the more so as the shortage of paper became more critical in 1919 and a severe reduction of publishing activity, including that of newspapers, had to be carried out. Private publishing, indeed all non-essential publishing, (as defined by the authorities) had a very low priority in this crisis.

Gosizdat was officially placed under the authority of the Ministry of Education. V. V. Vorovsky was its chairman and the editorial board consisted of Bukharin, Nevsky, Pokrovsky and I. I. Skvortsov–Stepanov.[68] After Vorovsky's departure to take up his post as ambassador to Italy in July 1920, Meshcheriakov became its chairman.[69] As is to be expected, given the conditions of the time – the civil war, the economic crisis and the acute paper shortage – much of its early activities were taken up with preliminary organisation in the metropolitan cities and only subsequently in the provinces. Even so, it soon had an effect on the shape of publishing and expanding its share largely at the expense of private publishing. Figures for the number of titles, size of editions and print runs for 1919 and 1920 show this clearly (see Table 4.1).

Gosizdat's disproportionate showing in the column for print runs, that is the percentage of the total output of printed material in terms of the number of copies of published items, is to be explained by the large number of agitational pamphlets, posters and calendars that it produced. The breakdown of its output according to subject matter and type of publication can be ascertained from the following. In 1920 its major areas of activity were agitational literature (165 titles for a total of 12 million copies) and 'official, calendars etc.' (133 titles, 10 million copies). By comparison, it produced, in other fields, textbooks (41 titles, 5.5 million copies), scientific (45 titles, 2.7 million copies), posters (75 titles, 3.2 million copies), artistic (42 titles, 1.2 million copies). It also produced, in smaller quantities, some journals and technical, agricultural and children's publications.[70]

The establishment of the censorship apparatus, Glavlit, also nominally a department of Narkompros, came some time after the establishment of the State Publishing House, of which it was a subsidiary, enabling Gosizdat to carry out its growing obligation to 'regulate and supervise' all private publishing activities. Initially, censorship appears to have been carried out in a rather haphazard way by Gosizdat and it is difficult to ascertain exactly how it operated and by what criteria certain items were published. A large proportion

TABLE 4.1

	No. of titles		Size of editions (printers Listy)		Print runs	
	1919	1920	1919	1920	1919	1920
Gosizdat	4.9	34.8	6.3	35.9	9.6	64.0
Official, party and trade union	65.5	57.6	63.0	52.2	68.7	29.7
Co-op and private	26.7	6.9	28.1	11.4	19.8	5.9

Figures in percentage of given category for each year.
SOURCE   Nazarov (1968) p. 191.

of the less orthodox output of the book presses of Russia at this time undoubtedly consisted of publications in Gorky's 'World Literature' (*Vsemirnaia literatura*) series, which was subject to a special agreement that had been thrashed out between Gorky and Lunacharsky. The list that it was able to publish was subject to constant bargaining with Narkompros and, on occasions, even with Lenin. In no way did its distinguished editorial board have a free hand to produce items for which the need was thought to be most pressing. Its rather odd opening publications of 1919 – a volume by D'Annunzio, two by Anatole France, some stories by Guy de Maupassant and one of Mirabeau's works – indicate something of its eclectic character and, perhaps, its difficulties.[71] As regards other publishers it is even more difficult to ascertain the way in which they operated. One can, however, speculate that continuous personal lobbying and shunting of proposals from committee to committee within Gosizdat was the most likely route. The anomalies of publishing at this time are also illustrated by the case of the collection of articles entitled *Iz glubiny* (*Out of the Depths*) which was highly critical of Bolshevism. This book was set up and produced in late 1918 and early 1919 and was ready for distribution before the authorities cottoned on and seized it, though not before the printers themselves had been able to put a small number of copies into circulation.[72]

Haphazard and inefficient though it may have been, the intention to control was already clear and the means to achieve this in a more systematic way were being developed. In spring 1921, in the first issue of the periodical *Pechat' i revoliutsiia* (*The Press and the Revolution*) – one of the first of the government's efforts to replace the pre-revolutionary 'bourgeois' intellectual journals with one of its own – Lunacharsky wrote a defence of currently existing censorship practices. His article was, typically, couched in the mildest terms possible that could also be consistent with supporting censorship. Reminding his readers, though they had probably not forgotten anyway, that 'The idea of revolution is, in the minds of many, firmly associated with the idea of freedom', he gradually moved round to arguing that temporary measures of censorship were necessary, even in the field of *belles-lettres*: if the party could use such literature for purposes of propaganda, then so can its opponents. It then follows, he went on, that it was the duty of the party to suppress artistic anti-propaganda. 'Censorship', he concluded, 'what a terrible word. But for us there are no less terrible words', in particular those referring to the weapons used by the conservative and liberal bourgeoisie.

However, in 'our' hands, according to Lunacharsky, 'bayonets and cannon, prisons themselves and *our* state' are means for the destruction of the bourgeois world.[73]

Far from being 'temporary', however, the censorship functions of Gosizdat were shortly to be strengthened and systematised, as indeed was the case, as we have seen, with all other mechanisms of intellectual control in these years. In this case, however, the issue was, initially at least, less clear cut than in the case of other areas: the tightening of regulations came about because a new situation, which might have given some benefit to private publishers, was about to come into existence in the form of NEP. In order to plug this gap before it widened a new set of regulations governing private presses was enacted by Sovnarkom on 12 December 1921. According to the decree all private publishers had to obtain the permission of Gosizdat's local branch, or an equivalent where none existed, before it could be set up. The local branch had to inform the Chief Administration of Gosizdat in order to obtain approval. As far as manuscripts were concerned, they also had to be submitted to the local Gosizdat or its equivalent to obtain permission for them to be published. Local decision again had to be communicated to the Editorial College of Gosizdat. Any unauthorised publication would be confiscated and the publisher prosecuted. Gosizdat also had to agree 'in each case' to proposed imports of books and it had the right to buy up the stocks of a privately produced book, including an entire edition, at an agreed price.[74] Clearly, as a result of this, Gosizdat had plenty of possibilities for making life difficult for private publishers. None the less, the months following the publication of these regulations were an Indian summer for private publishing to the extent that a number of privately produced books written by non-Bolshevik intellectuals still in Soviet Russia did see the light of day in the course of 1922. These included works by Sorokin, Izgoev, Berdiaev and others. A number of collections of articles appeared including *Partenon*, *Oswald Spengler and the Decline of the West* and *Feniks*. Journals such as *Ekonomist* published a few issues. But even this limited space for independent social comment had been closed down by the beginning of 1923.[75] It is not clear why this last flourish came about, or why it died away. One might surmise that private publishers were exploiting loopholes in the new NEP regulations and that these were closed off by a cumulation of administrative and financial measures once the apparatus realised what was happening. Lenin, for instance, was insistent that *Ekonomist* should be closed down as its editorial board was 'an obvious centre of White Guards' who should, Lenin said, be expelled.[76] This in itself was a result of concern that had grown earlier in the year. For example, at a meeting of the Agitprop section on 21 February 1922. Voronsky, backed by Meshcheriakov, had pointed to the growth of literary works from private publishers that exhibited 'various counter-revolutionary and petty-bourgeois ideas and did not have a single word favourable to Soviet Russia and the Bolsheviks. . . . The market was strewn with literature that was not only alien but directly hostile to us.'[77]

A rather more systematic picture of private publishing in 1922 can be formed from an article written by Meshcheriakov in the July–August issue of *Pechat' i revoliutsiia*. For Meshcheriakov the main problems facing the private publishing houses were social and economic. The disappearance of their former readership, the problems of distribution and establishing a sales apparatus in conditions of massive inflation, and the lack of funds for book purchase on the part of the new worker/peasant readership all imposed severe limits on the activities of private publishers. He did not mention the web of regulations that surrounded them as another factor. As a result of these problems the size of editions tended to be small, around 1000 copies as a rule. As far as content was concerned, according to Meshcheriakov, the journals that appeared concentrated on *belles-lettres*, art and philosophy without concerning themselves with directly political issues. Though he does not say so, book publishing appears to have followed the same course. His article also reveals the interest the possibility for independent publishing aroused as well as the difficulties it entailed. In Petrograd 99 private publishers had registered by the end of January 1922 and in Moscow 220 had registered (excluding Soviet and trade union publishing) by 26 May 1922. Of the 99 in Petrograd 44 had not yet presented any manuscripts, 21 had presented one and only 13 had presented more than six. Corresponding figures for Moscow were 133 had not presented a manuscript, 60 had presented between one and six, 17 had presented from six to ten. Ten had presented more than this, the highest figure for any one publisher being twenty-seven. Of the 190 manuscripts presented in Petrograd, ten had been refused for publication by what Meshcheriakov calls Gosizdat (*tsenzura*). In Moscow only 31 out of 813 manuscripts had been similarly refused.[78] Clearly most of the potential publishers were making very heavy weather of the enterprise. It is therefore surprising to learn that, according to a Soviet scholar, the share of private publishing for 1922 was 20 per cent of titles and 25 per cent of the total number of copies produced. In 1923 it was 25 per cent of titles but only 13.7 per cent of the total number of copies produced.[79] It is not clear, however, to what extent the figures for 'private' publishing are boosted by the inclusion of contract work undertaken on behalf of Gosizdat by the main private publishing houses such as Granat', Knebel', Sabashnikov and Mir, which are mentioned in this connection by Meshcheriakov.[80] It seems probable that the true figure for private publishing was much lower. A great deal of what was left, after allowing for this, is probably accounted for by the publications of the *Smena vekh* movement, the only significant non-revolutionary intelligentsia grouping sponsored by the Soviet authorities.[81]

It is possible that even the limited degree of press freedom that can be deduced from the facts and figures presented above had been allowed to come into existence by default. Certainly, 1922 saw great strides towards its further limitation. In the first place the mass expulsion of intellectuals[82] had deprived private publishing of many of its leading authors and some of its entrepreneurs. Even more serious were steps taken in June to tighten up the censorship system. In addition to Gosizdat, by mid 1922 censorship functions were also being exercised by the GPU, Narkompros and other bodies, according to a leading Soviet authority on the period. In his words 'It was necessary to unify and systematise all forms of censorship.'[83] Though the actual processes at work bringing these changes about are hard to trace, some sources are available that throw some light on them. In an important letter to Dzherzhinsky, the head of the secret police, of 19 May 1922, Lenin linked these various processes together. In it he called for careful preliminary work, especially by writer communists such as Steklov, Olminsky, Skvortsov and Bukharin, to delineate counter-revolutionary intellectuals from the less harmful ones. They would gather evidence on 'the political record [*stazh*], work and literary activities of professors and writers'. Those deemed to be counter-revolutionary would be exiled. In the same letter Lenin argued that *Novaia Rossiia* had been closed down prematurely and that 'by no means all of its collaborators are candidates for exile', but that *Ekonomist* was 'an obvious centre of White guards', and should be closed forthwith.[84] It was against this background of concern at the highest level that, on 6 July, Sovnarkom set up the Chief Administration for Literary and Publishing Affairs, known as Glavlit for short, which from that time on became the basic institution of Soviet censorship. On 9 February 1923 a separate branch, Glavrepertkom, was set up to control public performances including music which had 'to be purged of its religious content', among other things.[85] Glavlit was attached to Narkompros. Its head was said to be Meshcheriakov with the former Proletkul't chairman Lebedev–Poliansky as his deputy, though one could assume that this simply indicates that Glavlit was a beefing up of the already existing Gosizdat censorship committee and that Meshcheriakov was head of it through his position as head of Gosizdat with Lebedev–Poliansky acting as day-to-day organiser of the censorship. The precise scope and impact of the censorship apparatus is hard to judge. Figures for items rejected can only give a very loose indication since the chief effect of censorship is the very primary one of discouraging, by its very existence, potential authors and publishers from producing and presenting materials that they think will be refused. Soviet scholars invariably emphasise that its targets were 'bourgeois ideology, religious-mystical and pornographic literature [these last two categories usually being bracketed together] and racism'. They sometimes point to instructions emanating from the Central Committee and the Politburo to Glavlit's predecessors that Marxist and revolutionary works should not be forbidden. It is not clear what authority Glavlit had to control Soviet and party publishing and the output of dissident Marxist tendencies. In its early years it does not appear to have been active in this field. This does not, of course, mean that party, soviet, trade union and co-operative publishing was uncontrolled. These areas continue to have their own control apparatus of committees that had to approve or refer publication projects. In short, by the end of 1922, spontaneous publishing, which had scratched a small, marginal existence from the hostile soil of the civil war, was at an end. The necessity to unify and systematise, mentioned by Fediukin, had taken firm root in this field as in all other aspects of Soviet intellectual life. A survey of the remaining key sectors reveals exactly the same process at work.

The frontal assault on higher education in the summer of 1918, which had perforce given way to the 'salami tactics' proposed by Reisner and followed by Pokrovsky, was resumed in 1921. The combined tactics of undermining the professoriat and, primarily for political reasons, swamping the student body with underqualified, politically vetted working-class candidates from the Workers' Faculties (*rabfaky*) brought about the final submission of higher education and the ending of university autonomy. Nothing illustrates better the difference of atmosphere separating 1921 from 1918 than a comparison of the conferences on higher education held in those years. As we have already seen, the relatively mild proposals of Narkompros in 1918, themselves a testimony to the low expectations of the Soviet authorities, even allowed each university to retain its own press. None the less, the massed ranks of professors were able to throw the proposals out unceremoniously. At the 1921 conference, however, the situation was very different. This time it was a number of professors who were thrown out unceremoniously as a consequence.[86]

The new constitution for higher education was approved by Sovnarkom on 2 September 1921 and went into effect for the new academic year. It shifted control out of the hands of the professors and put it into those of the Soviet and party authorities. The aims of the higher education institutions were defined as:

1. the creation of specialists for all branches of the RSFSR;
2. the preparation of scientific workers to serve in the scientific and scientific-technical and productive institutions of the Republic, and in particular in higher-education institutions themselves;
3. the diffusion of knowledge among the broad worker and peasant masses whose interests should be in the forefront of all the activities of higher-education institutions.[87]

Compared to the draft and even more the version approved in 1918 this new definition was uncompromising. The class principle was firmly embedded in it. References to university 'autonomy' were dropped. The political situation had changed so much that the meeting between the state, party and university authorities held in June to 'discuss' the draft did not even vote on these vital clauses because 'there were no amendments'.[88] There were, altogether, some forty amendments proposed to the other more detailed clauses, none of which was passed. The voting record on these amendments shows a consistent vote of about 50 in their favour and about 130 against, suggesting very strongly the existence of blocks and the packing of the conference. The composition of the delegates to the conference confirms this suspicion. According to the journal of Narkompros, the conference consisted of 89 rectors and professors, 71 government representatives and 136 students; 165 delegates, which tallies well with the majority votes, were communists.[89]

The contrast between the 1918 and 1921 conferences and the ensuing decress is striking. In 1921 the government decreed what it wished without fear of contradiction. Opposition at the conference

was purely token and no amendments were accepted. A boycott by
Moscow University professors was completely ineffective. Repression
was stepped up and their 'trade union' was broken up. Narkompros
introduced its tried and tested tactic of replacing it with a pro-
government union called 'The Union of Workers in Education and
Socialist Culture'.[90] All in all it represents an excellent example of
how the situation had developed in the intervening three years. As
elsewhere, the boundaries of toleration, which had been defined by
the power of resistance to government and party encroachment, had
narrowed substantially. The enforced 'pluralism' of the early years
was once more giving way to a considerable extension of centralised
control. The process of control was not yet complete, of course, but
the consistent feature of developments was that the authorities were
attempting to extend their control as far as they thought possible and
were held back, not by any uncharacteristic 'liberal' scruples on their
part, but by structural limitations on their power.

As the authorities gathered strength, so the limits of toleration
were narrowed. The 1921 conference and the ensuing decree were
the beginning of the end for the old professoriate. A final decisive
blow came in late summer of the following year when, at short notice,
a number of leading intellectuals, heavily weighted towards those who
had attempted to defend university autonomy and had participated in
the ill-starred academic strike of 1922, were forcibly expelled. The
precise number involved is difficult to ascertain. Most sources claim
that about 150 people were expelled, but the *émigré* press went as
high as 200 to 250 in its estimates though it is not known what their
sources were for this high number.[91] What is beyond dispute is that
it ripped the heart out of the remaining non-socialist intelligentsia
and even included some who were sympathetic to the revolution,
though highly critical of Bolshevism. Given the doubts about numbers
it is difficult to give a full list of those expelled, but a list of the best
known of them is sufficient to show the nature and purpose of this
action. Not surprisingly, S. Prokopovich and E. Kuskova, opponents
of revolutionary social-democracy since 1900, when they had been
leading representatives of a sort of Bersteinian revisionism in Russia,
were included, although, like a number of others, the authorities had
included them only a year before in the committee that had been set
up to combat the famine. A number of religious philosophers and
some contributors to *Vekhi* were prominent on the list, in particular,
Berdiaev, Frank, S. Bulgakov, Izgoev, Il'in, Lossky, Karsavin,
Fedotov and Florovksy. Other prominent intellectual enterpreneurs

and professors expelled included Novikov, Mel'gunov, Kizevetter and Sorokin. The dividing line between those expelled and others who remained, such as the editor of *Vekhi*, Mikhail Gershenzon, was a very fine one and may have reflected expectations that some of the old intelligentsia, other than the close collaborators who had emerged from it, might be more favourable to Soviet power than those expelled. In addition, one should not overlook the possibility that there was more than a little arbitrariness in making the division. Finally, those expelled were not in any way associated with subjects the authorities wanted to protect for productionist reasons; in fact, quite the reverse since a number of them taught philosophy and theology. The official reason, still echoed today by Soviet historians,[92] that they were the most active proponents of 'bourgeois ideology' has some truth in it, but equally active bourgeois ideologists were allowed to stay. The effect of the expulsions, however, was to deliver a decisive blow to the critics of the authorities, especially those who had continued to fight for university autonomy. Even so, this issue was not entirely killed off and as late as 1925 even non-Marxist academics who were closest to the party, notably Sakulin, revived the call for academic freedom,[93] which the authorities claimed had only been 'temporarily' suppressed.[94] None the less, the tide had turned decisively.

If the publishing house and the university were central institutions for the material and intellectual survival of the intelligentsia, they were not the only ones. The others, with the sole exception of the Academy of Sciences whose hour had not yet come, were also being controlled or broken up. Lower down the educational ladder, the Ministry of Education and the party had begun to exert their authority over schools. There were still very few communist teachers, but firm control of the school apparatus and finances, and the destruction of private and religious schools plus the disappearance of the classes on whom these schools depended, had had their effect. Organised resistance to Bolshevisation among teachers had been outflanked by use of the state's instruments of coercion, including the Cheka. The authorities also continued to use the tactics of co-opting the support of progressive, but not necessarily communist, teachers in militant minority organisations formed around a hard core of party members, and of letting the hopelessness of further resistance and the promise of improving conditions after the end of the civil war sink into the minds of teachers. The abandonment of the most vigorous experimental projects, desired in any case by some party leaders, was part of the price paid for this truce. Attempts were made to bolster the political content of school education, which ran into the usual difficulties of the lack of personnel qualified to teach Marxism, a shortage of textbooks and division, reflecting political struggles among the party leaders, as to the pace and scope of political education. Also, a more productionist mentality was inserted into education although the principles of the unified labour school, fought over so bitterly in the summer of 1919, were never implemented and dropped from view.

If party- and state-sponsored unions and organisations had been decisive in winning control over the schools, one can identify the same process at work in other vital areas. The replacement of traditional intelligentsia groups, clubs and societies as well as the independent self-defence organisations set up since 1917, and the counter-attempts by the Soviet authorities to set up organisations of their own, was inevitably resulting in the incorporation of the former in the latter or in the total replacement of spontaneous organisations of intellectuals. The process was not entirely even across the board in that specialists whose skills were needed, including, above all, engineers of various kinds and economists and their associates, were treated with less hostility than those who were thought to belong to an 'unnecessary' part of the intellectual and artistic spectrum deemed to be irredeemably bourgeois.

As a result, by 1922 a revolution in the institutions of culture had already taken place. The autonomous intellectual institutions of tsarist society – universities, artistic groups, philosophical schools, the Imperial Free Economic Society, the Pirogov Society and so on – with the exception of the Academy of Sciences, had ceased to exist or had been thoroughly transformed. What is more, embryonic institutions and organisations more adapted to the new conditions – notably independent organisations defending intelligentsia interests – had been strangled at birth or been assimilated into government-sponsored equivalents. This applied to left-wing groups like Proletkul't as well as to liberal and right-wing ones. As a result, party hegemony (though far from complete) had spread to such an extent that the fledging civil society of post-revolutionary Russia had been effectively eliminated. The cultural possessions of the church had been nationalised. Even individuals had been dispossessed of cultural paraphernalia. Musical instruments, personal libraries and so on, as well as art collections, had been confiscated. Groupings that were still allowed to exist in the 1920s were subject to much more effective

184   *Culture and Power in Revolutionary Russia*

and organised supervision than their predecessors.

However, the question remains why were large and widely influential organisations, notably the 'Living Church' experiment and *Smena Vekh* ('Changing Landmarks'), allowed to continue to exist, even actively encouraged up to a point? Clearly, the answer is that, for a while, they were useful to the authorities. The same could be said for the phenomenon of 'fellow-travelling' in general. Its existence is not evidence of the strategic turn towards an uncharacteristic toleration on the part of the party, but an indication that a more restrained form of tactics was necessary given the need to utilise the skills of intellectuals and to achieve greater stability to facilitiate economic reconstruction. It would be quite wrong to imply that the party was opening the way to a permanent form of 'ideological coexistence'. In all such cases the compromises were said to be temporary and based on the hope that they would bring the target group over to the principles of the party and the revolution.

By 1922, such policies had been stumbled into without much forethought. Long-term strategy for intellectual and cultural life was non-existent. Those who had been most concerned to establish such long-term policies, those who saw the cultural, intellectual sphere as a vital additional dimension of the revolution, were on the retreat. Bogdanov had been broken, Lunacharsky was increasingly marginalised and only retained his position through his ability, arising out of his loyalty to the party, to sustain a series of defeats for the principles he had appeared to stand for in the early years of the revolution. Even Krupskaia, distracted by her own ill-health and her mission of nuturing and protecting an increasingly stricken Lenin, was marginalised in policy-making. Such policies as had come into effect by 1922 were guided by short-term and crude considerations of administrative convenience, economic necessity and the transfer of slogans of class war into the cultural field. These policies had been laid down by party administrators grouped around the Central Committee, the Secretariat and the Orgburo rather than its strategic thinkers. After 1922, when pressing economic and military pressures had temporarily receded, the major figures of the party – notably Lenin, Trotsky and Bukharin – began to turn their attention to the field of culture. While it might be argued that Lenin could yet have turned policy in this field into a new direction – where Trotsky and Bukharin, lacking the stature to do it, could not – it is more probable, particularly given Lenin's unremitting hostility and apparent contempt for the intelligentsia, that the foundations of party policy had become so entrenched by 1922 that a change of direction was unlikely in the extreme. The apparatus of control established by 1922 steadily increased its power through the 1920s. The NEP period in culture was not one of widespread relaxation. Rather it was one of a steadily rising tide of centralisation. The fact that there was a massive tidal wave of a much greater scale at the end should not blind us to this fact, particularly since, when that tidal wave of the 1928–31 cultural revolution receded, the principles of the earlier period were still being implemented. In many ways, 1931 on was a reassertion of what had begun in 1920–2. The final chapter attempts to give an overview of the early 1920s with a view to showing these processes in action.

5 Compromise or Confrontation? The Contours of Cultural Policy, 1923–5

Power is tolerable only on condition that it mask a substantial part of itself. Its success is proportional to its ability to hide its own mechanisms.

Michel Foucault, *The History of Sexuality*

The events of 1920 to 1922 had brought about a new balance of forces in culture that, it was widely assumed, would provide a basis for policy for the indefinite future. At the basis of this equilibrium was, on the one hand, the growth of a much more powerful and systematised apparatus of control in the hands of the party leadership, which gave it a lever to exert extensive pressure in the cultural and educational fields. The initial successes of this apparatus had broken the most entrenched organs of intelligentsia resistance, actual and potential, and replaced them with less threatening, but still partially independent, institutions and organisations. On the other hand, control through this apparatus had also to be limited from pragmatic considerations. What would the returns be on the investment of given amounts of energy devoted to the various options available? Given firm overall control, and the receding prospect of restoration or counter-revolution from within, there was space for a less direct confrontation, particularly since, having acquired the commanding heights of culture, there was no need to prolong the bombardment. Instead, a policy geared towards winning over, rather than annihilating, the remaining intelligentsia appeared to promise better returns, in that the 'bourgeois' intellectuals could be used to fill important roles in management and development of production during the period of reconstruction: they could be preserved for as long as necessary in order to transfer their knowledge and skills to more reliable 'proletarians'. While the focus of this study is not directly on the technical intelligentsia, it followed that concessions to this group implied a certain amount of freedom in other areas, including access to information from abroad and contact with foreign engineers and scientists. Access to appropriate cultural facilities was also part of the process. Indeed, the economic provisions of NEP allowed, within the limits defined by the censorship, the growth of commercial cultural activity, normally at its strongest in the theatre, and seriously confined with respect to the press, film and so on, to which the authorities gave a higher priority on account of their greater impact on the masses.

Additional factors of some importance also contributed to this new state of affairs. It would be wrong to overlook the continuing weakness of the Soviet state in the sense that active support for it remained confined to a limited, mostly urban, part of the population. Its ability to uphold its authority and to make its writ run throughout its territory was vastly greater than it had been in the civil war, but there were still large areas of the provinces that exerted some independence. This might even be found within the party where large regional parties, such as the Ukrainian, defended, in so far as they could, some independence from Moscow. The enforcement of law was, no doubt, also limited by traditional factors, such as corruption of officials and inefficiency and arbitrariness of the enforcement agencies, but these have been little studied or remarked on outside the pages of the literature of the period. In addition, it should be borne in mind that the party leadership was still learning its trade and had very little experience of peacetime policy-making at the outset of this period.

More important, and considerably more tangible than the impact of weakness and inexperience, though perhaps arising from the latter, was the continuation of the extraordinary vacuum at the centre of cultural policy. Nobody in charge of it had much idea of what it was for and continued to discuss it in agitprop terms and through the wielding of rather crude class slogans. After 1922, the weightiest figures in the party began to turn their attention to this vacuum but it remained unfilled, large because of increasingly serious disagreements over revolutionary strategy on the part of those same leaders. Their participation in the cultural debate will be considered below.

These limitations on the power of the cultural apparatus allowed the continued flourishing of a degree of independent, but increasingly atomised culture. It is this aspect of NEP that has attracted a good deal of attention and led to the over-optimistic picture of the degree of toleration allowed. Concentration on the achievements of a handful of immensely talented individuals in this period, the great names of Soviet culture in the 1920s such as Maiakovsky, Tatlin, Eisenstein, Vertov, Mandelstam, Gorky, Sholokhov, Shklovsky, Chukovsky, Pasternak and so on, can lead to some distortion, even though a closer look at the careers of many of these people shows the 1920s to have been 'tolerant' only against the most extreme of criteria – comparison with the 1930s. In practice, most of them experienced steadily increasing difficulties in the 1920s, not a stable degree of toleration on the party of the authorities.

The shape of cultural life in the 1920s was thus the outcome of the shifting balance of these forces. It would be inappropriate to refer to this as a relaxation. In many ways it was the opposite. After taking a town an army ceases shelling and bombardment but does not withdraw. Indeed, its grip tightens more during the ensuing 'peace' than it did during the process of capture itself. A town under occupation could not be said to experience a relaxation of pressure. From the cultural point of view NEP was more analogous to this situation than to any model of incipient pluralism. Though tactics changed, the authorities continued to pursue the goal of winning over, controlling and replacing the old intelligentsia. The insistence of Soviet historians, though their terminology is anachronistic, that there was no concession to 'ideological coexistence' at this time is perfectly justified, as is their assertion that the establishment of the leading role of the party was a major policy objective.[1] The remainder of this chapter is devoted to showing that 'relaxation' is an inappropriate term to use of Soviet cultural policy in the 1920s. With this in view the chapter focuses on three main areas. First, an account of one of the most extensive examples of apparent toleration, the *Smena vekh* ('Changing Landmarks') movement, to illustrate the degree and purpose of such toleration; secondly, an examination of the party debates about culture that took place in 1924 and 1925 in particular and produced, among other things, an important and controversial statement of party policy on literature in 1925; and, thirdly, to examine some of the actual policies being implemented, which throw some light on the aims of those who originated them. In all these fields one can observe a steady encroachment of institutional and administrative control by the kind of militants who had been behind the policies of 1920–2 and appeared in many cases to continue to be full of proletarian chauvinism and unsubtle self-confidence bred in the early stages of the revolution and the civil war. They, in particular, were not content to have captured the town and wanted to continue to exert their authority by, figuratively, continued force of arms and to pursue rapid and total victory. In many ways, during these years they were creating the policy tide that others were trying to stem, ride or divert. Those fighting the tide had no more success in their endeavours than King Canute.

SMENA VEKH AND NEP TOLERATION

If ever a movement was built on an illusion it was *Smena vekh*. Although, despite being a fairly small, it was divided into two wings with a less committed centre, all those associated with it believed that the revolution would have to 'normalise' itself in the sense of making a compromise with the mass of the population and give in to the petty bourgeois and proprietorial instincts of the peasantry in particular. The adoption of NEP, which was a partial restoration of just such a relationship between government and the market, appeared to be a step towards the fulfilment of their expectations and this gave them renewed confidence. They also believed that reconstruction would require an accommodation with another bourgeois and market-oriented social force – the technical white-collar intelligentsia. Many of the leaders of the movement were employees of the Soviet state whether, like Ustrialov, they remained outside the Soviet Union (in his case in the northern Chinese city of Harbin where he worked for the Chinese Eastern Railway, a company that the Soviet state had inherited from its predecessors); or, like Kliuchnikov, they returned to work in the upper levels of the Soviet bureaucracy, in his case Narkomindel (the Foreign Ministry), or Vesenkha (the State Economic Commission) which during the 1920s was a centre for all kinds of non-Bolshevik specialists including at least one Orthodox priest. Before this, Kliuchnikov had had two articles published in *Pravda* and had acted as an advisor to the Soviet delegation at the Genoa Conference.

The movement had also gestated in its various places of origin under other, shared influences. Most of its leaders had been members of the Liberal Constitutional Democratic Party (Kadets) and as such had been partially alienated from the tsarist élite, and had discovered they had less and less in common with the White cause in the civil war as it became more and more dominated, so they believed, by people who were determined to do the impossible and put the clock back. For *Smena vekh* it was as foolish to force history into a right-wing mould as it was to force it into a left-wing one.[2]

One of the first people to utter this heretical thought from within the White camp was N. V. Ustrialov (1890–1938), a lawyer by training, who was head of Admiral Kolchak's Press Bureau and a minister in his Siberian Government. By the end of 1918 and early 1919 Ustrialov had, thanks to his close acquaintance with its inner politics, begun to have doubts about the White cause. The Siberian stronghold of the Whites, Omsk, where Ustrialov was living at that time, appeared to him more and more as a focus of hopeless and unrealistic expectations and increasingly irrelevant squabbling. It is interesting to note that his criticisms preceded the catastrophic decline in the military fortunes of the Whites and were gestating at a time when White prospects seemed good. His unpublished memoirs *White Omsk* (*Belyi Omsk*)[3] show his disillusionment to be rooted in a comprehensive sense of Russian nationalism, which was, he thought, being compromised by the élite, sectarian infighting of the White leaders, and their complete reliance on foreign assistance. The example of popular energy shown by the Bolshevik and Red forces, which were entirely Russian, was, by contrast, impressive. In addition, the reactionary nature of some White supporters repelled him and he was also haunted by the marginalisation and provinciality of the Whites and longed to return to Moscow. Interestingly, he also mentions that he was impressed by early Bolshevik acts of reconcilation associated with Lunacharsky. In all this one can see a microcosm of his later ideas which were built on the assumption that a process of conciliation would have to be followed by the Bolsheviks. Finally, as the White cause foundered his alienation from it gathered strength.

Some confirmation that his doubts had been expressed early on is provided by a letter to him written by Iu. V. Kliuchnikov (1886–1938) who had passed through Omsk in winter 1918–19 on his way to Japan and, eventually, Paris. Writing from Vladivostok and Tokyo, he shared Ustrialov's 'doubts and sorrow displayed in one of our night-time meetings'.[4] The main drift of Ustrialov's thinking at this time was the irony of the humiliating dependence of Russian nationalism of the White variety on foreigners who, said Kliuchnikov, 'are not on our side'.[5]

Once in western Europe Kliuchnikov began to elaborate his ideas for himself and moved in directions that Ustrialov did not feel able to follow. Kliuchnikov became much more positive about the Bolsheviks. Ustrialov, on the other hand, defined his own position as being with the Bolsheviks but not of them.[6] Kliuchnikov declared himself to be 'a Bolshevik of the second day of the revolution'.[7] Ustrialov retorted that this position risked becoming merely that of 'a Bolshevik of the second class'.[8] In particular he was sceptical about Kliuchnikov's sympathy for internationalism and his neophilia. Indeed, Ustrialov always identified himself as a 'national Bolshevik' rather than as a 'Smenavekhovets', a title that strictly speaking only applies to the group around Kliuchnikov. None the less, all tendencies continued to publish their ideas in whatever journals and books any one of them was able to produce. Despite differences, the experience of emigration tended to strengthen the view of all of them that the clock could not be put back. Equally, the adoption of NEP by the Bolsheviks confirmed their belief that the left was no more capable of forcing history into a dogmatic mould and seemed to suggest that their third way – between Bolshevism and the emigration – might have a future. Their confidence was further strengthened by references in the Soviet press and warnings by high-ranking party leaders, especially Stalin, to the effect that the *Smena vekh* tendency was growing in the early 1920s, particularly among the technical intelligentsia whose assistance was being enlisted by the Soviet government in these years. Indeed, a rather rudimentary 'opinion poll' published in *Pravda* in September 1921 showed that among Moscow engineers the ideas of *Smena vekh* were more influential than any other ideology, be it Marxist or reactionary.[9] Overall, however, the strength of the *smenavekhovtsy* was never really of any significance either within Soviet Russia, where they simply trailed after events without ever influencing or even understanding them, or in the emigration, the leaders of which treated them as outcasts and Bolshevik agents. The *smenavekhovtsy* failed to make any significant converts among the *émigré* population. In fact, the monarchist assassination squads roaming Europe in a final, hopeless and callous fight to exterminate their enemies selected a number of followers of *Smena vekh* as their targets. A. M. Ageev was murdered in Sofia in autumn 1922 and D. I. Cherniavsky was killed in Harbin.[10]

Their significance lies less in their ideas and influence and more in their historical role at this time, in particular as the wing of the emigration most favourable to Bolshevism. This turned them into what Meshcheriakov called a 'bridge' from the emigration to the new Russia,[11] and it was as a bridge that they were able to assist and encourage the repatriation of tens of thousands of *émigrés* who wished to return to Russia. A number of leaders of the movement, notably Kliuchnikov and Potekhin, returned to live in Moscow, although

Ustrialov never did, apart from a visit in 1925. He turned down an offer to teach at Irkutsk University and angled for a post in the Law Faculty at Moscow University,[12] but his efforts in this direction were half-hearted and he continued to live in Harbin, teaching in the educational establishments of the Chinese Eastern Railway and in the local university, which had both *émigré* and Soviet constituents ranging from Fascists to young communists in its classes.[13]

None the less, this break in the united front of *émigré* opposition to the Soviet government offered an unparalleled tactical opportunity for the latter which they were not slow to exploit. While the *smenavekhovtsy* thought history was flowing in their direction, even to the extent of believing that, in some unspecified fashion, they would come to power,[14] the Soviet leadership, with considerably greater realism, saw that far from being a threat, *Smena vekh* enabled them to boost their skilled technical, engineering and managerial work-force at low cost and low risk, and set the emigration to fighting among themselves, though admittedly this last was not difficult to achieve. It was in this context that sympathisers with *Smena vekh* and related ideas were able to engage in public debate and even to publish in Russia and to circulate their newspapers published abroad. The central book of the movement, *Smena vekh*, from which it took its name, was published in two Soviet editions.[15] The journal *Nakanune* was, from June 1922, flown into Moscow from Berlin.[16] The limited extent of such circulation can be judged from the fact that even Lenin complained that he was having difficulty obtaining a copy of the journal *Smena vekh*.[17] Even so, these unique freedoms made the *Smena vekh* movement the most significant non-party intelligentsia grouping in these years and its history is an interesting case-study of the dimensions and purpose of NEP 'toleration'.

There were two attitudes to the *Smena vekh* movement among party and state leaders. One group shared Meshcheriakov's view that it was a bridge, permitting a useful, even necessary, function. For the others, any concessions of this sort were a betrayal of the proletariat and they argued that it should be wound up as soon as possible. Both sides shared the view that the concessions were, at best, temporary. No one was of the opinion that they could last indefinitely and no one believed that their existence excluded the continuation of direct pressure for conformity to the new ideals of communism, exerted by means of a monopoly of propaganda and the press, control of education, growing censorship, limitation on contacts abroad and the use of the law and the police to back up 'toleration'.

As soon as the *Smena vekh* movement appeared it was subjected to criticism, particularly from the core of party militants. An article in the agitational journal *Sputnik kommunista* (*The Communist's Companion*), published by the Moscow party committee, placed the struggle against the supporters of *Smena vekh* in the context of the bourgeoisie's drive for power, the 'game' they had been playing since 1916. The anonymous author was irreconcilably opposed to the steps being taken by the old intelligentsia to restore its position. The terms in which the hostility was expressed could hardly have been more emphatic. Before October the intelligentsia had called the workers their 'comrades' but afterwards the 'officials, engineers, doctors, professors, students and so on to a man sabotaged the institutions established by the proletariat; they deliberately interfered with and wrecked all initiatives aimed at restoring industry and the national economy'. Worse accusations followed:

> It was they, the Russian intelligentsia, in the form of mercenaries and officers in the armies of the various generals, who shot tens of thousands of workers and Red Army soldiers; it was they whose artillery fire wiped from the face of the earth entire villages which had risen against the Tsarist generals and landowners; while they slandered and accused the Bolsheviks of 'betrayal of the fatherland' they invited the whole foreign bourgeoisie to fight against Soviet Russia, French, English, Czechoslovak, American, Japanese and so on.

In addition, it was 'the intelligentsia who staffed the agitation and cultural-educational departments of the generals, they edited all the black hundred and pogrom-inspiring publications and newspapers'.[18] And so the accusations mounted. After this unpromising invective with which it had begun, the article went on, in much shrewder fashion, to analyse the *Smena vekh* movement and the apparent reconciliation with the revolution that it represented. *Smena vekh*'s main interest, the article concluded, was that Soviet power appeared to be the only possible route to the reconstruction of a viable national state. They considered the communist elements of Soviet power to be transitory and Utopian, a belief they thought was borne out by the adoption of NEP. For them, NEP was not a temporary retreat but a step towards the dilution of the class character of the Soviet state, a step on the road to the politics of democracy. Within this new context, their aim was to serve the NEP bourgeoisie. This account of their crimes concluded with the interesting view that the main tactic of their attack was to weaken the 'base fortress of the proletariat, its understanding of the world'. It followed, the article concluded, that 'the clerical counter-revolution and the attack on materialism should be met with an organised rebuff in the form of the militant materialism and militant atheism promoted by comrade Lenin'. The party, it concluded, somewhat paradoxically, 'should exert maximum energy in spreading Marxist knowledge among the masses and, in the first place, in the party itself', which seemed to suggest something of a weakness in the 'base fortress'.[19]

This article shows a number of interesting features, not least of which are the very high importance given to ideology and the portentious 'Stalinist' vocabulary of 'sabotage' and 'wrecking'. Arguing in the same crude fashion as the author, one might see this as an example of promoting the status and the vested interests of the party agitational apparatus from which the author may well have sprung. However, one should look more deeply into its roots. Its odd assumption that the framework of ideas among the bourgeois intelligentsia was idealist and religious must be unique in twentieth-century history, particularly since the basic code of the Russian intelligentsia had been anti-clerical and materialist since the mid nineteenth century. Clearly, the term intelligentsia was being used here in an increasingly frequent polemical form, to equate it with tsarism. A crude and undifferentiated picture of the intelligentsia as the general staff of tsarist society, a definition that had existed before the revolution but had been far from widespread, was becoming more and more useful to the militants and represented a consequence of the equating of the struggle against the intelligentsia with class war; the equating of the intelligentsia with Russia's missing bourgeoise.[20]

In addition, however, one should also see in such an attitude one of the consequences of the tsarist politicisation of culture. The simple assumption that there were only two tendencies possible – on the one hand tsarist clericalism and mysticism aimed at keeping the labouring classes under control, and on the other the socialist, scientific and materialist outlook of the revolutionaries – could only appear credible in a situation like that of Russia where the manipulation of the church and the attempt to maintain popular ignorance and superstition had been so sustained and so recent.

Be that as it may, the article also shows that any groups within the party that wished to compromise with the *smenavekhovtsy* and the old intelligentsia were going to encounter vigilant opposition. The debate was somewhat muted in the first year or two but became more prominent in 1923 and 1924. Defenders of the limited toleration afforded to the non-party intelligentsia began to find life more difficult in this respect. Meshcheriakov and Voronsky, for example, attempted to restate arguments for such toleration in these years. They had initially addressed the issues raised by the appearance of *Smena vekh* as early as 1921. For Voronsky, in a review of *Smena vekh*, the indications were that, since opposition to the October revolution no longer seemed to have much future, 'even in *émigré* circles' the intelligentsia 'had begun a re-evaluation of its values, which found its most acute expression in *Smena vekh*'.[21] Meschcheriakov took a similar point of view. The old choice between either Westernism or Slavophilism had been replaced, since 1917, with a third choice, that of proletarian revolution. The initial impulse of the intelligentsia was to be suspicious of the revolution and either to oppose it or stand to one side. However, it was the author's belief that it would abandon its current position, which was pointed out (in contrast to the writer in *Sputnik kommunista*) to be one of rejection of the old culture but reluctance to accept the new. 'A sense of self-preservation, a sense of life, must prompt the intelligentsia to overcome this apathy so that with its whole soul and its whole mind it will join the camp which is now constructing a new life, a new culture for a humanity freed from all exploitation.'[22] In 1923, Meshcheriakov tended to justify the policy of partially sponsoring the *smenavekhovtsy* by claiming that its function as a 'bridge' (*mostik*) had allowed many people from different groups, ranging from the Mensheviks to the Kadets, to reconcile themselves in their own time with the revolution. He quoted, with approval, the comment of one of them that the function of the intelligentsia was to be the errand-boy (*prikazchik*) of the people and their state.[23]

There is no doubt, judging from these defenders of the policy of permitting the *smenavekhovtsy* to operate, that the purpose of the policy was to strengthen the revolution and to win over important support. In no sense did it imply a form of 'ideological coexistence' or a weakening of faith in the values of the revolution. It was not a dialogue with the old intelligentsia, in the sense of a process leading to mutual compromise, but a tactic aimed at rallying such elements of the old intelligentsia as were redeemable, in communist eyes, and sowing division within the emigration. Even this, as we have seen, was too much for the more militant party members who wished to get on with the undiluted class struggle, purified of any temporising qualifications. The biggest obstacle for this latter group, however, was that, under the direct influence of Lenin, going back to February 1918, party policy had been directed to gaining as much material support as possible from the old intelligentsia, particularly, but by no means exclusively, the technical specialists. For as long as this policy continued, as it did under Lenin's patronage, then the policy of limited toleration could be defended. Its opponents, however, made no bones about their opposition and in the mid-1920s the arguments came out into the open once more, with the renewed energy arising from the fact that the big guns of the party were directly involved in a way they had not been earlier. Before turning to this debate, however, it is worth taking a look at the activities in which the *smenavekhovtsy* were able to engage while they, for the time being, enjoyed the continuation of the favourable conjuncture of circumstances that had allowed them to operate openly in Soviet Russia.

For the most part, the *smenavekhovtsy* were limited to organising meetings, holding discussions and setting up debates. Some of these, particularly in 1921–2, were widely reported in the Soviet press. They also worked in important positions in a number of state institutions including the economic apparatus, Vesenkha and the Ministry of Foreign Affairs. Activities of this kind were not particularly unusual in the years up to 1922 and there is nothing unique about them. A number of non-party intelligentsia groups were able to do the same and some more hostile ones also published books for a very short period as mentioned above. An interview with Potekhin and Kliuchnikov did appear in *Izvestiia VTsIK* during their exploratory visit to Soviet Russia in 1922.[24] Rather more unusual was the fact that Gosizdat twice reprinted *Smena vekh* – once in Tver and once in Smolensk – because the original Prague edition barely circulated in Russia, the entry of *émigré* publications being 'as is well known, strictly controlled'.[25] Organisation did not, for the most part, go beyond this. Requests to set up a better focused centre for their activities was rejected in 1921. Lunacharsky, for one, was unequivocal in his condemnation of the request, particularly since it involved the setting up of a newspaper. The apostle of toleration wrote in *Petrogradskaia pravda* that 'Any attempt to set up a competitor or party independent of Communism would be a significant mistake.'[26]

After the tightening of control in 1920–2 the likelihood of such a request being granted was remote. At least so it would appear. It is perhaps, then, all the more surprising that the *Smena vekh* movement – still defined in its loose sense to cover a wide spectrum of formerly hostile *intelligenty* who were increasingly prepared to make peace with the Soviet authorities – was allowed to circulate some of its literature and even to organise a newspaper in the Soviet Union and open an office for one of the *émigré* papers. As such, the movement provides a unique example of apparent toleration. A closer look at the available information, however, shows the limits of these concessions.

In June 1922 the *Smena vekh* tending, *émigré* newspaper *Nakanune* (*On the Eve*), set up by Kliuchinikov and Potekhin among others, was allowed to open an office in Moscow. Copies of the paper were flown by air from Berlin and circulated in the metropolitan and some provincial cities of Soviet Russia. In this respect, *Nakanune* was unique. Information presented by Soviet scholars in recent years has helped us to explain why this unique patronage was granted.[27] As in any newspaper office, the Moscow correspondents' task was to channel information about the country in which they found themselves. In this case it meant passing on items that the Soviet government wanted to bring to the attention of the *émigré* community to improve its image. For instance, according to one former employee's memoirs, Ivan Maisky, at that time head of the press department of the Foreign Ministry, would draw their attention to particular aspects of Soviet or foreign news to which the government attached priority or answer particular charges made by the *émigré* press and politicians.[28] According to the best Soviet account of the movement, most of the important employees in the Moscow office were close to the Soviet apparatus. One of them claimed never to have seen the volume *Smena vekh*; others, including the chief editor of the journal, G. L. Kirdetsov, worked for, or returned to, the Foreign Ministry once the journal closed down. Another, M. Levidov, took charge of the foreign section of TASS, the Soviet news agency that had succeeded ROSTA in July 1925. Thus, from the point of view of the Soviet authorities, *Nakanune* was staffed by trustworthy people to provide a useful channel of propaganda to the *émigré* intelligentsia. In particular, the wide range of non-party 'fellow-travelling' writers who were published in its literary section, edited by A. N. Tolstoi, who was himself to return to the Soviet Union in 1923, gave an impression of normality and progress. Among those published were M. Bulgakov, Mandel'stam, Ehrenburg, Pil'niak, Babel' and Zoshchenko. The hope was that, with this formula, it would reach parts of the emigration the regular Soviet press could not reach. Overall, the newspaper played on feelings, including nostalgia, that inspired thoughts favourable to the new regime, implied the hopelessness of struggle against it and promoted the idea of return. Although former employees of *Nakanune*, as well as of other non-party journals, for obvious reasons played down their unorthodox views in their memoirs, there can be no doubt that *Nakanune* was heavily supervised – to the point of dependency – by the Soviet authorities. According to a Central Committee Press Section report on its activities, *Nakanune* was 'sufficiently steadfast' and the information it contained 'for the most part coincided with that in our newspapers, and the ideological aspect of the newspaper was sufficiently firm and consistent with respect to its goodwill towards the Soviet authorities'.[29] Its dependence is indicated by the fact that its last issue was produced on 15 June 1924, just five months after the Thirteenth Party Conference had passed a resolution calling for a break with *Smena vekh* ideas. The view of its editors, echoed by Soviet commentators, that it closed down because it had 'fulfilled its basic task' now that the Soviet Union had regularised its foreign relations and that the *Smena vekh* ideology had been superseded, overlooks this coincidence. Its passing was noted in *Izvestiia VTsIK* which praised it for combating the hostile, anti-Soviet views of the emigration.[30] From the point of view of the Soviet authorities it had served its purpose well.

A similar venture within Soviet Russia was protected by the authorities because it performed the function of strengthening the Soviet government's legitimacy in the eyes of indifferent and potentially hostile intellectuals who had not emigrated. The first issue of the journal *Novaia rossiia* (*New Russia*) was published in Petrograd in March 1922. It soon ran into trouble with the local Soviet authorities and was closed down by them after publication of its second issue. The matter was brought to Lenin's attention and, in a letter to the head of the Cheka, Dzherzhinsky, he argued that it had been premature of the Petrograd authorities to take this step because it betrayed a certain lack of discrimination between degrees of hostility to Soviet power shown by different intelligentsia groups. Implicitly, Lenin wished to use the more sympathetic to isolate the more hostile. 'Of course', he wrote about *Novaia rossiia*, 'not all the collaborators on this journal are candidates for exile abroad.'[31] The question was brought before the Politburo on 26 May 1922 as a result of which the Chief Administration for Press Affairs was instructed to arrange ffort

for its continued publication. This did not sway the Petrograd Soviet authorities and they appealed against the decision. On 1 June the Politburo again ordered that it should appear and the Presidium of VTsIK was given the task of implementing the decision. As a result, the journal moved from Petrograd to Moscow where it reappeared under the title *Rossiia* (*Russia*) in Summer 1922. It continued until 1926 and reached a circulation of 15,000 in 1924.[32]

Rossiia, and its editor I. G. Lezhnev, represented a distinct and independent tendency that can only loosely be related to *Smena vekh*. Indeed, Lezhnev always claimed that his ideas on reconciliation between the intelligentsia and the Soviet authorities had preceded those of *Smena vekh* proper.[33] It seems quite likely that he had arrived at his position through a more independent line of evolution. A number of other non-party and even formerly anti-Bolshevik intellectuals had decided quite independently to make their peace with Bolshevism. Like his counterparts in *Nakanune*, Lezhnev was exaggerating somewhat in his later memoirs when he denied that the people working on the journal had been anything other than 'warm supporters of co-operation with the Soviet authorities and sincere sympathisers with the revolution and the communist party'.[34] Lezhnev was, however, correct in pointing out that, unlike participants in *Smena vekh*, he and his associates had not been White Guards. Like the *smenavekhovtsy* proper, however, the collaborators on *Rossiia* envisaged a future Russia of the 'third way' which would be neither communist nor White.[35] In the meantime, however, they believed the only way to achieve this end was to work through and with the party. In Lezhnev's words, 'serve according to decree, live in secret'.[36] By 1924 the position of Lezhnev was little different from that of Kliuchnikov and Potekhin, who considered themselves, to Ustrialov's disappointment, to be for all practical purposes supporters of the right wing of the Communist Party.[37]

The January 1924 decision of the party conference did not hit *Rossiia* with the same rapidity as it did *Nakanune*, perhaps because the former was a little bigger and was not as firmly under the thumb of the authorities as the latter. Perhaps the fact that it did not have a White Guard past helped it. Whatever the reason, the reprieve was temporary. In 1926 *Rossiia* was closed and, unlike the staff of *Nakanune*, who were allowed to continue other work in Soviet Russia, or even returned from Berlin, Lezhnev was exiled. This was not the only bizarre twist in his colourful career. According to a Soviet source, he had been in the Bolshevik underground but had left the party, becoming a Menshevik according to Potekhin,[38] and had fought with the Red Army during the civil war. In 1920–1 he worked as head of an unspecified department of the newspaper *Izvestiia VTsIK*. His exile was not the end of the tale. In 1930, he was not only allowed to return, but was admitted to the party on the recommendation of Stalin.[39] He thus provides an example of someone exiled in the years of 'toleration' allowed to return in the years of violent 'class struggle' on the cultural front. The closure of his journal in 1926 did, however, mark the end of the last remaining quasi-independent organ of political and social comment in Soviet Russia. Lezhnev claimed in the first issue that it had been the first such journal and it had gone on to outlive all similar enterprises. It was virtually the last private publication of any significance left in Soviet Russia. With its demise, institutional control over culture was further strengthened and, with the continued and very unworldly exception of the Academy of Sciences, only party-organised or party-dominated institutions survived, such as the journals *Krasnaia nov'* and *Novyi mir*, in which strictly controlled non-party writings could still be published. Direct political and social comment was completely excluded from these journals unless it came from sources sympathetic to the revolution. Even here, control was reaching further and further and the scope of publication and cultural activity was being eroded steadily. Party policy on culture and the debates around it in these years have been the subject of much discussion in the Soviet Union and in the West and it is not possible to give a full account of it here. However, an explanation of its main contours, in the light of the themes pursued in this and in previous chapters, shows that, as in the case of the various tendencies among the *smenavekhovtsy*, 'toleration' was very limited and instrumental from the party point of view and the space available for the expression of non-approved opinions was being steadily reduced throughout the 1920s. Such areas of expression as remained were more and more atomised. The institutions in which such discourse was possible were under ever-increasing party control.

THE EVOLUTION OF PARTY POLICY ON CULTURE IN THE MID 1920s

From the early years of NEP onwards, discussion of cultural policy and the related problem of the intelligentsia began to attract the attention of leading figures in the party. In his last writings Lenin gave considerable importance to what he understood by cultural revolution as a major strategy for completing the revolution. Other leading figures joined in. Trotsky, Bukharin, Zinoviev and Stalin all made significant contributions to the discussion. At lower levels, battles within the party broke out with greater force than ever. The fracture lines remained as they had been since the civil war but the intensity of the debate was much greater, perhaps as a result of the greater security of the revolution after the end of hostilities and the beginning of international agreements and treaties, often about trade that Kliuchnikov described as 'recognition *de pecuniae*'. The issues also became closely embroiled in the overriding questions of the mid-1920s, namely what strategy should the revolution pursue in the circumstances of international isolation in which it found itself, and who would, in the absence of Lenin, provide the appropriate leadership. The central cultural debates in these years revolved around literature and in 1924 and 1925 a number of high-level conferences were organised that culminated in July 1925 in the authoritative statement, endorsed by the Central Committee, of the party's policy on literature. Because of their centrality and their high profile these discussions have attracted much scholarly attention, especially in Western Europe and North America. The statement of party policy on literature has been variously interpreted as a victory for 'moderation' and a continuation of the toleration that was said to have existed prior to 1925, to the extent that crudely proletarian chauvinist tendencies were not granted a monopoly over party orthodoxy in literature, and the policy of attempted seduction of the non-party intelligentsia, as proposed by most of the leaders, was not to be transformed into rape, as the militant left wanted, as they had since 1918. More recently, the fact that the underlying principles of the proletarian chauvinists were at least in part endorsed by the party leadership and were in no way repudiated by them has been interpreted as a moral victory for the militants and a defeat for conciliation.[40]

Curiously, but far from uniquely, given the course of events in the Soviet Union and the nature of the historiography of the period, the debates of the 1920s have been interpreted in the light of what came after rather than what came before. As a result, the apparent toleration of the 1920s is contrasted with the rigid orthodoxies of the 1930s. The fact that in July 1925 the party did not impose a single orthodoxy in literature, as it is said to have done through the doctrine of socialist realism in the 1930s, is seen as evidence of the existence of a more acceptable, more liberal, perhaps more Leninist set of values, substantially different from those of the Stalinist 1930s. While there is no doubt that there was more toleration compared to the 1930s, this is not saying very much. It can also be misleading to look at the period with this as the prime assumption because it can distract from the processes observed prior to 1925, which show a continuous and irreversible erosion of toleration ever since 1919, the logical end-point of which could be seen as the imposition of an orthodoxy. Perhaps a second illusion arising from concentration on the mid 1920s and after is that, without paying attention to the instruments and institutions of cultural power, the way they were evolving prior to 1925 and the people involved in them, one can get a false impression of the significance of these debates. Energetic and stimulating the discussions may have been, but it is hard to see that they had very much impact. They arose because of the disjunction between the awesome cultural-institutional power wielded by the party and the shallow, propagandistic understanding of the strategy governing the use of that administrative power. None of those involved had any clear idea of what sort of cultural policy should be pursued. Those who had delved into this question, notably Bogdanov, had been quickly marginalised and the vacuum at the heart of party policy on culture was filled with slogans of class war and the reduction of culture, following a very crude interpretation of Marx, into a secondary, derivative, and superstructural phenomenon. Culture was increasingly identified with propaganda, a process that had begun very early in the revolution. In addition, the almost complete disappearance after 1917 of the capitalist bourgeoisie meant that the old cultural and professional intelligentsia was the most prominent, indeed the only significant, remnant that could be classified as 'bourgeois' left in urban Soviet society. The addition later of the 'nepman' (the type of small trader who flourished during NEP) and the *kulak* (the peasant who hired labour) diversified the class enemies available, but in the early 1920s the full fury of militant class enmity tended to fall on the intelligentsia. As we have seen, the fragile defence of the old intelligentsia, particularly by those Bolsheviks who had themselves been close to it before the revolution, had been unable to protect it fully from the proletarian chauvinists. The discussions of the middle of the decade attracted an impressive array of talent, often otherwise in opposition to one another, like Trotsky and Bukharin, who asserted that one could not apply crude class-based assumptions in the more delicate field of culture and that it was one area in which simple class barriers did not apply. Despite this, the tendency towards applying nothing beyond the clichés of class struggle to the cultural sphere continued without serious check. The growth of the institutional apparatus of cultural control meant that, in determined hands, orthodoxy could be imposed. The proletarian chauvinists who, for the most part, did not come from intelligentsia backgrounds, did not give the same weight to ideas as did their opponents, who followed the assumptions of many intellectuals that ideas have a power of their own. As a consequence, intelligentsia Bolsheviks tended to assume that, if one was right, the mechanisms of history would ensure a kind of Darwinian selection in favour of that position. Wittingly or unwittingly, the opponents of the intelligentsia Bolsheviks were elaborating their control of the actual mechanisms of cultural revolution – the press, censorship, school system, party schools, workers' faculties and so on. It is in this context that the development of party cultural policy in these years should be interpreted. Clearly, this approach demonstrates greater continuity between these years and those that followed.

The debates of the middle of the decade did not have a precise origin but grew out of growing tension with the policies and attitudes that had hitherto prevailed. As we have seen, institutional policy towards culture had run ahead of explicit formulation of principles in this sphere. As far as the latter are concerned, it was the breaking down of the assumptions – particularly about the degree of support that could be attracted to the new authorities – that had emerged very early on that was at the root of the change. This breakdown itself reflected the tensions and ambiguities of those initial assumptions, and since it was, above all, Lenin who was responsible for mediating and arbitrating both the policies and the assumptions, the ambiguity of his own views also has to be taken into account. Because of this, and because of the gap between debates about policy and actual implementation of policy, we have to turn our attention first to the content of the discussions starting with an examination of Lenin's views and then those of other leading participants – especially Zinoviev, Trotsky and Bukharin – before moving on to examining the impact of actually existing policies.

It is not possible to extract a consistent theory of culture from Lenin's life and works, though attempts have been made.[41] The axes of Lenin's attitudes to and interpretation of culture – understood both in the anthropological and high culture senses – are contradictory. The main elements are, in the first place, an unremitting contempt for the apparent feebleness and flabbiness of the Russian intelligentsia. Secondly, there is a great respect for what these people do, either as artists or, in the wider sense, as scientists and even as managers and administrators. This is complicated still further by the fact that Lenin himself, and many of the people whom he admired, were, by any standards, members of that very intelligentsia. Lenin's family lived lives close to the pattern of those of many other members of the intelligentsia, including his brother Alexander who was executed as a student terrorist. In addition, Lenin's deeply felt appreciation of the most 'bourgeois' high culture – the music of Beethoven and the acting of Sarah Bernhardt – coexisted with a crude materialism that refused to acknowledge the significance of spiritual, moral and ethical ideals other than as the result of direct material forces. For instance, he often expressed the view that high pay will win over the hearts and minds of waverers, while at the same time, of course, exhibiting in his own life and in the personal standards set within the party the most devoted and non-materialistic ideals of personal behaviour and motivation to strive for the success of the revolution on humanist grounds. Indeed, party members were expressly forbidden high salaries and careerism was attacked. Intellectuals who did not agree with Lenin, even those whose social background and underlying principles (though not their views on particular issues) were almost indistinguishable from those of Lenin, such as Martov and Sukhanov, were all 'petty-bourgeois' and those who supported him were the 'democratic intelligentsia' or, when referring to earlier generations, 'revolutionary democrats'. People jumped from one categorisation to the other according to their ideas at a given time, or, more precisely, according to the relationship of their ideas to those of Lenin at a given time. This association of intellectuals with the bourgeoisie was not, however, matched by an unequivocal assertion that there was a purely 'bourgeois' or purely 'proletarian' culture with a corresponding 'proletarian' intelligentsia.[42] In his arguments against Bogdanov, Lenin did say that, initially, the revolution should settle for 'real bourgeois culture' and not toy with ideas of an experimental and exclusively proletarian culture.[43] This casts some doubt on just how 'bourgeois' bourgeois culture was in Lenin's eyes since it was the most acceptable cultural form for transitional socialist society and indeed constituted one of the most important survivals of pre-revolutionary society. After carrying out the revolutionary assault on the tsarist state – the army, the landowners, the capitalists, the banks and so on – the revolutionary was, according to Lenin, supposed to pause when confronted with the culture of pre-revolutionary society, and, at least in the short term, absorb it rather than overthrow it (notwithstanding the fact that those who produced this culture were untrustworthy renegades and class enemies).

One also has to take into account that, like everyone else, Lenin used the word 'culture' in more than one sense. Most frequently, at least in his more important speeches and writings, he used it to mean a whole way of life, a way of administering affairs, a way of carrying on commerce. A 'cultured' society was a literate and well-mannered one. At other times culture referred to higher cultural activities, of writers for instance, though here, too, there was a tendency towards a reductionism that saw them first and foremost as ideologists of a class.

For all these reasons, Lenin's writings are unpromising material for anyone seeking a theory of culture within them, or perhaps one should say they provide rich material for a variety of different interpretations of what he meant. The ambiguity resident in them was never resolved, not least because Lenin did not often give the issues his full attention. None the less, on the question of the approach he adopted after the October revolution we are on surer ground. The stages of evolution of his policies are well established. In the first enthusiasm of the revolution many of his statements suggested that he was very optimistic that, once the revolution had seized power, it would unleash pent-up energies in all sections of society and realise the potential of the massive but still dormant 'spiritual' as well as 'material' forces. The lack of response on the part of the intelligentsia, and other sections of society, to this appeal swiftly destroyed these illusions and within months of October a new line, most unpopular with the left in the party, was being evolved according to which the issue of immediate survival was so great that any sacrifice of principle was justified if it served this overriding aim. This meant abandoning the principles of the Paris Commune and offering very high salaries to any technical experts prepared to work with the Soviet authorities to keep industry, the banks and the state bureaucracy running. This was soon extended to the military sphere also, though still over the protests of the party left. Essentially, this defence of the specialists (*spetsy*) remained in force throughout the rest of Lenin's life and the belief that improving living standards would reconcile them to the Soviet way of life, irrespective of its idiosyncratic view of democracy, its ideology of class struggle and so on, was never dimmed. Similarly, the conflict this change of direction brought was also a permanent feature of Lenin's years in power. As a result of it, his distrust of the ultra-left can be traced in the cultural sphere, notably his preference for real bourgeois culture rather than some chimerical and insubstantial, as he saw it, proletarian culture. There could never be a purely proletarian culture, he said, and ridiculed the idea of a specifically proletarian science.[44] He had also warned Lunacharsky against giving the militants their head within the Education Ministry for fear of the damage they might do.[45] As far as Proletkul't was concerned, his distrust of left-wing factionalism strengthened his hostility to their views on proletarian culture, and his opposition to their views strengthened his distrust of them as a faction.

At the same time as he was defending bourgeois culture and bourgeois specialists, Lenin stoked up an unremitting campaign of hostility against representatives of the bourgeoisie whose skills did not have any apparent utilitarian value. Bourgeois ideologists, as opposed to bourgeois culture, were being uprooted in the 1920–2 period, as we have seen, with the full knowledge and support of Lenin, who often spoke and wrote with the utmost contempt of people such as Sorokin, Miliukov, Sukhanov and many other intellectuals who expressed open hostility to Bolshevism. This in itself is scarcely surprising, but its existence alongside a defence of bourgeois culture does point up, once more, the ambiguity. What was supposed to be at the heart of this new cultural apparatus and in what name were bourgeois ideologists being expelled if not that of proletarian culture and proletarian cultural revolution? None the less, on the face of it, Lenin's position appeared to be one of using the full force of the proletarian state to impose bourgeois culture on the workers and peasants. It was only in his last writings, especially 'On Co-operation', in which he argued that only cultural revolution – meaning, roughly, a modernisation of outlook and attitudes in Russia, the establishment of Enlightenment principles of rationality and literacy rather than superstition and custom – was needed to save the revolution and bring the consciousness of the people into line with the consciousness of the party vanguard, did Lenin show a growing awareness of the contradictions. But even so he did not resolve them. In one of his very last works the ambiguous interplay of themes remained. A few lines from 'Pages from a Diary' show this:

Our schoolteacher should be raised to a standard he has never achieved, and cannot achieve, in bourgeois society. This is a truism and requires no proof. We must strive for this state of affairs by working steadily, methodically and persistently to raise the teacher to a higher cultural level, to train him thoroughly for his really high calling and – mainly, mainly and mainly – to improve his position materially.

We must step up our efforts to organise the schoolteachers so as to transform them from being bulwarks of the bourgeois system, as they still are in capitalist countries without exception, into bulwarks of the Soviet system, in order, through their agency, to divert the peasantry from alliance with the bourgeoisie and to bring them into alliance with the proletariat.

From the evidence of these words, written in January 1923, Lenin's underlying approach remained unchanged. There remained the firm conviction that 'we' have the truth and that the teachers' cultural level can be 'raised' in order that 'he' will be able to perceive this. At the same time, this intellectual process was underpinned by satisfying the material interests of the teacher. To see them purely as a substance for manipulation in this way, both by 'us' and, presumably by the bourgeoisie for whose domination they are 'bulwarks', suggests a rather considerable weight was attached to the apparently 'superstructural' phenomenon of the teaching profession. Finally, the immediate purpose of this transformation was the instrumental one of 'diverting' the peasantry (through conviction? not through *their* material interests?) from alliance with the bourgeoise. Clearly, right to the last, Lenin's views remained in a state of flux. The exigencies of immediate needs, practical and polemical, remained the driving force of his views on culture rather than any attempt to elaborate a comprehensive theory of culture. For Lenin, as for the administrators, cultural policy was an immediate weapon of class power with no long-term core or objective, indeed, with the explicit denial that the class possessing the power, the proletariat, was capable, at least in current circumstances, of elaborating its own culture. One cannot help but relate this to a fundamental theme of Lenin's political career, a distrust of, even a contempt for, the idea that the unaided and 'spontaneous' efforts of Russian workers could achieve the revolution.

Lenin's views, then, were not very much help to anyone trying to devise a consistent and penetrating approach to the role of culture in the transition from capitalism to socialism. His writings reflected only too well the inconsistencies and confusions of party policy in the early years and the contradictory tensions within it. This did not prevent participants in the debate of the mid 1920s from claiming Lenin's authority for their various positions. Indeed, 'Leninism' was invented in the course of these very arguments. While Lenin was still alive, however, no trace of this appeared, so that when the debate began in earnest his authority was not a central theme or point of reference.

An early, and rather unlikely entrant onto the cultural battlefield, where he firmly and unequivocally planted the banner of militant class struggle, was Grigory Zinoviev. He produced a pamphlet published under the title *The Intelligentsia and Revolution*.[46] The occasion of his unexpected selection of such a theme was a conference of scientific workers to whom he made the speech, reprinted in the pamphlet, on 23 November 1923. Not surprisingly, Zinoviev's contribution could not be said to have gone very far in providing a solution to the knotty problems associated with this theme. Perhaps the most significant point was his view that the intelligentsia, although he referred to it as though it was a recognisable group throughout his speech, was best understood as being 'divided in its turn into layers, groups and sub-groups which go with various classes of the population. Depending on the particular stage of the revolution, the intelligentsia played various roles, among others approaching the revolution and evaluating it.'[47] This dual definition of the intelligentsia – that it was an identifiable group but was also divided up between various classes – was an attractive one for a number of participants in the debate because it legitimised almost any arbitrary judgement about the intelligentsia to the extent that individuals could be pigeonholed subjectively as 'bourgeois', 'proletarian' or whatever, while at the same time the term intelligentsia could still be used.

Although he was an early entrant into the field, Zinoviev's contribution was marginal. The chief contributors were Trotsky and Bukharin. Curiously, they shared certain basic principles, above all a persistent respect for the values of high culture, no matter what its source, and a tenacious refusal to allow a narrow interpretation of the existing intelligentsia which would equate it with the bourgeoisie. Even as late as the mid 1930s, when he was vigorously attacking popular front policies on the grounds that they weakened the impact of class struggle, Trotsky was still arguing that, in the field of culture, alliances across class divides were not only possible but necessary. In

Trotsky was characteristically forthright in expressing his views. In his book *Literature and Revolution*, published in 1923 as the debate was taking off, he pointed out that the simple assumption that 'Every ruling class creates its own culture, and consequently, its own art'[52] needed to be modified in the case of the proletariat by two considerations. First, the cultural flowering of previous ruling classes had, he asserted, sometimes come centuries after their social, political and economic emergence. To back this up he pointed out, rather questionably, that the nineteenth century represented a greater period in bourgeois culture than the Renaissance. Secondly, it followed from this that since the proletariat was only in power temporarily in order to supervise the transition to a classless society, it would not have time to elaborate its own culture. The period of transition, according to Trotsky, 'will last not months and not years, but decades – decades, but not centuries, and certainly not thousands of years. Can the proletariat in this time create a new culture? It is legitimate to doubt this.'[53] The period of transition would, he said, be characterised by violent class struggle, 'in which destruction will occupy more room than new construction'.[54] 'This', he said,

> seems to lead to the conclusion that there is no proletarian culture and that there never will be any and in fact there is no reason to regret this. The proletariat acquires power for the purpose of doing away forever with class culture and to make way for human culture. We frequently seem to forget this.[55]

If this argument held true as a general principle for the international revolution and the international proletariat then it was even more applicable in specifically Russian conditions. 'Our task in Russia is complicated by the poverty of our entire cultural tradition and by the material destruction wrought by the events of the last decade. . . . Our proletariat is forced to turn all its energies towards the creation of the most elementary conditions of material existence.'[56] In particular, literacy was a key preliminary target. It was thus a question of laying the basis for the new culture, not a case of the new ruling class possessing a culture when it came to power as the bourgeoisie had done. 'The problem of a proletariat which has conquered power', he argued, going to the heart of the process as it had occurred in Russia, 'consists, first of all, in taking into its own hands the apparatus of culture – the industries, schools, publications, press, theatres, etc. – which did not serve it before, and thus to open up the path of culture for itself.'[57]

Curiously enough, given their differences in other key respects, Bukharin shared some of Trotsky's assumptions, especially about the immediate question of proletarian culture. For Bukharin, also, the proletariat, particularly in Russia, was too weak to have elaborated its own culture before it came to power. Intelligentsia tutelage of the fledgling proletariat was as essential to him as it was to Trotsky. In phraseology strikingly similar to that of Trotsky he said 'The bourgeoisie, in the womb of feudal society, was able to develop its cultural force much more highly than the proletariat in the bounds of bourgeois society so that culturally [the proletariat] is many, many times weaker than the class which it overthrows.'[58]

The theoretical lessons he drew from this, however, diverged from those of Trotsky. Far from dogmatically asserting that there was not going to be time for the proletariat to develop its culture, Bukharin was eager to see it taking such steps as it could in this direction. Its cultural weakness, he inferred, led to two consequences. First, it made it prone to error arising from inexperience and, secondly, it was necessary for it to call on socially hostile forces to help it overcome its weakness.[59] In actual practice this was not far removed from Trotsky's idea of what needed to be done immediately, even though the long-term analysis of the two men was quite different, perhaps as a reflection of their divergent views over the length of time that NEP could be expected to last and the nearness or otherwise of the swing back to more open and aggressive class struggle on the international scale. Bukharin, then, was not opposed to the idea of moving towards a proletarian culture but, like all the other leading figures we have looked at who were interested in this question, he understood that the first stage of this process had to be the acquisition of at least some aspects of bourgeois culture. Trotsky had said the same thing.

> The main task of the proletarian intelligentsia in the immediate future is not the abstract formation of a new culture regardless of the absence of a basis for it, but definite culture-bearing, that is, a systematic, planful and, of course, critical imparting to the backward masses of the essential elements of the culture which already exists.[60]

While the theoretical analysis on which their defence of current cultural policies was based rested on solid ground, Bukharin and

Trotsky had been drawn into tactically much more difficult terrain. To base one's policy on the long-term weakness and dependence of the Russian proletariat led them into head-on confrontation with the different varieties of proletarian chauvinism. If the proletariat was so weak, how could it have carried out the revolution? If so many powerful tsarist institutions had given way before it, why should it have to acknowledge bourgeois superiority in what many thought of as the marginal field of culture? Militant critics were not slow to seize on these points. They saw no reason to think that culture was a fortress the Bolsheviks could not storm. Most of their venom was directed at the non-proletarian elements who were making the running in many areas of Soviet cultural life. The debate was so intense that leading party institutions began to get involved. In May 1924 the Press Section of the Central Committee, headed by Iakovlev, arranged a debate to thrash out the issues as they affected the crucial field of literature. Far from settling the question, the situation continued much as before. In June the following year the Central Committee itself passed a resolution enumerating the principles governing its approach to literature – and, by implication to cultural revolution in general. Even this did little to change the direction in which events were moving. The process of drift towards aggressive assertion of class struggle continued. The debates do, however, provide a valuable crystallisation of the issues.

In the May 1924 debate, the main speakers were A. K. Voronsky, by then editor of the journal *Red Virgin Soil*, who represented the status quo, and I. Vardin representing the *On Guard* group (*Napostovtsy*), the main focus of proletarian militance. The essential point of Voronsky's speech was that, contrary to the assertions of its critics, the party did have a policy on literature, that of nurturing all those who accepted the October revolution. The point was to draw all such elements to the party, a difficult and arduous job, particularly given the fact, heavily emphasised by Voronsky, that the Russian working class was very close in outlook and habits to the peasantry. It had, he asserted 'firm roots' in the peasantry and was connected with it not only through the general environment and atmosphere but through its origin. This applied, he argued, to actual proletarian writers, not just the so-called fellow-travellers.[61] The party could not afford to stand for one single tendency in art. Its policy was to maintain relations with all pro-revolutionary tendencies.[62] He accused the *On Guard* group of being hostile to the use of specialists by the Soviet government in other spheres. In conclusion, he claimed that he was speaking not only for himself but for many fledgling literary tendencies, 'in the name of virtually all of young Soviet literature. This literature is moving towards us.'[63] This was the fundamental point in Voronsky's speech. To ignore it would, he said, be a great mistake.

Vardin was able to launch a vigorous attack on Voronsky's assumptions. Where was this movement towards the party? Did not Voronsky stand in 1924 on exactly the same spot he had stood on in 1921?[64] The situation had changed in the meantime. The political danger of restoration had increased by leaps and bounds. It was absolutely essential, he argued, that all forms of bourgeois ideology should be nipped in the bud. He took his stand on unashamedly political principles.[65] The literary question was a part of the wider political crisis. The fellow-travellers defended by Voronsky were a threat to the party. He quoted the recently published words of Pilniak that he was not a communist, that he did not recognise that he ought to be a communist and that he was 'For the communists to the extent that they are for Russia.' This, Vardin claimed with no uncharacteristic inaccuracy, was how Miliukov viewed the issue.[66] Vardin's answer to the problem was that the 'The Party should supervise VAPP [the All-Russian Association of Proletarian Writers – the group that published the journal *On Guard*] and all the non-party writers should be grouped around it.'[67]

Vardin's position was much more forcefully expressed than Voronsky's and, indeed, was based on attacking the anomaly whereby the party, having established a line in most other important spheres – usually along lines of party leadership and infiltration of communist cells as proposed for literature by Vardin – was reluctant to take analogous steps in the cultural sphere. For the first time in such arguments, both sides claimed the mantle of Lenin, who had died four months earlier. Iakovlev, who had actually been the mouthpiece of Lenin on other occasions – notably in the Proletkul't affair when he had drafted an article over his own name which was, in reality, a summary of Lenin's views written with the latter's approval[68] – intervened to support the status quo. The danger of the On Guardists' position, he argued, was that they might drive talented writers away from the party and the Soviet government, thereby stifling the growth of a healthy new literature. 'Comrade Lenin', he argued, 'had always fought against this path and it is our duty not to distort the Leninist line.'[69] Perhaps having foreseen this ploy, Vardin had himself claimed Lenin's authority for vigilance against bourgeois influence on the

masses. In particular, he had referred to recently published reminiscences of Lenin by Klara Zetkin from which Vardin extracted Leninist
sanction for the view that, while it might be permissible for leading
party figures to read and enjoy bourgeois writers, it was a very
different matter when it came to the masses. No doubt, Vardin
asserted, everyone taking part in the discussion had read White
literature but 'we have an appropriate immunity'. The masses did
not. 'When Comrade Kamenev reads Ehrenburg, that is one thing;
when a student from the Sverdlov University, particularly in the
current conditions of weariness and scepticism, reads this literature
that is something quite, quite different.'[70]

Indeed, both parties had no little grounds for rooting their outlook
in Lenin's ideas. As we have already seen, Lenin had simultaneously
defended the extensive use of specialists in key areas, including
literature, and warned against bourgeois influence. In particular,
the economic concessions of NEP were accompanied by increased
ideological vigilance. The insitutional revolution of those years,
especially 1922, was directed to achieving this effect. Lenin's legacy
in this respect was certainly ambiguous, due to at least in part to the
fact that he himself had been steering a middle course between the
militants and the conciliators in his own time.

In effect, his successors ended up acting in a similar fashion,
although the resolutions passed by the 1924 conference and by
the Central Committee in 1925 show significant differences. The
resolution of the 1924 conference, drafted by Iakovlev, was unequivocal in its defence of the fellow-travellers and condemned the *On
Guard* group by name. It even repeated charges Iakovlev had made
in his speech at the meeting that the On Guardists were infected with
the same faults of Bohemianism, sectarianism and pessimism they
criticised in others[71] and that, through incorrect understanding of the
fellow-travellers, they were driving them away and making the task
of creating proletarian writers more difficult. The final clause of the
resolution, however, illustrated once more the natural reflex towards
greater and greater party control that we have seen to have been
constantly at work since 1920. The first half of the clause, which is
frequently quoted, asserted that 'no single literary tendency or group
can or should speak in the name of the party'. The second half, more
often than not overlooked, called for regular meetings of writers and
communist critics to be organised under the auspices of the Central
Committee through its Press Section and that there should be 'more
systematic supervision of the work of party members and of party

he was speaking not only for himself but for many fled
tendencies, 'in the name of virtually all of young Sovi
This literature is moving towards us.'[63] This was the f
point in Voronsky's speech. To ignore it would, he said,
mistake.

Vardin was able to launch a vigorous attack on Voronsky's
assumptions. Where was this movement towards the party? Did not
Voronsky stand in 1924 on exactly the same spot he had stood on in
1921?[64] The situation had changed in the meantime. The political
danger of restoration had increased by leaps and bounds. It was
absolutely essential, he argued, that all forms of bourgeois ideology
should be nipped in the bud. He took his stand on unashamedly
political principles.[65] The literary question was a part of the wider
political crisis. The fellow-travellers defended by Voronsky were a
threat to the party. He quoted the recently published words of Pilniak
that he was not a communist, that he did not recognise that he ought
to be a communist and that he was 'For the communists to the extent
that they are for Russia.' This, Vardin claimed with no uncharacteristic
inaccuracy, was how Miliukov viewed the issue.[66] Vardin's answer to
the problem was that the 'The Party should supervise VAPP [the
All-Russian Association of Proletarian Writers – the group that
published the journal *On Guard*] and all the non-party writers should
be grouped around it.'[67]

Vardin's position was much more forcefully expressed than
Voronsky's and, indeed, was based on attacking the anomaly whereby
the party, having established a line in most other important spheres –
usually along lines of party leadership and infiltration of communist
cells as proposed for literature by Vardin – was reluctant to take
analogous steps in the cultural sphere. For the first time in such
arguments, both sides claimed the mantle of Lenin, who had died
four months earlier. Iakovlev, who had actually been the mouthpiece
of Lenin on other occasions – notably in the Proletkul't affair when
he had drafted an article over his own name which was, in reality, a
summary of Lenin's views written with the latter's approval[68] –
intervened to support the status quo. The danger of the On Guardists'
position, he argued, was that they might drive talented writers away
from the party and the Soviet government, thereby stifling the growth
of a healthy new literature. 'Comrade Lenin', he argued, 'had always
fought against this path and it is our duty not to distort the Leninist
line.'[69] Perhaps having foreseen this ploy, Vardin had himself claimed
Lenin's authority for vigilance against bourgeois influence on the

masses. In particular, he had referred to recently published reminiscences of Lenin by Klara Zetkin from which Vardin extracted Leninist sanction for the view that, while it might be permissible for leading party figures to read and enjoy bourgeois writers, it was a very different matter when it came to the masses. No doubt, Vardin asserted, everyone taking part in the discussion had read White literature but 'we have an appropriate immunity'. The masses did not. 'When Comrade Kamenev reads Ehrenburg, that is one thing; when a student from the Sverdlov University, particularly in the current conditions of weariness and scepticism, reads this literature that is something quite, quite different.'[70]

Indeed, both parties had no little grounds for rooting their outlook in Lenin's ideas. As we have already seen, Lenin had simultaneously defended the extensive use of specialists in key areas, including literature, and warned against bourgeois influence. In particular, the economic concessions of NEP were accompanied by increased ideological vigilance. The insitutional revolution of those years, especially 1922, was directed to achieving this effect. Lenin's legacy in this respect was certainly ambiguous, due to at least in part to the fact that he himself had been steering a middle course between the militants and the conciliators in his own time.

In effect, his successors ended up acting in a similar fashion, although the resolutions passed by the 1924 conference and by the Central Committee in 1925 show significant differences. The resolution of the 1924 conference, drafted by Iakovlev, was unequivocal in its defence of the fellow-travellers and condemned the *On Guard* group by name. It even repeated charges Iakovlev had made in his speech at the meeting that the On Guardists were infected with the same faults of Bohemianism, sectarianism and pessimism they criticised in others[71] and that, through incorrect understanding of the fellow-travellers, they were driving them away and making the task of creating proletarian writers more difficult. The final clause of the resolution, however, illustrated once more the natural reflex towards greater and greater party control that we have seen to have been constantly at work since 1920. The first half of the clause, which is frequently quoted, asserted that 'no single literary tendency or group can or should speak in the name of the party'. The second half, more often than not overlooked, called for regular meetings of writers and communist critics to be organised under the auspices of the Central Committee through its Press Section and that there should be 'more systematic supervision of the work of party members and of party press organs in the field of belles lettres'.[72] The main thrust of the resolution represented a major rebuff to the On Guardists. This was emphasised by the publication, together with the conference proceedings, of a letter signed by many prominent writers, mostly from among the fellow-travellers and including Esenin, Pilniak, Mandelstam, Babel, Voloshin, Kataev and Zoshchenko, which protested against the 'sweeping attacks' on them and of the tone of 'journals such as *On Guard*' which were 'knowingly biased and untrue' in their approach to 'our literary work'.[73]

Interestingly, among the signatories of the protest were the Proletkul't renegades Gerasimov and Kirillov, once more fulfilling their function as officially approved proletarian artists being used to bring a more independent-minded group to heel. This reminds us of the complexity, sometimes overlooked, in relations between various proletarian factions. The Bogdanovites, the party proletarians like Gerasimov and Kirillov, the On Guardists and the rump of Proletkul't all occupied substantially different positions on key issues and had complex relations with each other. They cannot be lumped together simply as an undifferentiated 'proletarian' group.

The aggressive tone of the On Guardists, who had not hesitated to insult their opponents, including Bukharin and Trotsky, and even to heckle their speeches – though this last was a somewhat hazardous procedure and they often came off worse in such exchanges, especially where the quick-witted Trotsky was concerned[74] – suggested that they would not accept their defeat meekly. After the conference they made yet greater efforts to get the party to recognise them as the hegemonic literary/cultural group.

A particularly energetic example of this continued aggression is shown in the resolution on Vardin's speech at the First All-Union Conference of Proletarian Writers, which was published in *Pravda* on 1 February 1925. Trotsky was accused of sharing Menshevik views in underestimating the power of the proletariat. Only resolute revolutionary activity in the cultural field would achieve proletarian victory. In the words of the resolution:

Without its own independent class culture, without its own literature, the proletariat cannot preserve its hegemony over the peasantry. Not only in the political and economic field but also in the cultural field the working class must draw non-proletarian layers to itself. But it resolves this task on condition that it promotes in the cultural field exactly that revolution which it has promoted in the economic and political field.[75]

If anything, the tone of proletarian chauvinism rang out even more strongly. The resolution ended by claiming that bourgeois culture throughout the world was undergoing a crisis of collapse and decay while, in the three years since the end of the civil war, Soviet proletarian literature had been growing by leaps and bounds. As a result, the resolution concluded:

> Proletarian literature in the Soviet Union sets itself a single goal – to serve the cause of world proletarian victory and to struggle mercilessly with all enemies of the proletarian revolution. Proletarian literature will defeat bourgeois literature because proletarian revolution inevitably annihilates capitalism.[76]

Such appeals were likely to strike a much more resonant cord amongst party proletarian militants than arguments based on reminding them of their own fundamental weakness.

The 1925 resolution of the Central Committee, drafted this time by Bukharin rather than Iakovlev, returned to some of the same themes as the 1924 one. At its heart, not surprisingly, was the question of correct relations between party and writers and, at much greater length than in the earlier document, a discussion of the theoretical base of party policy. What were the main principles enshrined in this resolution? Its emphasis on the leading role of the party, the goal of proletarian intellectual hegemony and the need, for the time being, to collaborate with non-proletarian groups, meant that all those involved could claim that it supported their point of view. For the proletarians there were reassuring phrases about class struggle taking place in art, proletarian writers as the future ideological leaders of Soviet literature, the impossibility of a neutral art, the leadership role of the proletariat in the intellectual sphere and even the need for it to capture new fields by establishing the domination of dialectical materialism in the natural sciences. In particular, the proletarians could take heart from the fact there was no explicit criticism of *On Guard* by name as there had been in 1924. For the more conciliatory minded there was a reminder that the essence of party policy was that wavering parts of the population – notably the peasantry – should be won over from the bourgeoisie rather than coerced and that the period of breaking society up had gone. In particular, the decree explicitly defended some of the fellow-travellers and repeated the warning against crude attacks on them. There was also an unambiguous reassertion that the party could not give its support to just one tendency or school. There should, it said, be free competition between all the tendencies deemed to be ideologically acceptable.[77]

Which of the groups was correct in drawing comfort from the resolution? For the fellow-travellers there was certainly the promise of a breathing space, but the proletarians could expect to grow in importance as the fellow-travellers were 'won over'. Although various shortcomings, notably their 'communist arrogance' (*komchvanstva*), were criticised, the absence of a direct condemnation could be seen as a kind of victory for the proletarians. But a closer reading of the complex document, in which so many themes, some of them almost contradictory, are fascinatingly interwoven, suggests, particularly in the light of the other developments we have been examining, that in the longer run neither side had a particularly bright future. If anything, the fundamental weight of the document is towards the assertion of greater and more effective supervision of intellectual life by the party leadership. Evidence for this within the document is plentiful. The central force mediating the literary and ideological processes identified in the document was, not surprisingly, the party. Amongst other things, it was to 'weed out anti-proletarian and anti-revolutionary elements'; 'fight against' new forms of bourgeois ideology such as *Smena vekh* which were beginning to form; 'assist' the emergence of proletarian writers; 'combat' communist arrogance at one extreme and underestimation of the need for proletarian hegemony at the other; nurture a responsible attitude towards the culture of the past; 'supervise literature as a whole, and point out' to all those working in the literary field the need for a correct demarcation of the functions of critics and writers. True, it also called for an end to 'self-appointed and incompetent interference in literary affairs' but, as the rest of the clause shows, the criticism was of the incompetence not the interfering because it called for a more careful vetting of people to work in the areas of supervision of the press in order to 'facilitate more correct, useful and tactful supervision of our literature'. Added to this, tasks allocated to 'the proletariat' in the resolution, such as 'preserving, strengthening and always broadening its leadership' and 'establishing a similar position in a whole series of new sectors on the ideological front', were, implicitly, tasks for the party, which exercised the dictatorship on behalf of the proletariat.

Weighed against this extremely active role for the party, the assertion (echoing Trotsky's phrase in *Literature and Revolution*[78]) 'communist criticism must banish from its everyday usage the tone of literary command' and that it would only prevail through its 'intellectual pre-eminence' rang rather hollow. In essence, the resolution was a blueprint for greater party intervention in all areas of intellectual life and for greater attention to be paid to this task which, it was pointed out, was 'infinitely more complex' than any other currently facing the proletariat. The unequivocal goal was proletarian intellectual hegemony. Concessions were only to be contemplated for as long as they were necessary. The specific attacks on *Smena vekh* were a clear example of what happened once tactical toleration of a specific group had run its course. The fact that in the document *Smena vekh* was described as part of the fellow-travelling movement and that it should be 'unmasked' showed what was likely to happen to fellow-travelling groups whose *rapprochement* with the party was not conducted with due speed. Indeed, the resolution itself differentiated between tactics of 'merciless struggle' against incorrigible opponents and those of patience with respect to those who could and would come closer to the proletariat. Beyond that, disagreement was tactical over where exactly the line should be drawn and how quickly the process of establishing hegemony should be achieved. Implicitly, the party was restrained, not by any semi-liberal scruples of vestigial tolerance, but only by the practical assessment of its strength and of what it had the power to achieve.

Considerations drawn from the circumstances surrounding the drawing up and the publication of the resolution point in the same direction. After all this was a resolution of the Central Committee and had been arrived at through the activities of Politburo appointees and had included some of its members. The 1924 resolution was much less authoritative and had been accompanied by public discussion of the issues by leading representatives of the conflicting party tendencies. The 1925 decision was reached behind closed doors and the only semi-open discussion of its principles had been at party conferences and congresses. In addition, the main publication of the decree and materials surrounding it came in the more authoritative form of a symposium entitled, somewhat unpromisingly, *Problems of Culture under the Dictatorship of the Proletariat* (*Voprosy kul'tury pri diktature proletariata*). The book included a number of articles, written by Bukharin, Iakovlev, Voronsky and Vareikis, supporting the positions outlined in the resolution. In many respects these articles went further than the resolution itself, particularly when it came to criticising the On Guardists whom Vareikis accused of being Trots-kyist in failing to support the necessity of a period of collaboration between the peasantry and the working class. They were also accused of failing to appreciate the inevitability 'in a peasant country like the USSR' of the presence, for a comparatively long period, of the fellow-travellers. This period was not to be measured in months, he said, but in years.[79] As a concession to the conflicting points of view the proceedings of the 1924 conference and the resolution on Vardin's speech at the First All-Union Conference of Proletarian Writers were reprinted *in toto*, but no additional material, apart from that emanating from the Central Committee itself, was included. Interestingly, the volume began with a facsimile reproduction of Lenin's copy of Pletnev's 1922 article on Proletkul't with Lenin's marginal comments. Since the handwriting was difficult to read as well as being cryptic at times, a printed version was also included. This document is familiar today, but its publication for the first time was very damaging to the proletarians. In one of the most outspoken, but by no means untypical comments, Lenin had underlined Pletnev's assertion that the first steps to create proletarian culture 'must be undertaken by the proletariat itself' and written the word 'rubbish' in the margin. The foreword to the book also pointed out that the article by Iakovlev on Proletkul't which was included in the collection had been written in the spirit of these marginal comments which Lenin had given to Iakovlev. Lenin, it was asserted, had looked over and edited Iakovlev's draft.[80] The aim of the collection as a whole, the editor said, was 'to acquaint the reader with basic materials characterising and criticising the recent deviation from the correct Leninist line on this question'. The text of the Central Committee resolution was said to 'define the party line in the literary sphere'.[81] Clearly, the hand of Bukharin could be seen behind this publication. The gloss on the issue was heavily tilted in the direction of his views. At the same time there was a significant coarsening of the argument and loading of the dice, phenomena gaining ground rapidly in the party at this time. The publication of Lenin's marginal notes was in itself something of a low blow, since Lenin himself had not wished them to be published. Significantly, none of Lenin's published works was included in the collection, presumably because none of them fitted, even though the foreword claims that Lenin had made his views on the question absolutely clear in a whole string of speeches and articles. After a certain amount of hesitation, the foreword said, the editors had decided to publish Lenin's notes with the aim of providing 'a precise clarification of the truth'.[82] The widening of the argument to include an attack on Trotskyism, plus the expanding net of guilt by association which lumped together Trotsky, Bogdanov, Pletnev and the On Guardists, suggested something more than 'precise clarification of the truth', was in the editors' minds.

Bukharin and Voronsky were no doubt of the opinion that they had won a famous victory on the cultural front. Certainly, the tone of the articles in *Problems of Culture under the Dictatorship of the Proletariat* would suggest that this was the case. As we have seen, there are substantial reasons for thinking, on the evidence of the resolution itself, that the position was not as clear cut as they were making out. The On Guardists, despite having undoubtedly suffered a shock, were not seriously damaged and regrouped themselves very rapidly.[83] In only two years' time, it was Voronsky who was being accused of Trotskyism and removed from his post as editor of *Red Virgin Soil*. Two years after that, Bukharin also fell from the heights, though chiefly for reasons only loosely connected with cultural policy. Both suffered from the same kind of crude manipulation and slanderous accusations they had been prepared to use against *Smena vekh* at one end of the spectrum and the On Guardists at the other. A full discussion of the processes surrounding these events in the late 1920s are beyond the scope of the present work, but one major current they had underestimated had already begun to make itself felt. An increasingly substantial group of unsophisticated and self-confident and semi-educated militants from the grass roots were beginning to make an impact. The final section of this chapter looks at other areas in which cultural politics was evolving in the middle years of the decade.

CULTURAL POLICY IN PRACTICE: THE WORKERS' FACULTIES (*RABFAKY*)

It is very hard to say what effect these debates about theory and the ensuing statement of party policy on literature had on the evolution of cultural policy as a whole. Certainly they provided a blueprint for greater central control and show the desire of the authorities to achieve it, but in many ways the basic underlying tendencies – namely the equating of cultural revolution with surrogate class war; its instrumental function in promoting the political stability of the regime and the party; the economic and productionist roots of many of the policies; the associated absence of any overriding theoretical principles, existing alongside very considerable achievements of providing basic education for wide areas of society who had never benefited from it before, and notable achievements of high culture – remained as much in evidence as ever, as did the continuing encroachment of administrative control in areas that had so far eluded it. The work of the various cultural institutions – Education Ministry, censorship, party schools, publishing houses, major newspapers, cultural trade unions and equivalent and so on – continued to be areas where a great deal of factionalism continued, not only in the sense of there being members of the retinue of leading contenders in the struggle for control of the party in most of these institutions but also that there were many disagreements on more mundane issues. How should adult education be conducted? Who was fit to be considered a fellow-traveller and who was an open counter-revolutionary? Was a particular work worthy of being published, exhibited or projected? Who should be held responsible if items transgressing the rules were published? On questions such as these, battles raged spontaneously. Pronouncements from the centre, such as the statement of policy on literature, were not treated as clear instructions – indeed, many of them were so ambiguous and contradictory that they could not be so treated – but as ammunition to be used by the factions in their conflicts with one another and, as a consequence, they were often subject to widely differing interpretations. Of course, most of these institutions were staffed by party members and these debates, and the ensuing power of decision-making, were increasingly confined to party circles. By the middle of the decade the relationship of the party to the outside world in matters of culture had resulted in the party holding the initiative. Within the party, factionalism was still rife and the indecisiveness and hollowness (in the sense that crucial issues of the content of culture were still glossed over) of party policy on culture were fully reflected in this state of affairs.

The crucibles in which the attitudes of many ordinary party members on cultural matters were being formed were the network of specifically Soviet institutions that were set up in parallel with or in place of the traditional cultural-educational institutions of Russia. We have already seen one of the earliest, the Sverdlov University. In addition to it a series of Proletarian Universities, which amounted to little more than elementary propaganda centres, also existed during the civil war. Once this war was over, more permanent and more ambitious institutions appeared. Party schools, such as the Zinoviev University in Petrograd, were regularised. At the highest level, a Socialist Academy was set up to foster the development of Marxist ideas. An Institute of Red Professors, consisting of personnel almost identical with those of the Socialist Academy, was set up in 1921 to train high-level Marxist teachers for higher education. A whole chain of Marxist organisations and research institutes, in the social and natural sciences in particular, began to emerge.[84] Most of these organisations show the dual nature of party cultural and intellectual life at this time in that they wielded increasingly authoritarian powers with respect to the non-party survivors in their field and were thereby agents of party encroachment, but, at the same time, they were battlegrounds for different interpretations of Marxism, the fundamental assumption of each school being that there was only one truth and that they possessed it. Associated with this was the involvement of leading figures in these organisations in the factional disputes of the leadership during the struggle for the succession in the mid 1920s. While the implications of these energetic disputes were significant they tended to be confined to a small party élite. Assumptions that, once revealed, Marxist truth would have a compelling attraction for all sincere intellectuals and scholars had proved to be naïve and illusory and mass conversions of formerly liberal and non-party intellectuals did not occur. The few who did become sympathisers, such as A. Tolstoi, N. Gredeskul' and P. Sakulin, were heavily publicised, but the roots of *rapprochement* were more akin to *Smena vekh* and national Bolshevik types of reasoning rather than endorsements of the Marxist world view. Marxists who had not been Bolsheviks were more likely to be found in these new Soviet institutions plus a few revolutionaries of different schools altogether, such as Kondrat'ev and Chaianov, a situation that did not make for harmony within them.[85] Thus, they tended to be marked by vigorous internal argument and an increasingly hostile and overbearing attitude to remaining non-Marxists, which grew in part out of the internal argument as each faction sought to show that it was not soft on non-communism.

If the atmosphere at the top of the intellectual-educational scale was one of intense debate, and these arguments were a breeding ground and arena of conflict for contending party views, they were not the only areas in which the struggle for cultural domination was being conducted. At lower levels the virtues and weaknesses of the a letter to André Breton he wrote that his defence of eclecticism in art might surprise those, such as Breton, who know that 'I'm scarcely a supporter of eclecticism.' He explained, echoing an open letter of the same time in which he asserted emphatically that 'the artist should be unwaveringly faithful to his inner self',[48] that in his view Marxism should not associate itself with a single artistic school but should have 'a critical and friendly attitude to different schools. But each artistic school must be faithful to itself.'[49] His experiences of literary politics in Russia in the 1920s was, no doubt, reflected in these later views. Although the emphasis is different, his contribution to these debates shows a greater respect for artists and artistic life than was shown by others, particularly in the 'proletarian' faction in these debates.

The growth in importance of cultural questions for the party, reflected in Lenin's last writings, continued after his death. In 1924 and 1925 important debates about it were conducted and decisions were made at the highest level. The main focus of these debates was literature and the precipitating cause was the rise of a militant faction of proletarian writers who increasingly claimed to speak, not just for themselves, but as the only authentic mouthpiece of the class. It followed from this that they should also claim to speak in the name of the party since it was supposed to be the instrument of true working-class consciousness. The proletarian writers seem to have spent considerably more time pursuing their political and institutional goals than they did in producing works of literature. None of their writing is remembered today but the effects of their institutional battles can still be traced. In particular, the aggression with which they pursued their aims and their immense, strident self-confidence created a major wound in the already divided Soviet cultural world. It would be wrong to attribute the increasing bitterness and, eventually, murderousness of Soviet cultural politics solely to them, but they did more than their share in bringing about this degradation of relations.

The challenge that they posed and the contempt and violence with which they pursued their aims provoked a major division of opinion within the party.[50] The central issue was, could there be an authentic, purely proletarian, culture as the proletarian faction understood it? Arrayed against them was an impressive team of often otherwise divided party leaders. For various reasons Bukharin, Trotsky and Lunacharsky fought against the pretensions of the proletarians as had Lenin before them. All of them had serious reservations about the concept of proletarian culture, at least in the short term.[51]

party's approach to culture can be found in the quintessentially Soviet innovations, the Workers' Faculties (*rabfaky*) and in other less 'élitist' organisations that were founded by people drawn to the revolution. An examination of these areas will help to illuminate some of the forces at work at a rather more grass-roots level.

Nothing exemplifies the many aspects, positive and negative, of Bolshevik cultural policy in this period better than the Workers' Faculties set up to provide crash-courses to enable poorly educated workers to enter higher education. They combined the highest idealism, opening the way to a first-class education for people who belonged to sections of the population who had not been able to contemplate such a possibility, with a short-term manipulative and instrumental function of being a Trojan horse for party objectives, notably the kindling of class struggle and the battle for complete institutional control in higher education. These two aims were contradictory in that, as a result of the development of the latter, the quality of education tended to fall rapidly making it difficult to achieve the former.

Precise figures for the number of students who took advantage of the Workers' Faculties, or even for the number of Workers' Faculties themselves, have not been established, but there is no doubt about the order of magnitude of these figures or about the rhythm of growth and contraction that they underwent from their origin to the end of the 1920s. Figures from the period show that in the 1920–1 academic year there were 54 Workers' Faculties with 18,005 students, rising to 85 with just over 27,000 students in 1921–2. In subsequent years the figure for students varied from around 40,000 to 48,000, the number of institutions fluctuating between 108 and 130. From 1928 there was a very sharp increase in both and, although the figures become even less reliable and the reality they purport to represent even more impenetrable, there can be no doubt that there was mass expansion with possibly as many as 1000 institutions with over a third of a million students in the peak year of 1932–3, after which they underwent a steady decline.[86] As far as social composition is concerned all sources agree that the overwhelming majority of students claimed to be workers or peasants and that about four-fifths of them were male. Some doubt is cast on the former figure by the frequency of complaints that students of concealed 'intelligentsia' or other privileged background were using Workers' Faculties as a back door into higher education. There is no evidence that such students were more than a minority though they may have had a disproportionately large place in Workers' Faculties compared to their size in the population as a whole. With respect to regional distribution, figures for 1928–9 show Workers' Faculties to have existed in eight republics, though out of the total of 176 no less than 155 were in Russia and the Ukraine.[87]

Clearly, the actual situation varied considerably between these institutions. A number of full and graphic accounts of life in them show, none the less, a number of fairly widespread similarities in the early years. Students had to put up with the most severe material shortages; they made considerable sacrifices to attend; relations with conventional university staff and students were variable but were most often bad; Workers' Faculty students were often the agents of increasing party and state control in higher education; the standard of education achieved was not high; their academic resources were inferior to those of the regular institutions of higher education; the motivation and revolutionary idealism of Workers' Faculty students was markedly greater.

The roots of these contrasts lie in the fact that Workers' Faculties were one of the most important channels drawing a class of people into higher education who had previously been almost totally excluded from it. The main constituency was workers and peasants, with the emphasis among the latter being placed on poor peasants. Substantial numbers of poor peasants were, indeed, drawn into them but they represented only 5–10 per cent of the total intake in Siberia, for instance, in the mid 1920s.[88] This feature of opening up the Workers' Faculties was ensured through the system of recruitment. In order to be admitted it was necessary for a candidate to be proposed by a local party or trade union branch. Typically, only 10–20 per cent of students would be outside the party and the Komsomol.[89] This in itself was no guarantee of admission, only a necessary precondition for an application to be accepted, for applicants outweighed the number of places available. This was true of full-time and evening courses. The more outlying Workers' Faculties, despite being small, drew their intakes from enormous areas and successful applicants often had hazardous journeys in order to reach them, particularly in the first years of their operation. On arrival their conditions of life would hardly be improved. Shortages of basic comforts and commodities were commonplace. One of the hostels in Leningrad was in a deplorable state. There were doors missing, windows without glass, no water, washrooms or lighting. All its inhabitants could expect from it, in 1921, was walls and a roof.[90] In the provinces comparable conditions could be found. Heating was a particular source of complaint and institutions reported that in the middle of the decade it was still the case that people had to wear their overcoats in the classroom during winter.[91] Overcrowding of rooms, in hostels and those in which teaching took place, was also common. Stipends were barely adequate to sustain life. According to a government report into conditions in the Siberian Workers' Faculties in the mid 1920s, almost a half of the stipend of 20 roubles a month was taken up by payments for lunch. In the morning and evening the students took only bread and water, a lucky 10 per cent being able to enjoy tea and, for a very few, the luxury of sugar. The bread cost 3–5 roubles a month, rent for the hostel 2–2.50 roubles per month. This left some 4–5 roubles for everything else. Under such circumstances reduced price tickets for theatres and cinema were useless, though many students took advantage of opportunities to obtain free tickets when they could.[92] As far as teaching was concerned, all the essentials – books, scientific equipment, dedicated teaching staff, adequate accommodation – were either lacking or in desperately short supply. Workers' Faculties often had to share their teaching personnel with local higher-education establishments and it was said that such teachers did not like working in the Workers' Faculty.[93] From the authorities' point of view this arrangement was far from satisfactory in that it gave non-party members – few established higher-education teachers being in the party – some influence in what were intended to be class-based institutions. The reticence of official statistics over teaching personnel is probably a result of this. The occasional glimpses that do exist confirm this, particularly if we assume that figures released were intended to be those showing the highest degree of party membership. Thus, to take the Siberian inquiry again, about two-thirds of social science teachers were party members in 1926–7. Since the term 'social science' tends to be a euphemism for 'Marxism' and party ideology, one is left with the conclusion that one-third of teachers of party policy were not members of the party.[94] It would also appear to be reasonable to assume that in technical subjects and basic education the presence of the party was even less marked, showing once again the consequences of the gap between those with expertise and those who were favourable to the party.

In Darwinian terms, the toughness of conditions seems to have encouraged the survival of a particularly hardy species of student, full of motivation to overcome the obstacles. The 'well-known antagonism', as one academic administrator put it, between the Workers' Faculties and the traditional higher-education institutions to which they were attached was also a school in the harsh realities of class struggle.[95] From the political point of view the Workers' Faculties had come into existence as the government's weapon to carry out the 'proletarianisation' of higher education following the reverses of 1918 and the adoption thereafter of 'salami tactics'. There can be little doubt that in this respect they succeeded. All existing accounts – official, eyewitness and *émigré* – agree that the Workers' Faculties were the advance guard of the party in its task of controlling higher education. Throughout the 1920s they grew in aggression and power. As such they are an excellent example of the erosion of traditional institutions that was taking place in Soviet intellectual life during NEP under the guise of toleration. A particularly graphic source for this is provided by accounts of the Workers' Faculty in the Leningrad Technological Institute. Accounts by the head of the institute, the head of the Workers' Faculty and a group of its students, published in 1928, give a very full picture of this process at work.

The decision to set up the Faculty was said to have come from the Oblprofsovet (the regional trade union committee) in 1919, at which time it was attached to the University.[96] It was only in autumn 1921 that it was established in the Institute, and it continued to hover between the two establishments until 1923.[97] The first stage of its life consisted purely of the struggle to exist, in particular to compete for already scare resources with the well-established Institute. In the words of the head of the Workers' Faculty 'A drawing table, standing on its legs, served as a desk, and the same table, lying on its side, served as our bench. Such were conditions during the first years of teaching activity within the walls of a splendidly equipped institution of higher education.'[98] The appalling conditions in the hostel at this time have already been referred to. The existence of such glaring inequality within the same institution could only lead to tension. In the first place, finding space for it continued to be difficult and even as late as 1926 it was rehoused yet again in a building separate from the main Institute.[99] Only in 1927, according to its director, M. A. Birzovich, did it have decent, permanent premises of its own. The struggle to obtain qualified teachers was equally difficult as the main body of the academic staff of the Institute were indifferent or hostile to the new faculty. It thus fitted in with existing divisions in the Institute, dating from the first attempts of the Soviet government at reforming higher education, divisions described by the rector as being between the representatives of the teaching staff and the old-style students on one hand and the employees of Narkompros and left-wing students on the other.[100] The evolution of the Workers' Faculty, which grew from an original 300 members to 1700 by 1927,[101] and which produced annually 100–200 graduates of whom 40–50 per cent went on to study in the Institute proper, gave weight to the government-oriented elements in the Institute. According to its students the workers' faculty was the 'bridgehead of proletarianis-ation' in the Institute.[102]

The mid 1920s appear to have been important years in establishing Soviet goals. The phases in which this occurred in the Institute fit in with wider national patterns. Broadly speaking there were three stages. Up to about 1920 the Institute, as has already been mentioned, continued to function 'from inertia'[103] in the midst of appalling shortages and difficulties but in the absence of direct political intervention. In 1921 new government provisions for elections enabled the establishing of a halfway house, in that less-hostile people, subject to government confirmation, were elected to leading administrative positions in the institute. According to the Rector, L. N. Veller, a beneficiary of this process, this period of compromise opened up the way to fruitful, democratic co-operation between teachers, students, the faculties and the administration.[104] It remained possible for institutions to frustrate or modify reform plans of the government, which were increasingly geared to adapting higher education to the needs of the economy. For example, the attempt to reduce technical courses to three years met opposition and a compromise figure of four and a half years was agreed, although, in actual fact, 'students, as before, continue to stay at the Institute for seven years or more'.[105] The period in which this balance of forces was maintained was very short at the Institute. By 1924, conflict, mainly emanating from the students, between traditional and proletarian factions was becoming increasingly acute. In Veller's words, there was a steady growth of influence of the proletarian students in all the student organisations. In 1924, he says, 'many' of the old student body with weak academic records were thrown out. In the light of 'the struggle between the old and new student bodies this is perfectly explicable', he continued, pointing out, however, that academic activities of all students were rather weak in 1924.[106] This oblique reference to a submerged purge of bourgeois elements in the Institute is confirmed by the accounts of members of the workers' faculty. The collective account by students talks of 'actual hegemony' in all the commissions of the mechanical engineering faculty falling into the hands of proletarian students in 1923–4.[107] According to the same source, by the beginning of the 1926–7 academic year 60 per cent of students at the Institute belonged to trade unions, rising to 71.8 per cent by the end of the year. Sixty-five per cent of students were said to be of worker–peasant origin.[108]

By 1925 the *rabfaky* had made a major impact on the higher-education system. Figures for the 1925 intake show that *rabfak* graduates made up two-thirds of entrants in science and technology courses and half for economics. They represented about a quarter of the agriculture intake, a fifth for medicine. Only in education and arts were they weakly represented with 15 and 6 per cent respectively.[109] In addition, many other *rabfak* students who followed shorter courses or who did not make the grade for higher education (about two-thirds of those attending *rabfaky* did not graduate or go on to higher education)[110] provided a significant leaven in other party, state and social organisations. Their impact can only be guessed at, but it must have been considerable, if only because their motivation had to be high. Competition to get in was fierce (only about a third of worker applicants were accepted in the mid 1920s)[111] and drop-out rates high. In many cases political idealism pulled candidates through. Comments by students at the Omsk *rabfak* illustrate this. One commented: 'I want to be an engineer and devote all my powers to the socialist construction front, since I am a worker and production is dear to me.' Another wanted, in a neo-populist way, to help 'with the solution of peasant problems in the ordering and perfecting of the rural economy', because she was herself from a peasant background. Another young woman wanted to be a lawyer in order to be 'a defender of the rights of women, in view of the backwardness of our women and their lack of skill in defending their rights'.[112] There seems little reason to disagree substantially with another former student, writing in 1934, who said 'the *rabfak* developed a hatred of capitalism and, instead of a spontaneous, rebellious mentality, forged a Marxist–Leninist world view. It raised me up to an understanding of the historic task of our revolution.'[113] In other words, the *rabfaky* were building an important core of activists devoted to socialist reconstruction, nurturing a hatred of the old élite (especially specialists and the remnants of the old intelligentsia) and were completely unaffected by liberal scruples. While we can exaggerate their importance, given the fact only some 43,000 workers and peasants graduated from them throughout the 1920s,[114] they formed an élite within the new élite and appear to have exerted an influence beyond mere numbers. In many ways, the *rabfaky* were a characteristically 'Stalinist' institution producing 'mini-Stalins' and it is no surprise that they expanded considerably in the 1930s. At this level, refined arguments between old Bolsheviks about literary policy seemed very remote. In the *rabfaky* and other proletarian institutions, the instruments for 'solving' cultural problems were being perfected.[115]

Conclusion

The revolution can be great without giving up respect for other people.
Marc Chagall, *My Life*

The unmaking of the Russian intelligentsia, like its making, cannot be reduced to simple explanations. One can no more accept the pro-Bolshevik view that it was undermined because it was actively counter-revolutionary than one can agree with the reverse explanation that it was Bolshevik persecution alone that brought about its transformation. Certainly, Bolshevik policies, direct and indirect, had their place but there were other factors to bear in mind. For instance, it was the war that had brought the 'Silver Age' to an end, not the October revolution. St Petersburg was not the only cultural centre for which this was true. Vienna never recovered. Even the inter-war artistic capitals of Munich and Paris took time to re-emerge after 1918. Consequently, one cannot say with any certainty what the fate of the intelligentsia might have been even if the Bolsheviks had not come to power. In addition, the state of disintegration that gave the Bolsheviks their chance was itself damaging to the intelligentsia, which was very vulnerable to economic collapse. As a result of these processes, which go much deeper into Russian society than the conscious policy acts of the Bolsheviks, the conditions that had brought the intelligentsia into existence had disappeared. The late nineteenth-century conjuncture on which it depended – a brutally repressive and unrepresentative regime in a socially polarised society; the growth of new employment opportunities for the more highly educated; and, above all, the diversity of patronage and broadening of the cultural market which were consequences of the emergence of new, Westernised, bourgeois industrialists and financiers, and of a relatively affluent stratum of educated professionals – these had all been transformed. Class relations had been reversed in that it was, for once, the wealthy who were being dispossessed by the poor. The urge to 'serve the people', now that they were nominally in charge, was much less irresistible for radical intellectuals. In addition, the confiscation of the surplus from below left few resources for old-style cultural and artistic activities. Even when a new élite was allowed to emerge under NEP it was a small-scale, entrepreneurial petty-bourgeoisie, spawning a cultural of seedy cafes, pornography and imported romantic, detective and adventure films, not the high culture of the educated past. In many ways it was these underlying factors of disintegration that made Bolshevik policies of remoulding the intelligentsia possible. In other words, the crisis of the intelligentsia (like the crisis of the rest of Russian society) opened up the opportunity for the Bolsheviks, it was not purely the outcome of Bolshevik initiatives.

This is not to say that Bolshevik policies were aimed at anything other than manipulating the intelligentsia crisis in the light of Bolshevik values and goals, but this aspect of the situation has been sufficiently emphasised by both the supporters and opponents of their policies not to require further exposition here. If anything, however, it is surprising that the old intelligentsia institutions such as universities took longer to deal with than apparently more powerful institutions of tsarist society such as the banks, the army, the state bureaucracy and so on. The explanation that culture was a marginal area is only partly true. If it was marginal, why spend considerable resources on universities and other Narkompros enterprises during the height of the civil war? To understand this anomaly one also has to take into account the peculiar nature of culture. One can reorganise its institutions, but its principles, lying deep inside the minds of its bearers, are not readily and instantly transformable. Other factors also had an impact. The Bolsheviks needed specialists in all areas. Finally, one also has to bear in mind that the Bolsheviks were almost totally unprepared to govern in this area.

This is not to say, however, that Bolshevik policy was an insignificant factor in the transformation of the old intelligentsia, far from it. The interesting features of Bolshevik policy that emerge are, however, rather unexpected. In particular, contrary to impressions derived from examining military/political and economic processes in the civil war, party policy on culture moved towards *greater* organisation and control as the civil war ended. NEP in culture cannot be described as a relaxation of control or be said to be based on liberalisation. Most areas of the old intelligentsia's intellectual/political spectrum – Slavophilism, liberalism, democratic socialism, populism, anarchism and even Bolshevik heresies such as 'Bogdanovism' – had been eliminated and were not revived. The undoubtedly great cultural achievements of the 1920s should not be allowed to conceal the fact that only those deemed to be on their way over to support the party were allowed to take advantage of the limited freedom of expression that existed. Even within the party, only tendencies with highly placed protectors could thrive. In any case, the Central Committee and its agencies played an increasing role in promoting and controlling acceptable intellectual discourse which, at its broadest, is exemplified in the party journals such as *Krasnaia nov* (*Red Virgin Soil*) and *Novy mir* (*New World*). The thinning out of the number of patrons at the top in the succession struggles of the 1920s was reflected in the narrowing of the already constrained limits of toleration. Although this study does not continue into the cultural revolution of the late 1920s, the implications of it are that it is dangerous to underestimate the degree of control from above in cultural matters since that which existed in the 1920s was already considerable. In cultural affairs, NEP was not a step backwards from centralisation to liberalisation but, rather, a halfway house between the confusion, arbitrariness, inexperience and lack of attention of the civil war and the much more rigid control characteristic of the 1930s. In other words, it was a step towards 'Stalinism' in culture, not away from it. From this perspective, control in culture grew steadily from 1920 to 1928, though this growth was uneven and by no means inevitable. From this viewpoint the aberration of 1928–31/2 looks more like a consciously guided attempt to break up the partially autonomous organisations that still existed and replace them with new ones still more firmly under the control of the party. While the old 'specialists' were often restored after 1932 their organisations were not and they had much less power in literature, art, education and science than had been the case even in the late 1920s.

One might even speculate that this pattern of steady encroachment of central control and organisation replacing arbitrariness fits the wider policies of NEP more happily than the centralisation–liberalisation–centralisation cycle usually associated with civil war–NEP–Stalinism. Instead, arbitrariness–limited control–rigid control (with the 1928–32 'Stalin revolution' as the watershed between the last two) fits better in many areas. The party became more organised and centralised in the 1920s; economic planning and co-ordination developed, albeit fitfully; party power began to infiltrate the countryside; the secret police was established on a permanent basis; the power of soviets continued to decline; the 1924 constitution regularised relations over the newly formed Soviet Union which reincorporated large areas and numerous national minorities over which control had been lost during the height of the civil war. In all these areas the underlying tendencies of the NEP period were at best only ambiguously liberal and tolerant, at worst aggressively centralising. In any case, the emergence of an incipient civil society was nipped in the bud whenever it showed signs of growth. While the period might be described as 'pluralist' or 'incipiently pluralist' by comparison with the 1930s, such a picture overlooks both its narrowness even compared to the civil war (and, even more emphatically, the brief pre-civil war period of Bolshevik government) and the steady erosion of vestigial and uncharacteristic 'toleration' not only in party–society relations but also in relations within the party in these years.

However, it would be wrong to conclude with these rather bleak considerations. The example of the civil war showed that even the most unfavourable external conditions will not necessarily extinguish intellectual life. And so it proves to be in considering the legacy of the old intelligentsia. While it had been destroyed as a social entity and dispersed to the four corners of the earth, some of its finest qualities were not forgotten. The courage, self-sacrifice and moral authenticity of its best representatives have inspired many contemporary Soviet intellectuals. Recent years have shown the extent to which any return to less controlled, 'normal' conditions of intellectual life in the Soviet Union leads immediately to people picking up the threads of pre-Stalinist and even pre-revolutionary cultural traditions. Even the groupings of current Soviet intellectual debates – Slavophiles, Westernising liberals, democratic socialists, Leninists, not to mention the echoes of populism in the speeches of President Gorbachev – mirror the pre-revolutionary spectrum. How is it that this can occur after the unimaginably disastrous experience of the 1930s, the war, continued severe censorship, political imprisonment, writers' trials, forced exile and so on? In a powerful analysis of Stalinism and its impact, the Ukrainian intellectual Valentyn Moroz pointed out the persistence of spontaneous thought despite all sorts of persecution.

How then, can this never-ending spontaneous thought process be stopped if, after all, it remains alive, having undergone all stages of standardisation and sterilisation? There is a last resort – freeze it – freeze it by ice cold terror, by building a giant refrigerator for human minds.[1]

The metaphor is particularly appropriate because a refrigerator does not destroy but preserves what it contains. When the power supply is interrupted, voluntarily or involuntarily, the contents thaw out.

That is what *glasnost'* has brought about. It also shows that while one can control public expression of ideas and control access to communications, even the Stalin system did not stamp out the flow of ideas among small groups. The writings of the past; the physical survival of many who remembered and embodied the values of the past, such as Nadezhda Mandelstam, Viktor Shklovsky, Boris Pasternak; the families who cherished memories of loved ones who had been active in earlier years, such as those of Lunacharsky and Bukharin, ensured the survival of tiny time capsules of immense importance when the moment came to reopen them. Of course, much else emerged. Who would have predicted that Nagorno–Karabakh was still a source of ethnic unrest capable of catalysing appalling communal violence? The burgeoning of religious, nationalist and many other persecuted cultural phenomena are eloquent testimony to the truth of Moroz's description. This is not to say that the past has survived unchanged, but its shaping influence is still felt everywhere. While the cultural revolution discussed above soon accumulated formidable institutional control, it is clear that it also came up against formidable, but much less readily visible, limitations. Winning over minds was a much more difficult, long-drawn-out and elusive task than the militants had thought in the early years. Seizing institutional power in culture was one thing. Establishing truly hegemonic values was quite another. The dilemma of the Soviet system has been that the methods used in the former task have made the latter much more difficult to attain. The authoritarian route to democracy is always going to be hazardous and circuitous.

Notes

Notes to Chapter 1: The Making of the Russian Intelligentsia

1. Preface to *A Contribution to the Critique of Political Economy* (1859).
2. N. Riasanovsky (1969) p. 74.
3. Ibid.
4. Ibid. It should, of course, be remembered that the education referred to was only available to a tiny fraction of the population.
5. Quoted by M. Polner in the introduction to K. P. Pobedonostsev (1965) p. vii.
6. Pobedonostsev (1965) p. 1. Though the faith is very different one can discern here echoes of the Stalinist obsession with dissent.
7. Ibid., p. 80.
8. G. Simon (1974) p. 16. Emphasis added.
9. Geoffrey Best (1982) p. 229.
10. H. Seton-Watson (1967) p. 247 and M. E. Falkus (1972) p. 54.
11. See pp. 21–38.
12. Leikina–Svirskaia (1971) pp. 69–70.
13. Leikina–Svirskaia (1981) p. 18. These figures are said to be based on incomplete data, though this is not explained.
14. Ibid., p. 16.
15. Ibid., p. 24.
16. Ibid., p. 25.
17. Kneen (1976) pp. 13–14.
18. Leikina–Svirskaia (1981) p. 60.
19. Ibid., p. 61.
20. Ibid., p. 62.
21. Ibid., p. 63. This expansion provides an interesting and largely unexplored precedent for post-revolutionary overstretching of available resources of qualified personnel in the interests of rapid industrial growth.
22. Leikina–Svirskaia (1971) p. 62.
23. Chutkerashvili (1968) p. 60.
24. Leikina–Svirskaia (1971) p. 60.
25. Chutkerashvili (1968) p. 60.
26. Figures for 1900 from Leikina–Svirskaia (1971) p. 64 and for 1914 from Chutkerashvili (1968) p. 60. I am indebted to P. H. Kneen's discussion paper for bringing these references together.
27. Leikina–Svirskaia (1981) pp. 60–1 and 64–5.
28. Ibid., pp. 60–1. There is little information about them. It would be fascinating to compare their background, qualifications, role and status with those of diamat (dialectical materialism) teachers in Soviet schools.
29. See, for example, A. Solzhenitsyn (1973) pp. 37–9; V. Nahirny (1983); A. Kelly (1983); A. Gouldner (1979); I. Volgin (1986) pp. 13 and 118.
30. For the sake of completeness it should be noted that there was a third

distinct use of the term to refer to people who patronised 'high culture'.
31. It is interesting to recall that Russia's awareness of economic backwardness can be traced back to the late seventeenth-century and Peter the Great's well-known attempts to import foreign methods of organisation and technology. However, the relatively low level of industrialisation in Western Europe and the restricted impact of Peter's innovations would make the terms 'development' and 'underdevelopment' anachronistic in that context since the terms imply a much greater gap in levels of industrialisation, normally revolving around the presence or absence of large-scale factory production, as well as a very large difference in per capita GNP. Neither of these criteria was operating at the time of Peter the Great. None the less, this did not prevent his example from being wheeled into and out of the arguments of the intelligentsia as an icon of good or evil depending on the arguer's standpoint.
32. The most comprehensive account is that by A. Walicki (1975).
33. Even the Bolshevik leadership felt the need to call in a fashionable British sculptress, Clare Sheridan, to make official busts of Lenin and others. See her memoirs including *Russian Portraits* (London, 1921).
34. For the broadest account of these developments see Camilla Gray (1971).
35. A few examples of this kind of activity on the part of supposedly apolitical intellectuals can be found in Read (1986).
36. The best accounts of this period are those of John Bowlt. See especially *The Silver Age* (1979).
37. The fact that in the Soviet Union the situation is the reverse might give pause for thought on the part of those resisting the idea of the avant-garde having political significance.
38. For a full discussion on the *Vekhi* debate see Read (1979) which is perhaps more successful in elaborating a taxonomy of intellectual life at this time than it is in analysing it or locating the debate in the wider social context. There is a full bibliography of the debate in this volume. The question of intellectual generations is raised in Read (1981). There are two English translations of *Vekhi*. See Shragin and Todd (1977) and Woehrlin (1986).
39. See Brooks (1983).
40. L. M. Kleinbort (1923). All refs below are to vol. I.
41. Ibid., p. 10.
42. Ibid., p. 14.
43. Ibid., p. 15.
44. Ibid., pp. 16–17.
45. Ibid., p. 29.
46. Ibid., p. 23.
47. Ibid., p. 30.
48. Ibid., p. 38.
49. Ibid., pp. 36–7.
50. Ibid., pp. 36–7.
51. Ibid., p. 39.
52. Ibid., p. 29.

53. Ibid., p. 55. Infuriatingly, but not uncharacteristically, Kleinbort does not say which year this was, though from the context one would assume that it was after 1905.
54. Gorky (1914).
55. See Glatzer–Rosenthal (1986).
56. Merezhkovsky (1907) no. 2, p. 65.
57. The social-democratic journal *Mir Bozhii* had a circulation of 13,000–15,000. The liberal *Russkaia mysl'* had a circulation of up to 13,000.
58. *Paris–Moscou* (1979) p. 26.

Notes to Chapter 2: The Intelligentsia in War and Revolution

1. Makovskii (1917) p. xvi.
2. Struve (1917) p. xii.
3. see F 2306.2.12.
4. Lapshin (1983).
5. Kleinbort (1923) p. 29.
6. McNeal (1973) p. 177 and Krupskaia (1970) pp. 299, 303 and 306–8.
7. Lapshin (1983) p. 138.
8. Ibid., p. 142.
9. Livshits (1977) p. 244.
10. Gray (1971) pp. 202–4.
11. Lapshin (1983) p. 27–8.
12. Ibid., p. 160.
13. Ibid., pp. 165–6.
14. Ibid., p. 166.
15. Ibid.
16. Ibid., p. 254.
17. Ibid., p. 256.
18. Ibid.
19. Ibid., pp. 259–62.
20. Ibid., pp. 274–80 has one of the fullest and most recent accounts of this early episode in relations between the Bolshevik government and the intellectuals.
21. Referred to below as *B.l.i.zh.*
22. *B.l.i.zh.*, October 1917, kn. V, pp. 22–6. Original source Iu. Nikolaev, 'Natsional'noe samoubiistvo', *Russkaia svoboda*, 18–19.
23. *B.l.i.zh.*, October 1917, kn. VI, pp. 20–7. Original source *Russkaia svoboda*, 16–17.
24. Ibid., p. 23. Original source, P. Sorokin, 'Zametki sotsiologa', *Volia naroda*, 116.
25. Ibid., p. 26. Original source, I. Kantorovich, *Rech'*, no. 150.
26. 'K kharakteristike russkoi revoliutsionnoi intelligentsii', *B.l.i.zh.*, November 1917, kn. IX–X, p. 44. Original source, S. Kondrushin, *Rech'* no. 236.
27. Ibid., p. 39.
28. Ibid., p. 44. Original source, K. Gorev, *Vol'nosti* (n.d.).
29. A. I. (1918) p. 3.

30. Red'ko (1918) p. 264.
31. Ibid., p. 261.
32. Ibid., p. 262.
33. Ibid., p. 266–7.
34. Ibid., p. 261.
35. Ibid., p. 266.
36. Ibid., p. 275.
37. Ibid., p. 263.
38. Ibid., pp. 267–74.
39. Ibid., p. 280.
40. Ibid., p. 278.
41. Ibid., p. 279.
42. Ibid.
43. Ibid., p. 281.
44. Izgoev (1910) pp. 63–72.
45. A. I. (1918) p. 3.
46. Lunacharsky's work at Narkompros is discussed later in the present chapter and in the next two chapters.
47. See below pp. 62–76.
48. *Letopis' dom literatorov*, no. 1–2 (5–6) (15–e ianv. 1922) p. 7.
49. A wide-ranging and informative account of intelligentsia reaction (mostly hostile) can be found in Burbank (1986).
50. Andreev (1985) p. 21.
51. Ibid., p. 99.
52. Ibid., p. 115.
53. Ms Coll/Polivanov (Crimea) p. 2.
54. See Williams (1972).
55. Miakotin (1923) p. 185.
56. Ibid., p. 188.
57. Ibid.
58. Ibid., p. 181.
59. Ibid., pp. 180–1 and p. 183.
60. Ibid., p. 183.
61. Ibid., p. 185.
62. Ibid., p. 196.
63. Ibid., p. 194.
64. Ibid., p. 195.
65. Ibid., pp. 196–7.
66. Ibid., p. 197.
67. Ibid.
68. Ibid., pp. 198–9.
69. Ibid., p. 194.
70. Ibid., p. 193.
71. Mel'gunov (1964) p. 85.
72. See Sorokin (1924) p. 279 and Krylenko (1923) pp. 28–56 and 369–404.
73. Osorgin (1928) p. 19.
74. Ibid., p. 21.
75. Ibid., p. 20.
76. Ibid., p. 23.

77. Ibid., p. 23.
78. Ibid., p. 32.
79. Lozinskii (1928) pp. 33–8.
80. Osorgin (1928) pp. 21–2.
81. Osorgin (1932) pp. 57 and 59. Shershenevich does not appear to have been good at arithmetic.
82. On the Petrograd clubs see the thoughtful and informative account by Scherr (1977).
83. Shirmakov (1958) pp. 455–6.
84. Ibid., p. 457.
85. Ibid., p. 464.
86. Ibid., pp. 464–5. See also Fitzpatrick (1970) pp. 113–16 for an account of the activities of the Arts Union (*Soiuz deiatelei iskusstv*) founded in May 1917.
87. F 5508.1.3.
88. F 5508.1.4.8.
89. F 5508.1.93.1.
90. F 5508.1.70.1.
91. Ibid., l. 1.
92. F 5508.1.66.14.
93. Minsky (1922) p. 136.
94. Berdiaev (1950) p. 222.
95. Ibid., p. 225.
96. Ibid.
97. Ibid., p. 229.
98. Ibid., p. 228.
99. Ibid., p. 231.
100. Ibid. pp. 231–2.
101. Ibid., p. 232.
102. Ibid.
103. See ibid., pp. 231–43 for his account of these activities.
104. This account is based on ibid., p. 239.
105. *Iz glubiny* (1918). There is an English translation. See Woehrlin (1986).
106. For a discussion of *Iz glubiny* see Burbank (1986) pp. 190–8.
107. An informative account of these groups can be found in Chagin and Klushin (1975).
108. Novikov (1930) p. 169.
109. Ibid., p. 170.
110. Ibid., p. 179.
111. Ibid., p. 180.
112. Novikov (1952) pp. 286 and 293.
113. Novikov (1930) p. 178.
114. Stratonov in Novikov (1930) pp. 193–242. The strike is described on pp. 219–35.
115. *Tekhnologicheskii institut. Sto let'* (1928) pp. 212–16.
116. Ibid., p. 212.
117. Kim (1968) p. 94.
118. F 2306.18.5.5.
119. Ibid.

240   *Culture and Power in Revolutionary Russia*

120. Beilin (1935) p. 70. One should allow considerable room for inaccuracy in all such figures relating to the chaotic civil war period, particularly those published in 1935, a period of peak distortion of statistics in the USSR. Statistical compilations since 1956 have been more accurate, by and large, but tend to give little information on the period 1917–21, perhaps because of the chaotic nature of the available information. Chutkerashvili (1961) gives corresponding figures of 204 institutions and 221,300 students for the 1919–20 academic year.
121. Nazarov (1968) p. 81.
122. Ibid., p. 83.
123. Ibid., p. 121.
124. Ibid.
125. Ibid., p. 129–30.
126. Novikov (1952) p. 289.
127. For further information see Bailes (1978) and Lewis (1979), though neither of these pays much attention to the early years.
128. Vserossiisskii Soiuz Inzhenerov, *Otchet o zaniiatiiakh 2-i Moskovskoi oblastnoi konferentsii 18–21 oktiabria 1918 g.* (Moscow 1918) p. 12.
129. Ibid.
130. *Zaniatiia 1-go Moskovskogo oblastnogo delegatskogo s'ezde, 4–6 ianv. 1918g. Biulleteni Moskovskogo oblastnogo biuro i Moskovskogo otdeleniia Vserossiisk. soiuz inzheneroz,* MOB no. 1 i MOVs SI No 3 (Moscow 1918) pp. 47–9.
131. Ioffe (1933) p. 21.
132. Ibid., p. 22.
133. Ibid.
134. RSFSR Nauchno-tekhnicheskii otdel VSNKh, *Rabota nauchno-tekhnicheskikh uchrezhdenii respublikh 1918–1919g,* Sostav. inzh. M. Ia. Lapirov-Skoblo, Moscow (n.d.). The cover in English and French and the high quality of the layout, printing and paper indicate that this list was produced for purposes of international propaganda.
135. F 2306.18.5.
136. Graham (1967) p. 24.
137. Bardin (1938) p. 46.
138. Ibid., p. 108.
139. See Bailes (1978) p. 149.
140. See ibid., p. 56. An interesting account by a major participant can be found in Novikov (1952) pp. 303–28.
141. *Stenograficheskii otchet rabot 1-go Vserossiiskogo s'ezda Inzhenerov, chlenov profsoiuzov 16–22 dekabriia 1922* (Moscow, 1923) p. 25.
142. An excellent description of Lunacharsky's problems at this time in the sphere of the arts is to be found in Fitzpatrick (1970) ch. 6 *passim*.
143. See below pp. 115–18.
144. *Novaia zhizn',* 14 (27) July 1917. Translated by H. Ermolaev in Gorky (1968) p. 74.
145. Ibid., pp. 115–16.
146. Ibid., p. 119, 31 December (17 January).
147. Mandel'stam (1971) p. 110.
148. 'Mitingi trudiashcheisia intelligentsii', *Severnaia kommuna,* no. 167 (30-go Noiabria 1918) p. 3.

149. 'O volnykh izdatel'stvakh', *Vestnik literatury*, no. 3 (27) p. 11.
150. 'Maksim Gorky o bol'shevikhakh i intelligentsii' in *Poslednie novosti*, no. 746 (23 sentabria 1922) p. 2.
151. See, for instance, Fitzpatrick (1970), Lodder (1983), Milner (1983), Bowlt (1976), Williams (1977), Nilsson (1979), Barron and Tuchmann (1980), *Paris–Moscou* (1979), Gleason (1985), and many others.
152. See below for a fuller discussion of relations between government and Proletkul't.
153. Lodder (1983) p. 109.
154. There is a very good account of these developments in Lodder (1983) pp. 109–13.
155. Gronskii and Perel'man (1973) pp. 80–1.
156. Lodder, (1983) p. 112.
157. Meyer, pp. 243–4.
158. Chagall (1965) p. 131.
159. Ibid., p. 134.
160. Meyer, p. 265.
161. Chagall (1965) p. 137.
162. Ibid., p. 142.
163. Ibid. p. 167.
164. Ibid., p. 171. For a fuller account of Chagall's life at this time see Meyer pp. 217–313.
165. For a full account of the controversy around Blok see the essay in Schapiro (1986). Although this is an excellent weighing up of the evidence, the author discusses the issue in terms of whether or not Blok retained his enthusiasm or disavowed it later on. He does not take into account that Blok's position was more one of seeing hope in the revolution rather than of identifying with and defending the Soviet authorities.
166. Belyi (1922) p. 2.
167. Belyi (1923) pp. 233–4.
168. Ibid., p. 232.
169. Khodasevich (1954) p. 326.
170. Ibid., p. 330.
171. Belyi (1922) p. 6.
172. Khodasevich (1954) p. 326.
173. Belyi (1922) p. 4.

Notes to Chapter 3: The Bolsheviks and Cultural Life During the Civil War

1. See in particular Fitzpatrick (1970) which presents an excellent account of the institutional history of Narkompros in the period 1917–21.
2. See Tait (n.d.) and his article in Rosenthal (1986).
3. For an account of God-building see Read (1979) pp. 77–94 (reprinted in Obelkevich (1987) pp. 450–66).
4. O'Connor (1983) p. 44.
5. Quoted in ibid., p. 44.

6. Lunacharsky (1918) p. 10. This theme recurs in his dialogue with Proletkul't around this time. See below p. 124.
7. See below pp. 115–18.
8. On Pokrovsky see Enteen (1978) and Barber (1981).
9. The purpose of the following discussion of these two issues is to show how Narkompros dealt with such matters and the divisions revealed within it rather than to deal fully with the debates surrounding these questions. For fuller accounts the reader is referred to Anweiler (1964), Fitzpatrick (1970) and (1979), Hans and Hessen (1930) and Witt (1961).
10. F 2306. 2.141.1–3.
11. Ibid., 1.5.
12. Ibid., 1.8.
13. Ibid.
14. Ibid., 1.9.
15. Ibid., 1.10.
16. Sheila Fitzpatrick (1970) pp. 31 and 334 n.154 refers to a meeting of the State Education Commission on 10 August which was not included or referred to in the copies of the minutes to which I was given access in the archives. On the other hand, she does not refer in her discussion of the Unified Labour School to the meetings of 20 July or 17 and 19 August at which major discussions of the issue took place.
17. F 2306.2.141.1.47ob.
18. Ibid., 1.21.
19. Ibid., 1.22.
20. Ibid., 1.25 and 1.27.
21. Ibid., 1.33.
22. Ibid., 1.47ob. The records are not consistent in giving initials. I have assumed that the Kalinin whose vote is recorded is F. I. Kalinin.
23. Ibid.
24. Fitzpatrick (1970) p. 31.
25. F 2306.2.141.1.22.
26. F 2306.2.12.227.
27. Ibid., 1.285–92.
28. Fitzpatrick (1970) p. 76.
29. F 2306.18.65.22 and 26-28.
30. Ibid. One name, which appeared to be that of Trotsky's wife, was crossed out in the record.
31. Ibid., 1.19ob–19 (*sic*: the page was bound back to front in the archive). The speaker is identified as 'Chicherin'.
32. Ibid., 1.11.
33. Ibid. 1.12–13.
34. Fitzpatrick (1970) p. 78.
35. F 2306.2.141.60–2.
36. Ibid., 1.64–5.
37. F 2306.18.92.20.
38. Ibid., 1.19 and 1.20ob.
39. F 2306.18.48.34.
40. F 2306.18.210.4.
41. Fitzpatrick (1970) p. 78.

42. F 2306.18.48 1.9.
43. Ibid., 1.10.
44. Ibid.
45. See below pp. 179–82.
46. See, for instance, Shmidt's theses on mass preparation of specialists and scientific workers approved by Narkompros probably in 1919 although they are undated in the archive. F 2306.10.31.1.
47. See Read (1979) pp. 42–56 and Read (1981).
48. Bogdanov (1911).
49. Ibid., p. 3.
50. Ibid., pp. 14–15.
51. Ibid., p. 21.
52. Ibid., p. 57.
53. Ibid., p. 70.
54. Ibid., p. 30.
55. Ibid., p. 76.
56. Ibid., p. 77.
57. Bogdanov (1923) p. 16.
58. S. A. S. (Sokolov) (1923) p. 19.
59. Ibid. For an excellent and thorough account of Bogdanov in Tula see J. D. White's article of that title, White (1981).
60. For an account of Bogdanov's developed ideas on these issues see Read (1979) pp. 42–6, Vucinich (1976), Putnam (1977) and Sochor in Rosenthal (1986) pp. 293–314.
61. White (1981) pp. 43–6 and 49–51.
62. See above p. 98.
63. See Scherrer (1978) and Biggart (1981).
64. An account of the political conflicts involved can be found in Schapiro (1970) pp. 110–13.
65. Aleksinskii, box 8, Capri School, *Obshchii otchet*.
66. *Otchet Vysshei Sots–Dem. Propagandistsko–agitatorskoi shkoly dliia rabochikh* (hereafter *Otchet*).
67. *Otchet* p. 10.
68. *Obshchii otchet*.
69. Aleksinskii, box 8.
70. Aleksinskii, box 6.
71. Aleksinskii, box 8.
72. See Read (1979) pp. 77–90.
73. Aleksinskii, box 8.
74. Aleksinskii, box 8. Lenin's School in Longjumeau.
75. Kosarev p. 66. According to this source there were ten students who had come from Moscow, five from elsewhere in the Russia Empire and twelve from the emigration who wished to go back on party work.
76. Kosarev, p. 71.
77. Ibid., p. 67.
78. Ibid.
79. Ibid., p. 72.
80. Ibid., pp. 74–5.
81. Lapshin (1983) p. 142. Sheila Fitzpartick, like Gorbunov, describes the

244   *Culture and Power in Revolutionary Russia*

conference as having been 'called by Lunacharsky' (Fitzpatrick (1970) pp. 89–90). Lapshin, more plausibly, simply mentions Lunacharsky as 'one of the organisers'.

82. *Protokoly* (1918) p. 31.
83. Literature, too, had an organising function in Bogdanov's view. He develops his ideas on this in Bogdanov (1918a) pp. 3–31 and 44–6. They resemble his views on the encyclopaedia referred to above, pp. 113–14.
84. Ibid.
85. Bogdanov (1918b) p. 23.
86. *Protokoly* (1918) pp. 101–2. A more detailed outline can be found in Bogdanov (1920).
87. Bogdanov develops this theme in (1918a) pp. 12–14.
88. Ibid., p. 21.
89. See below pp. 149–50.
90. See Bogdanov (1984).
91. Bogdanov (1918a) pp. 77–8.
92. Ibid., p. 31. The other task was 'independent creativity'.
93. Ibid., p. 36.
94. *Protokoly* (1918) p. 7.
95. Ibid.
96. Ibid, p. 7.
97. Ibid., p. 66.
98. *Proletarskaia Kul'tura*, no. 4, pp. 23–5.
99. Ibid, no. 2 p. 23.
100. Ibid, no. 7–8, pp. 1–3.
101. *Protokoly* (1918) p. 30.
102. Ibid., p. 23.
103. Ibid., p. 22.
104. Ibid. p. 21.
105. Ibid., p. 26.
106. Ibid., p. 28. Lunacharsky had made this statement to the Executive Bureau of Moscow Proletkul't.
107. Ibid., p. 21.
108. *Proletarskaia Kul'tura*, no. 1, p. 8.
109. Ibid.
110. Gorbunov (1974) pp. 124–5. Gorbunov gives an archive reference for this: TsPA IML F 17.60.43.19.
111. *Protokoly* (1918) p. 21.
112. Ibid.
113. Ibid.
114. Ibid., p. 51.
115. Ibid., pp. 20–1.
116. Ibid., p. 20.
117. F 1230.1.3.1.93 and 1.95.
118. Ibid., 1.10.
119. Ibid., 1.88.
120. F 2306.17.4.8–9.
121. F 1230.1.3.10.

122. Ibid., January 1919.
123. F 1230.1.1.2 and 9.
124. F 1230.1.3.38.
125. Ibid., 1.70 and 1.26ob.
126. See above pp. 123–6.
127. F 1230.1.137.7.
128. F 1230.1.3.95.
129. F 1230.1.1.12ob.
130. F 1230.1.1.9ob.
131. F 1230.1.6.1.
132. F 1230.1.138.17–24.
133. Bogdanov (1919) pp. 9–22.
134. Fitzpatrick (1970) pp. 101–2.
135. F 1230.1.3.103.
136. F 1230.1.3.71.
137. Ibid., 1.101. The text of this order has been published in Gorbunov (1974) p. 108. Some students had already been transferred to the Central Party School and to the localities (F 1230.1.3.71).
138. F 1230.1.3 1.101.
139. *Proletarskaia kul'tura*, no. 9–10, p. 59.
140. F 1230.1.3.69ob.
141. F 1230.1.7.57ob.
142. F 1230.1.6.36.
143. There is only one substantial reference to him in Fitzpatrick (1970) for example. Soviet works rarely mention him.
144. Nevsky (1920a).
145. Nevsky and Khersonskaia (1920).
146. Nevsky (1922b).
147. Nevsky, (1922 b).
148. F 5221.3.63.28–9.
149. Ibid., 1.67–8.
150. Ibid., 1.9–10.
151. F 5221.1.1.225.
152. F 5221.3.63.45.
153. Ibid., 1.10. Clearly these categories are not mutually exclusive.
154. F 5221.1.15.95.
155. Nevsky (1920a).
156. F 5221.1.1.225.
157. F 5221.1.1.4–10.
158. F 5221.1.15.64.
159. Ibid., 1.67.
160. F 5221.1.15.95.
161. F 5221.1.15.86.
162. F 5221.1.15.68. This was in October 1920.
163. Fitzpatrick, p. 251. Lenin was speaking to the Second All-Russian Conference of Political Education Departments, 17 October 1921.
164. 'An Integrated Economic Plan', *Pravda*, 22 February 1921.

246   *Culture and Power in Revolutionary Russia*

Notes to Chapter 4: Laying the Foundations of Cultural Power

1. Schapiro (1970) p. 348.
2. Fitzpatrick (1974).
3. Kemp-Welch (1978).
4. See above pp. 131–3.
5. F 1230.1.6.36.
6. F 5221.1.15.86. Mentioned above in chapter 3.
7. The concept was not, however, forgotten. In one of the last issues of *Proletarskaia Kul'tura*, S. Zander argued for a Proletarian University growing from and being associated with existing institutions from *rabfaky* to the Socialist Academy. See Zander (1921) pp. 19–27.
8. F 1230.1.1.38.
9. F 1230.1.6.1.
10. Quoted in Fitzpatrick (1970) p. 137.
11. F 1230.1.6.27.
12. F 1230.1.3.108.
13. F 1230.1.6.14.
14. F 1230.1.2.1ob.
15. F 1230.1.6.14ob.
16. F 1230.1.6.48.
17. See above chapter 3, pp. 121–2.
18. It is interesting to note that the most thorough Soviet investigation of these issues puts Proletkul't's refusal to accept the leading role of party and state as first in a list of its 'errors'. Gorbunov (1974) p. 5.
19. F 1230.1.6.71–2.
20. F 1230.1.6.88.
21. F 1230.1.6.101.
22. F 1230.1.6.82, 5, 67, 77, 92, 95 respectively.
23. F 1230.1.6.58.
24. F 1230.1.6.39 (10 May).
25. F 1230.1.6.80.
26. Some reflections on Proletkul't can be found in Eden and Cedar Paul (1921) which is mainly about British worker education.
27. An account of the Proletkul't Institute founded in Turin in January 1921 can be found in *Gorn* Kniga 1(6) (Moscow 1922) pp. 121–7, Gramsci may have written this account. His name appears first in the list of organisers.
28. V. Kunavin 'Vserossisskii s'ezd Proletkul'ta', *Proletarskaia kul'tura*, no. 17–19 (1920) pp. 74–84. Unless indicated otherwise the account of the conference given here is based on this article.
29. Gorbunov (1974) pp. 137–8.
30. Kunavin (1920) p. 78.
31. Gorbunov (1974) p. 134.
32. Ibid., pp. 139–40.
33. Ibid., pp. 142–52 has a very informative account of these meetings. Here, and elsewhere in his interpretation, Gorbunov stresses that Lenin was most concerned to prevent Proletkul't being, in any sense, autonomous with respect to party and state control and this was, in fact, his chief anxiety about Proletkul't.

34. Ibid., pp. 139–40.
35. Ibid., pp. 83–4.
36. For an account of the events surrounding the decision see Schapiro (1955) pp. 314–23, Daniels (1969) pp. 137–53 and McNeal (1974) pp. 114–26.
37. The best available account of the work of these commissions and of politics within Narkompros at this time is to be found in Fitzpatrick (1970) pp. 162–209. I have drawn heavily on this for much of the information used here on this topic but differ in substantial points of analysis of its significance.
38. Quoted in Fitzpatrick (1970) p. 192.
39. According to Fitzpatrick the majority of the Central Committee may have wanted to sack Lunacharsky. No source is given for this. Ibid. p. 190.
40. *Pravda*, 16 July 1921.
41. Ibid.
42. Quoted in Fitzpatrick (1970) pp. 244–5.
43. Fitzpatrick (1970) p. 216.
44. Lenin and other party leaders were themselves concerned, at this time, about a phenomenon described as 'communist arrogance' (*Komchvanstvo*) which differs from 'proletarian chauvinism' in that it applies to heavy-handedness in the implementation of policy, whereas the latter is a more extensive mentality shaping the way policy was framed. In addition, 'proletarian chauvinism' spread beyond the party itself and had roots in Russian society. Clearly, the two things could go together but not all manifestations of proletarian chauvinism were necessarily accompanied by communist arrogance. The latter is a subset of the former.
45. Quoted in Fitzpatrick (1970) p. 72–3.
46. This is how it is described by Fitzpatrick (1970) p. 208.
47. Ibid., p. 187.
48. Ibid., p. 200.
49. *Intelligentsiia i revoliutsiia*, p. 43.
50. Ibid., p. 44.
51. Ibid., p. 49.
52. Ibid., p. 147.
53. Ibid., p. 3.
54. Ibid.
55. Even such an assiduous chronicler of Bolshevik 'totalitarianism' as Robert Conquest does not begin to trace Bolshevik 'politics of ideas', in his book of that name, before the later 1920s, the earlier years being described as exhibiting 'relaxation' and 'a certain tolerance' in the literary and other fields. See Conquest (1967) p. 33.
56. See above pp. 52, 159 and 203–8.
57. See Fitzpatrick (1970) pp. 201–2.
58. Schapiro (1970) p. 251.
59. Andreeva in V. G. Chufarov (1974) p. 486. The source quoted here is from the party archive, TsPA 17.60.1.34.
60. Ibid.

61. Ibid.
62. Ibid., p. 487 quoting TsGA RSFSR 2313.1.1.494.
63. Ibid. p. 489.
64. Ibid, p. 487. The source is vague about dates for these developments but implies that they occurred prior to or simultaneously with its expansion in 1922.
65. Nazarov (1968) p. 140.
66. Ibid., p. 168.
67. Ibid., p. 137.
68. Ibid., p. 142.
69. Ibid., p. 144.
70. Ibid., p. 197.
71. Ibid. p. 156.
72. See above Chapter 2 and Burbank (1986) pp. 190–8.
73. Lunacharsky (1921) pp. 3 and 7.
74. Nazarov (1968) pp. 250–1 reproduces the regulations.
75. A little information on this last phase can be gleaned from Fediukin (1977) pp. 64–99.
76. Letter of Lenin to Dzherzhinsky, 19 May 1922, in *V. I. Lenin i VCHK* (1987) p. 540.
77. Fediukin (1977) p. 78. The original source is TsPA IML. 17.60.141.16.
78. Meshcheriakov (1922) pp. 128–34.
79. N. F. Ianitskii quoted in Nazarov (1968) p. 254.
80. Meshcheriakov (1922) p. 132.
81. See below Chapter 5, pp. 189–200.
82. See below pp. 181–2.
83. Fediukin (1977) p. 164.
84. *Lenin i VCHK* (1987) p. 540. *Novaia Rossiia* is discussed below (pp. 198–200).
85. Fediukin (1977) pp. 164–5.
86. For earlier references see Chapter 2, pp. 71–3 and Chapter 3, pp. 104–8.
87. F 2306.1.595. It was published in *SU* no. 742, p. 7. RSFSR stands for Russian Soviet Federative Socialist Republic.
88. F 2306.1.597.7.
89. Quoted in Fitzpatrick (1970) p. 224.
90. Stratonov (1930) pp. 215–16.
91. One of those involved, S. P. Mel'gunov, says that 70 intellectuals were expelled from Moscow and 60–70 from Petrograd. Mel'gunov (1964) pp. 81–2.
92. See, for instance, Fediukin (1977) pp. 177–80.
93. Fediukin comments that if someone close to Marxism like Sakulin did not understand the danger of 'ideological co-existence' then what must anti-Marxists think? Ibid., p. 96.
94. Lunacharsky, for example, had tried to win over support at the 1921 meeting on higher education by saying that the chains on freedom would have to be borne 'for the time being'. Fitzpatrick (1970) p. 223.

Notes to Chapter 5: Compromise or Confrontation? The Contours

1. See, for example, various works of Fediukin in the bibliography. See also Pethybridge (1982).
2. An interesting but unsystematic account of *Smena vekh* and the ideas around it can be found in Agursky (1980).
3. Ustrialov Archive (hereafter UA), Hoover Institution, Stanford, CA.
4. UA, Letter from Kliuchnikov to Ustrialov, 25 February 1919. Ustrialov referred to this meeting in his article 'Vpered ot *vekh*' in Ustrialov (1927).
5. Ibid.
6. UA Moia perepiska so Smenovekhovtsami Item 11, diary entry for 24 October 1921, p. 15.
7. Ibid., item 12. Letter from Kliuchnikov to Ustrialov of 8 November 1921, p. 18.
8. Ibid., item 40. Letter to S. S. Luk'ianov, early October 1922, p. 68.
9. *Pravda*, 3 September 1922.
10. Fediukin (1977) p. 124.
11. Meshcheriakov (1923) p. 88.
12. UA, Moia Perepiska s raznymi liudmi, items 37 and 38 (1923).
13. UA, Moia perepiska P. P. Suvchinskim, item 9, 30 January 1928, item 13, 19 October, 1928.
14. See, for example, ibid., item 3, 21 February 1927, p. 12, which shows that even at this late date Ustrialov believed things were still 'very slowly and step-by-step moving in our direction' though he did now recognise that there would not be a revolution in this respect.
15. Fediukin (1977) pp. 286–7.
16. Ibid., p. 130.
17. Ibid., p. 289.
18. *Sputnik kommunista*, no. 15 (1922) pp. 48–9.
19. Ibid., pp. 56 and 59.
20. This identification persisted. In the archetypical 'Stalinist' film *Chapaev* (1934), the élite squadron of White officers bearing down on the Reds are described as '*intelligenty*' by one of the Red soldiers.
21. Voronsky (1921) p. 28.
22. Meshcheriakov (1921) p. 43.
23. Meshcheriakov (1923) p. 88.
24. Fediukin (1977) p. 286.
25. Fediukin (1977) pp. 286 and 288.
26. Fediukin (1977) pp. 289–90.
27. See especially Fediukin (1977) pp. 127–32.
28. Mindlin (1968) p. 129.
29. TsPA IML F 17.60.263.74, quoted in Fediukin (1977) p. 131.
30. *Izvestiia VTsIK*, 25 June 1924, quoted in Fediukin (1977) pp. 131–2.
31. Letter to Dzerzhinsky, 19 May 1922, in *Lenin i VChK* (1987) pp. 540–1.
32. Fediukin (1977) pp. 301–2.
33. See, for example, his articles in the March 1922 and January and May, June 1923 issues.

34. Lezhnev (1936) p. 240.
35. See S. Adrianov, 'Tret'ia Rossiia' in the March 1922 edition of *Novaia rossiia*.
36. 'Sluzhit po dekretu, zhivet po sekretu' in the original. Lezhnev 'Pis'mo Prof. N. V. Ustrialovu', *Rossiia*, no. 9 (May–June 1923) p. 8.
37. See Potekhin's letter to Ustrialov of May 1923 and Ustrialov's reply in UA, 'Moia perepiska so smenovekhovtsami', item 53, p. 94 and item 54, p. 100. In the former, Potekhin argued that the task of the *smenavekhovtsy* was to shift the basis of the state from worker–peasant to peasant–worker, the Right Communists, Rykov and Kamenev, being the most likely allies. He added that Lezhnev did not believe the basis of the Soviet state would shift in this way. In his reply, Ustrialov vainly tried to remind Potekhin that 'we are not revolutionaries'.
38. Ibid., item 52, p. 93.
39. Fediukin (1977) pp. 272 and 300.
40. See, for instance, Maguire (1968), Ermolaev (1963), Kemp-Welch (1978) and James (1973) pp. 63–8. See also Metcalf (1987).
41. At greatest length by Gorbunov (1980, 1985). See also Claudin–Urondo (1977).
42. Read (1989) discusses definitions of the intelligentsia used by Lenin and others at this time.
43. Lenin 'Better Fewer, But Better'.
44. See, for instance, his marginal comments on Pletnev's article 'Na ideologicheskom fronte' (1922) or his 'Rough Draft of a Resolution on Proletarian Culture' of 9 October 1920, where he refers to 'Not the *invention* of a new proletarian culture, but the *development* of the best models, traditions and results of the *existing* culture, *from the point of view* of the Marxist world outlook.'
45. See Chapter 4, p. 161.
46. Zinoviev (1923).
47. Zinoviev (1923) p. 10.
48. Trotsky Achive, bMS Russ 13 T4493, pp. 2–3.
49. Ibid., bMS Russ 13.1 7429. This letter was dated 27 October 1938.
50. To say nothing of their effect beyond it. It is outside the scope of the present work to examine their influence on Soviet cultural life as a whole at this period. There are numerous studies of the Soviet literary scene in the mid 1920s. The most balanced and judicious is Hermann Ermolaev (1963). On the proletarians, see Brown (1953). For a bitter, but not necessarily inaccurate, view of the impact of the proletarian faction see the memoirs of Nadezhda Mandelstam, especially the earlier volume (1971).
51. A fuller account of Trotsky's ideas can be found in Deutscher (1959) pp. 163–200 and Knei-Paz (1978) pp. 445–94. For Bukharin see Cohen (1974) pp. 204–6 and 237–8 and Biggart (1987).
52. Trotsky (1960) p. 184.
53. Ibid., p. 185.
54. Ibid.
55. Ibid., pp. 185–6.
56. Ibid., pp. 192.

57. Ibid. pp. 191–2.
58. Bukharin (1923) p. 32. These lines are emphasised in the original.
59. Ibid., p. 33.
60. Trotsky (1960) p. 193.
61. *K voprosu* (1924) pp. 5–6.
62. Ibid., p. 7.
63. Ibid., pp. 12–13.
64. Ibid., p. 14.
65. Interestingly, Vardin quoted theses of Molotov, recently approved by Central Committee, which pointed to the danger of the growth of the *kulak* class in the countryside and of private capital in the towns. Ibid. p. 15.
66. Ibid., p. 18.
67. Ibid., p. 23.
68. See *Voprosy kul'tury* (1925) p. 3.
69. Ibid., p. 45.
70. Ibid., p. 17.
71. Though the 'October' and 'Smithy' (*Kuznitsa*) groups were mentioned by name here the inference was that the On Guardists were in the same category, as Iakovlev had said in his speech. Ibid., p. 46.
72. Ibid., p. 109.
73. Ibid., pp. 106–7.
74. Vardin, for instance, complained from the floor that Trotsky had not heard his speech but was deigning to reply to it. Trotsky amused the audience by saying that you didn't have to listen to Vardin to know what he was going to say. Ibid., p. 52.
75. *Voprosy kul'tury* (1925) p. 211.
76. Ibid., pp. 213–14.
77. The resolution was published, with accompanying materials, in *Voprosy kul'tury pri dikature proletariata* (1925) pp. 215–20. There is an English translation in James (1973) pp. 116–19 and a thoughtful discussion of its contents, pp. 63–8.
78. Trotsky (1960) p. 218, wrote that, in the literary field, the party was not called upon to command.
79. *Voprosy kul'tury* (1925) pp. 184–5.
80. Ibid., p. 3.
81. Ibid., p. 4.
82. Ibid., p. 3.
84. Metcalf (1987) shows this clearly.
84. See Katz (1956) for an account of some of these developments.
85. The classic study of these individuals and groups remains Jasny (1972).
86. Figures for 1920–6 from Podzemskii (1927) Table 28. Figures for 1927 and after from *Kul'turnoe stroitel'stvo* (1940) p. 100. Kim (1968) pp. 171–3 quotes similar figures.
87. *Kul'turnoe stroitel'stvo*, (1940) p. 100.
88. *Rabochie fakul'tety* (1928) p. 11.
89. Ibid., p. 12. For comparison, the national figure for 1927–8 was 30 per cent of *rabfak* students in the party, 40 per cent in the Komsomol. *Podgotovka kadrov* (1934) p. 21.

90. *Tekhnologicheshii institut* (hereafter *T.i.s.l.*) p. 464.
91. *Rabochie fakul'tety* (1928) p. 7 and *T.i.s.l*, p. 231.
92. *Rabochie fakul'tety* (1928) pp. 9–11.
93. Ibid., pp. 12–13.
94. Ibid., p. 13.
95. *T.i.s.l.,* p. 219.
96. Ibid., p. 462.
97. Ibid., p. 217.
98. Ibid., p. 463.
99. Ibid., p. 219.
100. Ibid., p. 226.
101. Ibid., p. 465.
102. Ibid., p. 318.
103. See above Chapter 2, p. 73.
104. *T.i.s.l.,* p. 230.
105. Ibid., p. 227.
106. Ibid., p. 246.
107. Ibid., p. 320.
108. Ibid., p. 323.
109. Katuntseva (1966) p. 173. For a fuller discussion of the proletarianis-ation of higher education in this period see the article by McLelland (1978).
110. Katuntseva (1966) p. 171.
111. Ibid., p. 127.
112. Ibid., pp. 175–6.
113. Ibid., pp. 180–1.
114. Ibid., p. 171.
115. For the later 'cultural revolution' see Fitzpatrick (1974, 1978, 1979).

Note to the Conclusion

1. Moroz (1974) p. 21.

Bibliography

(A full bibliography of works consulted in connection with a topic as broad as the current one would require a publication of its own. I have therefore restricted the bibliography to the provision of full details of items quoted in the text or referred to in the notes.)

ARCHIVE SOURCES
Bakhmetev Archive (Columbia University)
MS/Coll Aleksinskii
MS/Coll Polivanov (Crimea)

Houghton Library (Harvard University)
Trotsky Archive

Hoover Institution Archive (Stanford University)
Ustrialov Archive

Central State Literary Archive (Moscow)
F 1230.1 Proletkul't (Praesidium of Central Committee)

Central State Historical Archive (Moscow)
F 2306.1 Narkompros
F 2306.2 Narkompros (State Commission for Education)
F 2306.2.12 Narkompros (Reform of Higher Education)
F 2306.17 Narkompros (Proletkul't)
F 2306.18 Narkompros (Higher Education)
F 5221.1 Sverdlov University
F 5221.3 Sverdlov University
F 5508.1 Union of Workers in the Arts (Rabis)

(Soviet archive references are annotated according to the increasingly standardised form with the number of the collection, followed by the section, folder and page numbers – in Russian fond.opis'.delo.list [e.g. F 2306.2.12.2].)

PRINTED SOURCES
A. I., 'Tragediia russkoi intelligentsii. (Na mitinge soiuza pisatelei)', *Vechernyie ogni* 1 April (19 March) 1918.
Agursky, M., *Ideologiia Natsional-Bolshevizma* (Paris, 1980).
Andreev, L., *Pered zadachami vremeni* (Benson, Vt, 1985).
Andreeva, M. S., 'Glavpolitprosvet – organ gosudarstvennoi propagandy kommunizma', in V. G. Chufarov (ed.), *Kul'turnaia revoliutsiia v SSSR i dukhovnoe razvitie Sovetskogo obshchestva* (Sverdlovsk, 1974).
Anweiler, O., *Geschichte der Schules und Pädagogik in Russland vom Ende*

des Zarenreiches bis zum Beginn der Stalin-ara (Berlin, 1964).
Bailes, K. E. *Technology and Society under Lenin and Stalin: Origins of the Soviet Technical Intelligentsia, 1917–1941* (Princetown, NJ, 1978).
Barber, J., *Soviet Historians in Crisis, 1928–1932* (London, 1981).
Bardin, I., *Zhizn' inzhenera* (Moscow, 1938).
Barron, S. and Tuchmann, M., *The Avant-garde in Russia, 1910–1930: New Perspectives* (Cambridge, Mass. and London, 1980).
Beilin, A. F., *Kadry spetsialistov SSSR: ikh formirovanie i rost* (Moscow, 1935).
Belyi, A., 'Kul'tura v sovremennoi Rossii', *Novaia russkaia kniga* no. 1 (1922).
Belyi, A., 'O "Rossii" v Rossii i o "Rossii" v Berline', *Beseda*, no. 1 (mai–iiun 1923).
Berdiaev, N., *Dream and Reality* (London, 1950).
Berdiaev, N., *The Origin of Russian Communism* (Ann Arbor, Mich., 1960).
Best, Geoffrey, *War and Society in Revolutionary Europe, 1770–1870* (1982).
Biggart, J., 'Anti-Leninist Bolshevism: the *Forward* Group of the RSDRP', *Canadian Slavonic Papers*, 23 (June 1981) pp. 134–53.
Biggart, J., 'Bukharin and the Origins of the "Proletarian Culture" Debate', *Soviet Studies*, vol. XXXIX no. 2 (April, 1987) pp. 229–46.
Biulleteni Literatury i Zhizni.
Bogdanov, A. A., *Kul'turnyia zadachi nashego vremeni* (Moscow, 1911).
Bogdanov, A. A., *Iskusstvo i rabochii klass* (Moscow, 1918a).
Bogdanov, A. A., *Sotsializm nauki* (Moscow 1918b).
Bogdanov, A. A., 'Proletarskii universitet', *Proletarskaia kul'tura*, no. 5 (1919) pp. 9–22.
Bogdanov, A. A., *Element proletarskoi kul'tury* (Moscow, 1920).
Bogdanov, A. A., 'Moia prebyvanie v Tule', *Revoliutsionnoe bylo*, no. 2 (1923) pp. 16–18.
Bogdanov, A. A., (trans. J. Biggart), 'Fortunes of the Workers' Party in the Present Revolution', Appendix to a paper presented to the Study Group on the Russian Revolution, Oxford, January 1984.
Bowlt, J., *Russian Art of the Avant-garde; Theory and Criticism, 1902–1934* (New York, 1976).
Bowlt, J. *The Silver Age: Russian Art of the Early Twentieth Century and the 'World of Art' Group* (Newtonville, Mass., 1979).
Brooks, J., *When Russia Learned to Read* (London, 1983).
Brown, E. J., *The Proletarian Episode in Russian Literature* (New York, 1953).
Bukharin, N. I., quoted in 'K zakrytiiu proletarskogo universiteta', *Proletarskaia kul'tura*, no. 9–10 (1920) p. 59.
Bukharin, N. I., *Proletarskaia revoliutsiia i kul'tura* (Moscow, 1923).
Burbank, J., *The Intelligentsia and Revolution: Russian Views of Bolshevism, 1917–1922* (New York and London, 1986).
Chagall, M., *My Life* (London, 1965).
Chagin, B.A. and Klushin, V. I., *Bor'ba za istoricheskii materializm v SSSR* (Leningrad, 1975).
Chufarov, V. G., *Kul'turnaia revoliutsiia v SSSR i dukhovnoe razvitie sovetskogo obshchestva* (Sverdlovsk, 1974).

Chutkerashvili, E. V., *Razvitie vysshego obrazovanie v SSSR* (Moscow, 1961).
Chutkerashvili, E. V., *Kadry dlia nauki* (Moscow, 1968).
Claudin-Urondo, C., *Lenin and the Cultural Revolution* (Hassocks, Sussex, 1977).
Cohen, S., *Bukharin and the Bolshevik Revolution: A Political Biography, 1888–1938* (London, 1974).
Conquest, R., *The Politics of Ideas in the USSR* (London, 1967).
Daniels, R. V., *The Conscience of the Revolution*, 2nd edn (New York, 1969).
Deutscher, I., *The Prophet Unarmed: Trotsky 1921–1929* (Oxford, 1959).
Enteen, G., *The Soviet Scholar Bureaucrat: M. N. Pokrovskii and the Society of Marxist Historians* (University Park, Penn., 1978).
Ermolaev, H., *Soviet Literary Theories 1917–1934: The Genesis of Socialist Realism* (Berkeley, Calif., 1963, reprinted New York, 1977).
Falkus, M. E., *The Industrialisation of Russia 1700–1914* (London, 1972).
Fediukin, S. A., *Privlechenie burzhuaznoi tekhnicheskoi intelligentsii k sotsialisticheskomu stroitel'stvu v SSSR* (Moscow, 1960).
Fediukin, S. A., *Sovetskaia vlast' i burzhuaznye spetsialisty* (Moscow, 1965).
Fediukin, S. A. *The Great October Socialist Revolution and the Intelligentsia: How the Old Intelligentsia was Drawn into the Building of Socialism* (Moscow, 1975).
Fediukin, S. A., *Bor'ba s burzhuaznoi ideologii v usloviiakh perekhoda k NEPu* (Moscow, 1977).
Fediukin, S. A., *Partiia i intelligentsiia* (Moscow, 1983).
Fitzpatrick, S., *The Commissariat of Enlightenment: Soviet Organisation of Education and the Arts under Lunacharsky* (Cambridge, 1970).
Fitzpatrick, S, 'The Emergence of Glaviskusstvo: Class War on the Cultural Front, Moscow 1928–9', *Soviet Studies*, vol. XXIII, no. 2 (October 1971) pp. 236–53.
Fitzpatrick, S. 'The "Soft" Line on Culture and its Enemies; Soviet Cultural Policy 1922–7', *Slavic Review*, vol. 33, no. 2 (June 1974) pp. 267–87.
Fitzpatrick, S. (ed.), *Culture Revolution in Russia, 1928–1931* (Bloomington, Ind., and London, 1978).
Fitzpatrick, S., *Education and Social Mobility in the Soviet Union, 1921–1934* (London, 1979).
Getty, J. A., *Origins of the Great Purges: The Soviet Communist Party Reconsidered, 1933–38* (Cambridge, 1985).
Glatzer-Rosenthal, B. (ed.), *Nietzsche in Russia* (Princeton, NJ, 1986).
Gleason, A., Kenez, P. and Stites, R. (eds), *Bolshevik Culture* (Bloomington, Ind., 1985).
Gorbunov, V. V., *V. I. Lenin i Proletkul't* (Moscow, 1974).
Gorbunov, V. V., *Razvitie V. I. Leninym Marksistskoi teorii kul'tury*, vol. 1, dooktiabrskoi period (Moscow, 1980); vol. 2, Sovetskii period (Moscow, 1985).
Gorky, M., *Sbornik proletarskikh pisatelei* (St Petersburg, 1914).
Gorky, M. (trans H. Ermolaev), *Untimely Thoughts* (London, 1968).
Gorzka, G., *A. Bogdanov und der Russische Proletkul't. Theorie und Praxis einer sozialistischen Kultur-revolution* (Frankfurt and New York, 1980).

256   *Culture and Power in Revolutionary Russia*

Gorzka, G., 'Proletarian Cultural Revolution: The Conception of A. A. Bogdanov', *Sbornik*, no. 9 (1983).
Gouldner, A., *The Future of the Intellectuals and the Rise of the New Class* (London, 1979).
Graham, L. R., *The Soviet Academy of Sciences and the Communist Party, 1927–1932* (Princeton, NJ, 1967).
Gray, C., *The Russian Experiment in Art, 1863–1922* (London, 1971).
Gronskii, I. M. and Perel'man, V. N., *Assotsiatsiia khudozhnikov revoliutsionnoi Rossii – AKhRR – sbornik vospominanii, statei, dokumentov* (Moscow, 1973).
Hans, N. and Hessen, S., *Education Policy in Soviet Russia* (London, 1930).
Ilf and Petrov, *The Golden Calf* (New York, 1962).
Ilf and Petrov, *The Twelve Chairs* (New York, 1961).
Intelligentsia i revoliutsiia: sbornik statei, contrib. M. N. Pokrovskii, N. L. Meshcheriakov, A. K. Voronsky, V. Polonsky (Moscow, 1922).
'Intelligentskie nastroenie i chaianiia ot oktiabrskikh dnei do porazheniia belogvardeishchiny', *Sputnik kommunista*, no. 15 (1922) pp. 48–59.
Ioffe, A. I., *Moia zhizn' i rabota – avtobiograficheskii ocherk* (Moscow and Leningrad, 1933).
Iskander, F., *Sandro of Chegem* (London, 1983).
Iz glubiny: sbornik statei o Russkoi revoliutsii (contrib. S. A. Askol'dov, N. A. Berdiaev, A. S. Izgoev, S. A. Kotliarevskii, V. Murav'ev, P. Novgorodtsev, I. Pokrovskii, Petr Struve, S. L. Frank).
Izgoev, A. S., 'Na perevale VII. "Vekhist" sredi marksistov', *Russkaia mysl'*, no. 8 (1910) pp. 63–72.
James, C. V., *Soviet Socialist Realism* (London, 1973).
Jasny, N., *Soviet Economists of the Twenties: Names to be Remembered* (Cambridge, 1972).
Joravsky, D., *Soviet Marxism and Natural Science, 1917–1932* (New York, 1961).
Joravsky, D., 'The Stalinist Mentality and the Higher Learning', *Slavic Review*, vol. 45 (1986) pp. 575–600.
K voprosu o politike RKP(b) v khudozhestvennoi literature (Moscow, 1924).
Katuntseva, N. M., *Rol' rabochikh fakul'tetov v formirovanie kadrov narodnoi intelligentsii v SSSR* (Moscow, 1966).
Katz, Z., 'Party Political Education in Soviet Russia 1918–35', *Soviet Studies*, vol. 7 (1956) pp. 237–47.
Kelly, A., *Mikhail Bakunin* (Oxford, 1983).
Kemp-Welch, A., '"New Economic Policy in Culture" and its Enemies', *Journal of Contemporary History*, vol. 13 (1978) pp. 449–65.
Kenez, P., *The Propaganda State* (Oxford, 1986).
Khodasevich, V., *Literaturnye stat'i i vospominaniia* (New York, 1954).
Kim, M. P., (ed.), *Sovetskaiia intelligentsiia – istoriia formirovaniia i rosta 1917–1965gg.* (Moscow, 1968).
Kleinbort, L. M., *Ocherki rabochei intelligentsii: tom pervyi 1905–16; tom vtoroi Teatr, zhivopis', muzyka* (Petrograd, 1923).
Kneen, P., *Higher Education and Cultural Revolution in the USSR*, CREES Discussion Papers, Soviet Industrialisation Project Series, no. 5 (Birmingham, 1976).

Knei-Paz, B., *The Social and Political Thought of Leon Trotsky* (Oxford, 1978).

Kosarev, V., 'Partiinaia shkola na ostrove Kapri. Pochemu voznykla mysla o zagranichnoi part-shkole', *Sibirskie ogni*, no. 2 (mai-iiun 1922) pp. 62–75.

Krupskaia, N. K., 'Chem dolzhen byt rabochii klub', *Proletarskaia kul'tura*, no. 4 (1919) pp. 23–25.

Krupskaia, N. K. *Memories of Lenin* (London, 1970).

Krylenko, N. V., *Za piat' let 1918–22gg: obvinitelnyi rechi* (Moscow and Leningrad, 1923).

Kul'turnoe stroitel'stvo SSSR: Statisticheskii Sbornik (Moscow and Leningrad, 1940).

Kunavin, V., 'Vserossiiskii s'ezd Proletkul'ta', *Proletarskaia kul'tura*, no. 17–19 (1920), pp. 74–84.

Lapirov-Skoblo, M. Ia (ed.), (RSFSR Nauchno-tekhnicheskii otdel VSNKh) *Rabota Nauchno – tekhnicheskikh uchrezhdenii respubliki 1918–1919gg.* (Moscow, n.d.).

Lapshin, V. P., *Khudozhestvennaia zhizn' Moskvy i Petrograda v 1917 godu* (Moscow, 1983).

Leikina-Svirskaia, V. R., *Intelligentsiia v Rossii vo vtoroi polovine XIX veka* (Moscow, 1971).

Leikina-Svirskaia, V. R., *Russkaia intelligentsia v 1900–1917 godakh* (Moscow, 1981).

Lenin, V. I., *Between the Two Revolutions: Articles and Speeches of 1917* (Moscow, 1971).

Lenin, V. I., *V. I. Lenin i VCkK: sbornik dokumentov, izdanie vtoroe, dopolnennoe* (Moscow, 1987).

Letopis' dom literatorov.

Lewis, R., *Science and Industrialisation in the USSR: Industrial Research and Development, 1917–1940* (London, 1979).

Lezhnev, I. G., *Zapiski sovremennika*, vol. 1 (Moscow, 1936).

Livshits, B., *The One and a Half Eyed Archer* (Newtonville, Mass. 1977).

Lodder, Christina, *Russian Constructivism* (New Haven, Conn., and London, 1983).

Lozinskii, G., 'Petropolis', *Vremennik obshchestva druzei russkoi knigi*, vol. II (Paris, 1928) pp. 33–8.

Lunacharsky, A., *Kul'turnyia zadachi rabochego klassa* (Moscow, 1918).

Lunacharsky, A. V., 'Svoboda knigi i revoliutsiia', *Pechat' i revoliutsiia*, no. 1 (May–June 1921).

McLelland, J., 'Proletarianising the Student Body: the Soviet Experience during the New Economic Policy', *Past and Present*, no. 80 (August 1978) pp. 122–46.

McNeal, R., *Bride of the Revolution: Krupskaia and Lenin* (London, 1973).

McNeal, R. H. (ed.), *Resolutions and Decisions of the Communist Party of the Soviet Union*, vol. ii, *The Early Soviet Period: 1917–1929* (ed. R. Gregor) (Toronto, 1974).

Maguire, R. M., *Red Virgin Soil* (New York, 1968).

Makovskii, S., 'Ministerstvo iskusstv', *Apollon*, no. 2–3 (fevr.–mart. 1917) pp. i–xvi.

Mandelstam, N., *Hope against Hope* (London, 1971).
Mandelstam, N., *Hope Abandoned* (London, 1974).
Mel'gunov, S. P., *Vospominaniia i Dnevniki*, vypusk II (chast' tret'ia) (Paris, 1964).
Merezhkovsky, D. S., 'Revoliutsiia i religiia', *Russkaia mysl'*, (1907) no. 2, pp. 64–85 and no. 3, pp. 17–34.
Meshcheriakov, N. L., 'O novykh nastroeniiakh russkoi intelligentsii', *Pechat' i revoliutsiia*, no. 3 (1921)
Meshcheriakov, N. L., 'O chastnykh izdatel'stvakh', *Pechat' i revoliutsiia*, no. 6 July–August 1922 pp. 128–34.
Meshcheriakov, N. L., 'Mechty smenavekhovstva i ikh sud'bi', *Na ideologicheskom fronte bor'by s kontrrevoliutsii: sbornik statei* (Moscow, 1923).
Metcalf, A., 'The Founding of the Federation of Soviet Writers: The Forgotten Factor in Soviet Literature of the Late Twenties', *Slavonic and East European Review*, vol. 65, no. 4 (October 1987) pp. 609–616.
Meyer, F., *Marc Chagall* (New York, n.d.).
Miakotin, V., 'Iz nedalekago proshlago (otryvki vospominanii)', (Golos Minuvshago), *Na chuzhoi storony*, vol. II (1923) pp. 178–99.
Milner, John, *Vladimir Tatlin and the Russian Avant-garde* (New Haven, Conn., and London, 1983).
Mindlin, Em., *Neobyknovennye sobesedniki* (Moscow, 1968).
Minsky, N. M., 'Manifest intelligentnykh rabotnikov', *Sovremennyia problemy: sbornik statei* (Paris, 1922).
Moroz, V. (ed. and trans. by J. Kolasky), *Report from the Beria Reserve: The Protest Writings of Valentyn Moroz* (Toronto and London, 1974).
Na ideologicheskom fronte bor'by s kontrrevoliutsiei: sbornik statei (Moscow, 1923).
Nahirny, V., *The Russian Intelligentsia: From Torment to Silence* (Totowa, N.J., 1983).
Nazarov, A. I., *Oktiabr' i kniga: sozdanie sovetskikh izdatel'stv i formirovanie massovogo chitatelia 1917–1923* (Moscow, 1968).
Nevsky, V. I., *Otchet raboche – krestianskogo kommunicheskogo universiteta imeni Ia. M. Sverdlova za period iiun' 1918g.–ianvaria 1920 goda*, Chast' l-ia (Moscow, 1920a).
Nevsky, V. I., *Rabota v derevne i Tsentropechat'* (Moscow, 1920b).
Nevsky, V. I., 'Nostradamusy XX-go veka', *Pod znamenem marksizma*, no. 4 (April 1922a) pp. 95–100.
Nevsky, V. I., 'Restavratsiia idealizma i bor'ba s "novoi" burzhuazei', *Pod znamenem marksizma*, no. 7–8 (July–August 1922b) pp. 117–31.
Nevsky, V. I. and Khersonskaia, N., *Kul'turnaia rabota gorodskikh bibliotek* (Moscow, 1920).
Nilsson, N. A., *Art, Society, Revolution: Russia 1917–1921* (Stockholm, 1979).
Novikov, M. M., *Moskovskii Universitet 1755–1930* (Paris, 1930).
Novikov, M. M., *Ot Moskvy do Niu-Iorka: Moia zhizn' v nauke i politike* (New York, 1952).
Novikov, M. M., *Dvukhsotletie Moskovskogo Universiteta: Prazdnovanie v Amerike* (New York, 1956).
Obelkevich, J., Roper, L. and Samuel, R. (eds), *Disciplines of Faith: Studies in Religion, Politics and Patriarchy* (London and New York, 1987).

O'Connor, T. E., *The Politics of Soviet Culture: Anatolii Lunacharskii* (Ann Arbor, Mich., 1983).
Osorgin, M., 'Knizhnaia lavka pisatelei', *Vremennik obshchestva druzei russkoi knigi*, vol. II (Paris, 1928) pp. 19–32.
Osorgin, M., 'Rukopisnyia knigi Moskovskoi Lavki Pisatelei 1919–21', *Vremennik obshchestva druzei russkoi knigi* (Paris, 1932), pp. 49–60.
Paris–Moscou 1900–1930: Catalogue de l'Exposition, 2nd edn (Paris, 1979).
Paul, E. and Paul, C., *Proletkul't* (London, 1921).
Pethybridge, R. W., 'Concern for Bolshevik Ideological Predominance at the Start of NEP', *Russian Review*, no. 41 (October 1982) pp. 445–53.
Pobedonostsev, K. P., *Reflections of a Russian Statesman* (Ann Arbor, Mich., 1965).
Podgotovka kadrov v SSSR, vypusk II (Moscow 1934).
Podzemskii, A. Ia. *Kul'turnoe stroitel'stvo SSSR: K dokladu A. V. Lunacharskogo na 2-1 sessii tsentral'nogo ispolnitel'nogo komiteta SSSR, IV sozyv, oktiabr' 1927 Leningrad* (Moscow and Leningrad, 1927).
Protokoly pervyi vserossisskii konferentsii proletarskikh kul'turno – prosvetitelnykh organizatsii 15–20 sentiabria 1918gg. (Moscow, 1918).
Putnam, G., *Russian Alternatives to Marxism; Christian Socialism and Idealistic Liberalism in Twentieth-century Russia* (Knoxville, Tenn., 1977).
Rabochie fakul'tety i professional'noe obrazovanie sibirskogo kraia (Moscow, 1928).
Read, C. J., *Religion, Revolution and the Russian Intelligentsia: The Vekhi Debate and its Intellectual Background* (London, 1979).
Read, C. J., 'New Directions in the Russian Intelligentsia: Idealists and Marxists in the Early Twentieth Century', *Renaissance and Modern Studies* no. 4 (1981) pp. 1–17.
Read, C. J., 'The 1905 Revolution and the Intelligentsia', in Coquin, F.-X. and Gervais-Francelle, C. (eds), *1905: La Première Revolution Russe* (Paris, 1986) pp. 385–96.
Read, C. J., 'Some Early Twentieth Century Russian Definitions of the Intelligentsia', in *Intelligentsias: Contemporary Research and Methods* (Sofia, 1989, forthcoming).
Red'ko, A., 'Tragediia russkoi intelligentsii', *Russkoe bogatstvo*, no. 1–3 (ianv.–mart. 1918) pp. 261–83.
Riasanovsky, N., *Nicholas I and Official Nationality in Russia, 1825–1855* (Berkeley and Los Angeles, 1969).
Rosenthal, B. G. (ed.), *Nietzsche in Russia* (Princeton, NJ, 1986).
S.A.S. (Sokolov), 'Moia vstrecha s Bogdanovym', *Revoliutsionnoe bylo*, no. 2 (1923) pp. 18–20.
Schapiro, L., *The Origin of the Communist Autocracy* (London, 1955).
Schapiro, L., *The Communist Party of the Soviet Union*, 2nd edn (London, 1970).
Schapiro, L., *Russian Studies* (London, 1986).
Scherr, B., 'Notes on Literary Life in Petrograd 1918–1922: A Tale of Three Houses', *Slavic Review*, vol. XXXVI, no. 2 (June 1977) pp. 256–267.
Scherrer, J., 'Les Ecoles du Parti de Capri et de Bologne', *Cahiers du Monde Russe et Sovietique*, no. 19 (July–September 1978) pp. 258–84.
Selden, J. H., 'The Petrashevtsy: A Re-appraisal', *Slavic Review*, vol. 43, no. 3 (1986) pp. 434–52.

Seton-Watson, H., *The Russian Empire, 1801–1917* (Oxford, 1967).
Shatz, M. S. and Zimmerman, J. E. (trans. and ed.), *Signposts: A Collection of Articles on the Russian Intelligentsia* (Irvine, Calif. 1986).
Sheridan, C., *Russian Portraits* (London, 1921).
Shirmakov, P., 'Soiuz deiatelei Khudozhestvennoi literatury', *Uchenie zapiski Leningradskogo universiteta* (Filologiia) no. 3 (1958) pp. 445–63.
Shragin, B. and Todd, A. (eds), *Landmarks: A Collection of Essays on the Russian Intelligentsia, 1909* (New York, 1977).
Smena vekh: sbornik statei, contrib. Iu. V. Kliuchnikov, N. V. Ustrialov, A. V. Bobrishchev-Pushkin, S. S. Luk'ianov, S. S. Chakhotin, Iu. N. Potekhin (Prague, 1921).
Sochor, Z. A., 'A. A. Bogdanov: In Search of Cultural Liberation', in Rosenthal (1986) pp. 293–314.
Sochor, Z. A., 'Was Bogdanov Russia's Answer to Gramsci?', *Studies in Soviet Thought*, vol. 22 (February 1981) pp. 59–81.
Solzhenitsyn, A., *Nobel Prize Lecture* (London, 1973).
Sorokin, P., *Leaves From a Russian Diary* (New York, 1924).
Stenograficheskii otchet rabot l-go Vserossiiskogo s'ezda Inzhenerov, Chlenov Profsoiuzov, 16–22 dekabria 1922 (Moscow, 1923).
Stratonov, V., 'Poteria Moskovskim Universitetom svobody', in Novikov (1930) pp. 193–242.
Struve, P., 'Osvobozhdenaia Rossiia', *Russkaia mysl'* no. 2 (1917) pp. 3–4.
Tait, A. L., *Lunacharsky: Poet of the Revolution, 1875–1907* (Birmingham, n.d.).
Tekhnologicheskii Institut imeni Leningradskogo Soveta Rabochikh, Krest'ianskikh i Krasnoarmeiskikh Deputatov. Sto let, tom 1 (Leningrad, 1928).
Timiriazev, K., *Demokraticheskaia Reforma Vyshei Shkoly* (Moscow, 1918).
Trotsky, L., *Literature and Revolution* (New York, 1960).
Ustrialov, N. V. *Pod znakom revoliutsii*, 2nd edn (Harbin, 1927).
Volgin, I. *Poslednii god Dostoevskogo* (Moscow, 1986).
Voprosy kul'tury pri diktature proletariata (Moscow and Leningrad, 1925).
Voronsky, A., 'Na novom puti', *Pechat' i revoliutsiia* no. 3 (1921).
Vserossiiskii Soiuz Inzhenerov, *Otchet o zaniiatiakh 2-i Moskovskoi oblastnoi konferentsii 18–21go oktiabria 1918g.* (Moscow, 1918).
Vucinich, A., *Social Thought in Tsarist Russia: The Quest for a General Science of Society, 1861–1917* (Chicago, 1976).
Walicki, A., *The Slavophile Controversy: History of a Conservative Utopia in Nineteenth Century Thought* (Oxford, 1975).
White, J. D., 'Bogdanov in Tula', *Studies in Soviet Thought*, vol. 22 (February 1981) pp. 43–58.
Williams, R. C. *Culture in Exile: Russian Emigres in Germany, 1881–1941* (Ithaca, NY, and London, 1972).
Williams, R. C., *Artists in Revolution: Portraits of the Russian Avant-garde, 1905–1925* (Bloomington, Ind., 1977).
Witt, N. de, *Education and Professional Employment in the USSR* (Washington, 1961).
Woehrlin, W. F. (ed.), *Out of the Depths (De Profundis): A Collection of Articles on the Russian Revolution* (Irvine, Calif. 1986).

Zander, S. 'Vysshaia shkola i proletarskii universitet', *Proletarskaia kul'tura*, no. 20–21 (January–June 1921) pp. 19–27.

Zaniatiia l-go Moskovskogo oblast'nogo delegatskogo s'ezda 4–6 ianv. 1918g. Biulleteni Moskovskogo oblast'nogo biuro i Moskovskogo otdeleniia vserossiiskii soiuza inzhenerov, MOB no. 1 i MOVsSI no. 3 (Moscow, 1918).

Zinoviev, G. *Intelligentsiia i revoliutsiia* (Moscow, 1923).

Znumensky, O. N., *Intelligentsiia naka nune velikogo oktiabriia (Fevral' – oktiabr' 1917g.)* (Leningrad, 1988).

Index

Academy of Sciences, 62, 79, 80,
  145, 161, 164, 168, 182, 183, 200
Agitpropotdel, *see* Central
  Committee of the Communist
  Party
Alexander II, Tsar, 3
Alexander III, Tsar, 3, 4
Andreev, L., 57–8
Antony Volynsky, Archbishop, 29
Apollo (*Apollon*), 41
Aquinas, Thomas, St, 136
Association of Artists of
  Revolutionary Russia, 88

Bardin, I., 80
Belinsky, V. (1810–48), 17–18
Belyi, A. (1880–1934), 26, 51, 70–1,
  76, 89, 92–3, 127
Benois, A. (1870–1960), 23, 75
Berdiaev, N. (1874–1948), 1, 28, 48,
  68–70, 94, 176, 181
Bilibin, I. (1876–1942), 23
Blok, A. (1880–1921), 24, 26, 46, 51,
  52, 64, 75, 76, 89, 91–2, 93, 241
Bogdanov, A. (1873–1928), 43, 75,
  82, 108, 134, 135, 139, 140, 145–
  7, 153, 155, 160, 163, 184, 202,
  204, 220
  and principles of cultural
    revolution, 112–23
  on science, 119–20
  opposes iconoclasm, 121–3, 149–
    50
Bologna party school, 115, 116
Bolshevism
  and reform of human nature, 1
  policies affect intelligentsia and
    culture, 46, 52–5, 94–5, 142–
    5, 155–6, 159–62, 183–5, 186–
    9, 200–20, 230–4
Briusov, V. (1873–1924), 24, 75, 103,
  127
Buchanan, Sir G., 11

Bukharin, N. (1888–1938), 108, 111,
  132, 138, 140, 144, 170, 173,
  178, 184, 201, 208, 209, 216,
  218, 220
  views on intelligentsia and culture,
    211–12
Bulgakov, S. (1871–1944), 28, 58,
  181

Capri party school, 83, 99, 115–18,
  123, 146
censorship (Glavlit), 142, 162, 164,
  172, 175–6, 178–9
Central Committee of the
  Communist Party, 94, 198
  Agitation and Propaganda
    Department (Agitpropotdel),
    94, 162, 164, 169, 170–1, 177
  cultural apparatus of, 162–85
  Organisation Bureau (Orgburo),
    131–3, 138–9, 146–7, 158–9,
    184
  Press Section debate on literature
    (May 1924), 212–15, 218–19
  resolution on literature (July
    1925), 201–2, 216–20
Chagall, M. (1887–1984), 21, 23–4,
  44, 51, 89–91, 93
Chekhov, A. (1860–1904), 14, 31
China, 11
Comintern (Third Communist
  International), 152
Communist Party of the Soviet
  Union, *see* Bolshevism; Central
  Committee of the Communist
  Party
Comte, A., 9
Crimean War, 5

Danielson, N., 10
Darwin, C., 9
Diaghilev, S., 21
Dobuzhinsky, M. (1875–1957), 23
Dodonova, A., 148–9, 154

262

Index   265

Orthodox Church, Russian, 2, 18
political use of, 2–5
Osorgin, M., 63–4
Ouspensky, P., 27
Out of the Depths (*Iz glubiny*), 70,
175

Pasternak, B., 58, 188, 234
Paul, E., 152
peasantry
idealisation of, 19
image of in 1917, 47
Peter the Great, Tsar, 2, 236
Petrashevsky circle, 18
Petrograd, 5, 8, 23, 24, 31, 32, 44,
45–6, 54, 59, 70, 75, 99, 126,
177, 199, 224, 230
Petrograd Institute of Technology,
73
rabfak, 224, 226–8
Petropolis co-operative, 63
Plekhanov, G., 29, 33, 114
Pletnev, V., 145, 219, 220
Pobedonostsev, K. (1827–1907), 2–
4, 23, 40
Pokrovsky, M. (1868–1932), 77, 99–
100, 101–2, 103, 106, 108, 109,
134, 157, 160, 161, 163, 167,
173, 179
Poland, 5, 133, 146, 147
Polonsky, V. (1886–1932), 162, 164–
5, 166
popular culture, 30–2, 42–3
Potekhin, N., 191, 196, 197, 199
Potresov, A., 50–1
Pozner, V., 101, 103–4, 106
Preobrazhensky, E., 103, 158, 159,
161, 169
*Problems of Culture under the
Dictatorship of the Proletariat*
(*Voprosy kul'tury pri diktature
proletariata*), 218–20
Prokopovich, S., 108, 181
proletarian chauvinism, 160, 188,
201, 215–16, 247
Proletarian University, 146, 153, 246
Bogdanov's concept of, 113–14,
121, 131–2, 139
closed by Orgburo, 131–3

merged with Sverdlov University,
138–9, 146–7
Proletkul't (Proletarian Cultural
Educational Association), 43,
67, 87, 92–3, 94, 111–33, 134,
142, 164, 169, 183, 206, 213,
215
First All-Russian Conference,
124, 125–7
Second All-Russian Conference,
152–4
Moscow Proletkul't, 129, 151
and Narkompros, 123–4, 125, 126,
130–1, 143–51, 154–6
origins of, 118–19
Petrograd Proletkul't, 129–30
and provinces, 151, 155
restriction of (1920), 145–56
publishing
private, 74–5, 173, 176–8
state, 75, 85, 174–5
see also State Publishing House
(Gosizdat)
Pushkin, A. (1799–1837), 17, 34, 92,
93

Rabis (Union of Workers in the
Arts: *Soiuz rabotnikov
iskusstv*), 65–8
Radishchev, A. (1749–1802), 16–17
Red'ko, A., 49–50, 68, 69, 75
Reisner, M., 100, 106, 107, 108, 179
Repin, I. (1844–1930), 22–3
Rerich, N. (1874–1947), 23
Riabushchinsky, N., 36
Rogozinsky, N., 132
Rossiia (*Russia*), 199
Rozanov, V. (1856–1919), 26, 34,
35, 51
Russification, 3–4
Rykov, A., 72–3, 76

St Petersburg, *see* Petrograd
St Petersburg Religious and
Philosophical Society, 28
Sakulin, P., 75, 182, 222
Scales, The (*Vesy*), 24, 25
Serafim of Sarov, St, 11
Shchukin, S., 36

266 *Index*